Trading Up

Trading Up

Consumer and Environmental Regulation in a Global Economy

David Vogel

Harvard University Press
Cambridge, Massachusetts
London, England
1995

To Virginia

with love

Library of Congress Cataloging-in-Publication Data

Vogel, David, 1947–
　　Trading up : consumer and environmental regulation in a global
　economy / David Vogel.
　　　p. cm.
　　Includes bibliographical references and index.
　　ISBN 0–674–90083–9 (alk, paper)
　　1. Consumer protection—Law and legislation. 2. Environmental
　law. 　　I. Title.
　K3842.V64 1995
　343′.071—dc20
　[342.371] 　　95–11865

Contents

Preface

The subject of this book grows out of my longstanding interest in government regulation of business. This is my third book on the politics of consumer and environmental regulation. In my first book on the subject, *National Styles of Regulation: Environmental Policy in Great Britain and the United States,* I explored government regulation from the perspective of comparative politics. *Fluctuating Fortunes: The Political Power of Business in America* examined the politics of protective regulation in the United States. This book moves beyond the realm of national politics to explore the relationship between protective regulations and international politics.

The origins of this project lie in a paper I wrote in 1989 that compared consumer protection policies in the United States and Japan. While researching this paper, I became aware that the impact of Japanese consumer protection standards extended beyond Japan's borders. To the extent that these regulations served as nontariff trade barriers, they affected not only Japanese companies and consumers but also American firms seeking to export to Japan. American trade officials were pressuring Japan to change its regulatory policies on the grounds that they imposed disproportionate burdens on non-Japanese firms. The American effort was in turn vigorously opposed not only by Japanese domestic producers—for whom these regulations were a source of competitive advantage—but also by a number of Japanese consumer groups who claimed that the American demands threatened the health and safety of the Japanese public. During the following two years, my research on the politics of food safety and environmental standards within the European Community exposed similar linkages between international trade and national regulation.

Until recently, students of environmental and consumer regulation paid little attention to the international dimensions of national regulatory policies. Virtually all studies of protective regulation, including my own, have been either national or comparative in focus. With the exception of the literature on international environmental issues and agreements, there have been few efforts to place the making of national regulatory policies in an international context. Likewise, relatively few studies of trade policy have examined the significance of consumer and environmental regulations as nontariff trade barriers, or explored the role of environmental and consumer organizations in shaping the debate over and the terms of trade agreements. Both these omissions are understandable since it is only relatively recently that the linkages between these formerly distinctive policy areas have become politically salient.

Thanks in large measure to the controversial 1991 General Agreement on Tariffs and Trade (GATT) tuna-dolphin decision and the 1990–94 debate in the United States over the environmental impacts of the North American Free Trade Agreement (NAFTA), the linkages between trade and regulatory policies have moved to a more prominent place on both the policy and scholarly agenda.

Since 1991, reports and papers on this subject have been issued by the United States Office of Technology Assessment, the U.S. Environmental Protection Agency, the Organization for Economic Co-Operation and Development (OECD), The International Institute for Applied Systems Analysis, and the World Bank.[1] There have also been three edited volumes and two policy-oriented books.[2] Since 1992, numerous scholarly articles have been published on the subject of trade and regulation, mostly in law reviews.[3]

This book both draws upon and seeks to contribute to this rapidly growing literature on the relationship between trade policy and protective regulations. It is also distinctive in a number of respects. Most writing in this topic has focused on environmental issues, primarily in the context of a specfiic trade agreement, most frequently the GATT. The scope of this study is considerably broader. It focuses on the relationship between trade policy and both consumer and environmental regulation. In addition, it describes and compares the regulatory dimensions of a number of different trade agreements, including the

GATT, the GATT Standards Code, the Free Trade Agreement (FTA) between the United States and Canada, and the North American Free Trade Agreement among the United States, Canada, and Mexico. It also examines the regulatory policies of the European Union (EU, formerly the European Community) in considerable detail.* It treats the EU as an important case study on the relationship between economic integration and protective regulation, one with important implications for other agreements to reduce trade barriers, most notably NAFTA. In addition, it explores the ways in which the increasingly salient relationship between regulatory and trade policies have affected American politics and policies.

Virtually the entire scholarly literature on trade and regulation has been written by either lawyers or economists. This is the first extensive study of the subject by a political scientist. As such, it places particular emphasis on the role of nonstate actors—producers and environment and consumer organizations—in shaping national preferences and international policy outcomes. It examines the interaction of two policy regimes, one of which, namely, trade policy, has always had an international dimension, while the other, regulatory policy, is rapidly acquiring one.

While I do address the debate over the impact of trade on environmental quality, that is not the central theme of this book. Rather, my primary focus is on the relationship between trade agreements, treaties, and conflicts and regulatory *standards,* especially those which directly affect the movement of goods across national borders. I do explore international environmental issues and treaties, but only in the context of their relationship to trade policies. This book is essentially a comparative study of six trade agreements and treaties and their relationship to national environmental and consumer regulations.

Although I do not offer any explicit policy suggestions, my analysis does have important political implications. I show that the incompatibility between freer trade and more effective regulation has been exaggerated. The fear on the part of many environmental and consumer

---

*On November 1, 1994, following ratification of the Maastricht Treaty, the name of the European Community (EC) was officially changed to the European Union (EU). This book primarily uses the former term to describe specific developments that occurred prior to November 1994, and the latter to refer to European integration in historical or comparative terms.

groups, especially in the United States, that trade liberalization and agreements to promote that liberalization will weaken national regulatory standards is misplaced. On the contrary, I demonstrate how the former can, and frequently has, strengthened the latter. Rather than weakening the power of nongovernmental organizations in "greener" nations, trade liberalization and agreements to promote it can enhance the ability of NGOs to strengthen the regulatory standards of their nation's trading partners. In fact, increased economic interdependence has been associated with stronger, not weaker, consumer and environmental regulations. By contrast, "ecoprotectionism" threatens both free trade and, ironically, the improvement of environmental quality and consumer protection as well.

Because numerous consumer and environmental regulations have implications for trade agreements and policies, and vice versa, the scope of this book is potentially large. I have chosen to describe and assess the relationship between trade policy and protective regulation by emphasizing those linkages which either have become politically salient or which illustrate broader political trends. My logic of case selection is thus both broad and selective.

To explore the impact of the Treaty of Rome and the Single European Act on consumer protection in Europe, I examine one policy area in depth, namely, food safety regulation. This decision reflects not only the political and economic importance of trade in agricultural products within the EU, but also the critically important way in which the Union's efforts to reduce nontariff barriers in this sector have affected the legal and political development of the single market. I discuss the relationship between environmental protection and European economic integration by examining the development of national and Union standards for automobile emissions, chemical safety, and recycling. The highly contentious and prolonged debate over the formation of each of these regulatory policies illustrates the interaction of national economic interests and national regulatory preferences; together, these three case studies provide an overview of the impact of national and Union environmental regulations on intra-European trade. They also demonstrate how and why trade liberalization within the EU has contributed to the strengthening of environmental standards for traded goods.

My treatment of the GATT and environmental regulation is more exhaustive. I analyze each of the trade disputes that have come before dispute panels due to the (alleged) use of national environmental regulations as trade barriers. I also discuss a number of other trade disputes stemming from the divergence in national regulatory standards. In addition, I review and assess the growing debate over the impact of trade liberalization in general, and the GATT in particular, on both national and global environmental standards.

No formal dispute settlement proceedings have taken place under the Standards Code, which was adopted as part of the Tokyo Round GATT agreement in 1979. There has been, however, one highly acrimonious trade dispute involving differences in consumer protection standards in the EU and the United States which the Standards Code failed to resolve. It stemmed from the 1986 decision of the (then) European Community to ban the sale of beef from cows that had been fed growth hormones, which in turn severely restricted beef exports from the United States. Because of the political significance of this dispute and the economic importance of international trade in agricultural products, I examine in detail the role of food safety standards as trade barriers by reviewing a number of trade disputes between the United States and the EU, as well as between Japan and its trading partners.

There have been a number of both formal and informal trade disputes stemming from the role of national consumer and environmental regulations as nontariff barriers under the Free Trade Agreement. I examine each of them and assess the impact of their settlement on both American and Canadian regulatory policies. Since no dispute settlement proceedings have taken place under the North American Free Trade Agreement, I focus instead on the role of public interest groups in affecting the debate over the approval of NAFTA by the U.S. Congress and in shaping the terms of the final agreement.

I have benefited from the opportunity to present various portions of this book at a number of workshops, conferences, and conventions. The chapters on EU environmental policy, and the GATT and environmental regulation, as well as the material on Japanese consumer regulations, were presented at the annual meetings of the American Political Science Association. The chapter on EU consumer policy was presented at a biennial conference of the European Community Studies Association. The material on the EC-United States beef hormone dispute was originally prepared for a conference on "Reconciling Regulation and Free Trade," organized by the Centre for European Policy

Studies in Brussels. In addition, I presented drafts of both chapters on EU regulatory policies at workshops sponsored by the Center for European Studies at Harvard University organized by Nicholas Zeigler. I also presented drafts of the first and last chapters at the Workshop on Institutional Analysis at the Haas School of Business, directed by Oliver Williamson. The comments I received from participants at each of these presentations helped me to develop and clarify my analysis.

A number of my colleagues at Berkeley and other universities have been generous enough to read through all or sections of this manuscript and offer me the benefits of their comments and criticisms. I am pleased to acknowledge the assistance of Vinod Aggarwal, H. Landis Gabel, John Goodman, Ernst Haas, Peter Haas, Robert Kagan, Jonah Levy, Richard Lyons, Thomas McCraw, Francis Van Loo, and Steven Weber. I particularly wish to express my appreciation for the careful and critical readings of the entire manuscript by Steve Charnovitz of the Competitiveness Policy Council, Abram Chayes of the Harvard Law School, David Mowery, my colleague at the Haas School, Richard Steinberg of the Berkeley Roundtable on the International Economy, and David Yoffie of the Harvard Business School. This book in no small measure reflects the knowledge and insights of each of these individuals, and I am very much in their debt.

I am especially pleased to acknowledge the contribution of my research assistant and friend, Tim Kessler, a graduate student in political science at the University of California, Berkeley. He competently and cheerfully assisted me at every stage of this project, from the original research through the various drafts. Whatever coherence this book possesses owes much to his valuable assistance. Serena Joe of the staff of the Haas School also provided much-appreciated assistance in manuscript preparation. David Stuligross and Susan Wallace Boehmer assisted with the final editing.

As always, my deepest thanks go to my wife, Virginia, for her editorial assistance, encouragement, and endurance. As she can amply testify, writing books doesn't seem to be getting any easier.

The research and writing of this book were primarily supported by a series of grants from the Alfred P. Sloan Foundation, administrated through the Consortium On Competitiveness and Cooperation at the University of California, Berkeley, Center for Research in Management. I wish to express my appreciation to the Center's director, David Teece, for recognizing the importance of this project and for helping me to secure the funding needed to pursue it. Financial assistance was also provided by the Social Science Research Council, the UC Berkeley Committee on Research, and the Haas School of Business.

A version of the material on Japan in Chapter 5 was originally published in the *Journal of Japanese Studies*, 18, no. 1 (1992), under the title "Consumer Protection and Protectionism in Japan." Versions of the material on EC environmental policy in Chapter 3 have been published as "Environmental Policy in the European Community," in *International Environmental Politics and Policies,* edited by Sheldon Kamienieki (New York: SUNY Press, 1993); "Environmental Protection and the Creation of a Single European Market," in *Business and the Contemporary World*, Winter 1993; and "The Making of EC Environmental Policy," in *Making Policy in Europe: The Europeification of National Policy-making*, edited by Svein S. Anderson and Kjell A. Eliassen (London: Sage Publications, 1993). An earlier version of Chapter 6 was published under the title "The Public Interest Movement and American Trade Policy" in *Environmental Politics: Public Costs, Private Rewards,* edited by Michael Greve and Fred Smith (Westport, Conn.: Praeger, 1992).

-1-

National Regulation in the Global Economy

This book describes how the making of trade policy and the making of regulatory policy are influencing one another. It examines how international and regional trade negotiations, agreements, and disputes are affecting and being affected by national consumer and environmental regulations. It analyzes the growing political linkages between the formerly distinctive policy areas of trade and protective regulation within the European Union, in North America, and around the world. The main theoretical contribution of this work is to link the comparative study of regulatory policy to that of international political economy. It makes this contribution by demonstrating the connection among the domestic roots of national regulatory policies and preferences, national political and economic power, and regulatory outcomes.

Three themes are interwoven throughout this analysis.

First, the steady expansion of domestic health, safety, and environmental regulations, combined with the reduction of other forms of trade restrictions, most notably tariffs, has increased the relative importance of protective regulations as nontariff barriers. Consequently, agreements to liberalize both regional and international trade are attempting to reduce the role of consumer and environmental standards as obstacles to trade. Trade liberalization is thus undermining national regulatory sovereignty.

Second, it is no longer possible to understand the making of environmental and consumer regulation exclusively in national terms. Regulation, like so many other areas of public policy, is being shaped more and more by political and economic forces outside the nation

1

state. A number of political scientists have explored the increasingly important role of international environmental agreements and treaties in affecting national regulatory standards.[1] But these treaties and agreements represent only one source of international influence on domestic regulatory policies.

The role of trade and trade agreements in promoting both the regionalization and the globalization of regulatory policy-making are much more important. Trade and agreements to promote it affect not only the flow of goods among nations, but also the movement of regulations across national boundaries. Nations are thus increasingly importing and exporting standards as well as goods. Trade and trade agreements represent transmission belts by which producers, and environmental and consumer groups, can influence the regulatory policies of their trading partners, and in turn be influenced by them. Consequently, many of the conflicts over environmental and consumer regulation that formerly took place exclusively *within* nations are now also taking place *among* them.

Third, a new set of constituencies, namely, consumer and environmental organizations, have become active participants in the making of trade policy. Unlike producers or workers, these nongovernmental organizations (NGOs) are interested not in the economic impact of trade policies, but rather in the way they affect consumer health and safety and environmental quality in their own countries, and often in others as well. In many cases, NGOs have transferred their suspicion of domestic markets to global ones. Alliances between protectionist producers and NGOs have become commonplace in the United States, western Europe, and Japan, and these coalitions represent an important source of opposition to trade liberalization.

At the same time, consumer and environmental organizations are also playing a more important role in influencing the terms of particular trade agreements, attempting to make them more compatible with either the maintenance or strengthening of both domestic and international regulatory standards. Their impact has been particularly important within the European Union; both the Single European Act and the Maastricht Treaty reflect the influence of European NGOs, especially in Germany, Denmark, and the Netherlands—the EU's "greener" member states. In America, environmental groups were responsible for adding a Supplemental Agreement on the Environment to the North American Free Trade Agreement (NAFTA). American consumer organizations also had an impact on the final terms of the 1994 GATT (General Agreement on Tariffs and Trade) Uruguay Round's treatment of technical barriers to trade. In addition, environmental groups in Europe and America have helped place the linkages between trade and environmental policies on the agenda of the World Trade Organization (WTO), which was established in 1995 as the successor organization to the GATT.

These three related developments have made the relationship between trade and regulation much more contentious. Free trade advocates want to limit the use of regulations as barriers to trade, while environmentalists and consumer advocates want to prevent trade agreements from serving as barriers to regulation. While the trade community worries about an upsurge of "eco-protectionism"—the justification of trade barriers on environmental grounds—consumer and environmental organizations fear that trade liberalization will weaken both their own country's regulatory standards and those of their nation's trading partners.

However, while conflicts between trade and regulation are becoming both more numerous and more important, the policy goals of liberal trade and more effective protective regulations are not incompatible. This book demonstrates how trade liberalization and agreements to promote it, rather than undermining effective regulatory standards, have often served to strengthen them.

The Impact of Regulation on Trade

Since many national regulations disadvantage importers—either intentionally or unintentionally—the steady growth of protective regulations over the last three decades has made trade more difficult. Hence the growing number of trade disputes stemming from the alleged discriminatory impact of national environmental and consumer regulations on imports within the European Union and North America, and around the world. At the same time the undermining of trade liberalization by the expansion of environmental and consumer protection has also been limited by three factors: the role of international institutions, the power of internationally oriented producers, and the increasing number of international environmental agreements.

The international institutions created by the EU have played an especially important role in reducing the use of national protective regulations as trade barriers. The European Court of Justice (ECJ), the world's most powerful extranational judicial body, has struck down numerous national regulations which protected producers rather than consumers or the environment. Under the ECJ's interpretation of the principle of mutual recognition, each member state is required to permit the sale of products lawfully produced in any of the others. In addition, the Union's primary decision-making body, the Council of Ministers, has harmonized a significant number of national environmental and consumer regulations, thus preventing them from disrupting intra-Union trade. Much of the political support for EU rather than national regulatory standards has come from Europe's export-oriented producers, who want to reduce the role of protective regulations as obstacles to intra-Union trade. They have successfully challenged nationally oriented firms who often had relied upon distinctive national regulations to protect domestic markets.

The removal of national regulations as obstacles to intra-Union trade remains incomplete. In some cases, the Union has simply been unable to arrive at a consensus regarding the level at which standards should be harmonized. Thus it has permitted member states to maintain their own distinctive standards, even though they interfere with the single market. As the agenda of government regulation expands, so does the number of potential nontariff barriers: reducing the ability of consumer and environmental regulations to interfere with trade is an endless process. Nonetheless, over the last decade the EU has made substantial progress in creating a single market for a wide variety of products whose trade had historically been restricted by national regulations.

The General Agreement on Tariffs and Trade (GATT) is a much weaker institution than the EU, and accordingly the ability of national protective regulations to interfere with trade remains much greater at the global level. To date, the GATT has affected relatively few of the regulatory standards of its signatories. However, its rules and dispute settlement procedures have played a role in limiting the use of unilateral trade restrictions for the purpose of influencing the environmental policies of other countries. Equally importantly, the commitment of its signatories to trade liberalization has helped prevent the imposition of tariffs on goods from nations with laxer domestic regulatory standards—in spite of substantial domestic support for such measures from both NGOs and many domestic-oriented producers. In addition, internationally oriented agricultural producers succeeded in expanding the authority of the newly organized World Trade Organization to restrict the use of food safety and processing standards as trade barriers. At the international level, the growing number of international environmental agreements have also served to reduce trade tensions by creating a floor for a number of national regulatory standards that affect the global commons.

The Free Trade Agreement (FTA) between the United States and Canada has not significantly affected either nation's regulatory standards. However, NAFTA is likely to play a more important role in reducing the use of protective regulations as disguised forms of protectionism, especially for agricultural products. In addition, the United States has entered into environmental agreements with both its neighbors to address a number of cross-border environmental problems, thus reducing a potential source of trade conflict.

The "California Effect"

Agreements and treaties to promote liberal trade policies have contributed to limiting the role of national regulations as trade barriers. And their authority over national regulatory standards is increasing. But trade liberalization can just as easily be achieved by forcing nations with lower standards to raise them as by forcing nations with higher standards to lower them. While both have in fact occurred, the former has been more common than the latter. To the extent that trade liberalization has affected the level of consumer and environmental protection, it has more often strengthened than weakened it. There is, however, nothing automatic about this process. The impact of trade liberalization on regulatory standards is primarily dependent on the preferences of wealthy, powerful states and the degree of economic integration among them and their trading partners.

The notion that economic competition among political jurisdictions will lead to a regulatory "race to the bottom" has been labeled the "Delaware effect." This derives from the experience of the United States with corporate chartering.[2] Because corporate charters are given by an individual state and all states are legally required to recognize the legitimacy of one another's charters (an American version of mutual recognition), states have tended to compete with one another by liberalizing their chartering requirements. The state which has been most successful in this competition has been Delaware, whose corporate chartering law is generally considered the most responsive to the interests of management.

However, this book demonstrates that regulatory competition can lead to a rather different outcome. A number of national patterns of health, safety, and environmental regulation illustrate the "California effect," named for the state that has been on the cutting edge of environmental regulation, both nationally and globally, for nearly three decades.[3] The California effect refers to the critical role of powerful and wealthy "green" political jurisdictions in promoting a regulatory "race to the top" among their trading partners. Thus, just as California's relative size and wealth within the American economy has helped drive many American environmental regulations upward, so has Germany's relative size and wealth contributed to the strengthening of the European Union's regulatory standards. Both globally and within North America, the California effect has occurred primarily through the influence of the United States.

The Delaware effect assumes that stricter regulatory standards represent a source of competitive disadvantage. But, in contrast to labor standards, the costs of complying with stricter consumer and environmental standards has not been sufficiently large to force political jurisdictions to lower their standards in order to keep domestic firms or plants competitive. On the contrary: in the case of many environmental and consumer regulations, stricter standards represent a source of competitive *advantage* for domestic producers, in part because it is often easier for them to comply with them. Hence domestic producers often compete with firms from other political jurisdictions by raising rather than lowering their standards.

Equally significantly, when rich nations with large domestic markets such as the United States and Germany enact stricter product standards, their trading partners are forced to meet those standards in order to maintain their export markets. This in turn often encourages consumer or environmental organizations in the exporting country to demand similar standards for products sold in their domestic markets—a demand that internationally oriented producers are now more willing to support since their exports to greener markets already meet them.

Thus the disparity in national regulations is not only an ongoing source of trade tensions; it also represents a mechanism by which national standards can be driven upward. However, the role of greener markets in raising the regulatory standards of the nations with whom they trade is primarily confined to *product* standards. Trade liberalization, by itself, is less likely to strengthen domestic regulations governing how goods and natural resources are produced.

The impact of trade liberalization on regulatory standards is also affected by another factor: the degree of economic integration. The stronger the role of international institutions in promoting liberal trade policies, the more extensive the leverage of rich, powerful states over the regulatory powers of their trading partners. Thus it is precisely the EU's commitment to the creation of a single European market that has enabled Germany and its influential green pressure groups to exercise so much influence over the environmental policies of other member states. By contrast, because the GATT is a much weaker institution, the ability of a greener nation like the United States to affect the domestic regulatory policies of its trading partners has been much more limited. Unlike the EU, neither the GATT nor the WTO contains any legal mechanisms that would enable its most powerful members to strengthen the regulatory standards of other signatories.

NAFTA falls roughly in between. Like the EU, it subjects national environmental standards to extranational scrutiny: a nation can be disciplined either for not enforcing existing regulatory standards or for lowering them to attract investment. But compared to the EU, the institutions established by NAFTA have much less authority to harmonize regulatory standards within North America; NAFTA is essentially a trade agreement, albeit a relatively green one. It thus provides the United States with more opportunity to affect Mexican regulatory policies than America had under the GATT, but less than Germany has been able to exercise within the EU.

But it is important not to equate stricter standards with more effective regulations. Many environmental and consumer regulations contribute little or nothing to enhancing consumer or environmental protection. To the extent that these regulations have been successfully challenged through trade agreements and treaties, public welfare has been enhanced. However, efforts to remove trade barriers to promote economic integration have at times prevented greener nations from establishing regulations as strict as its citizens and producers would prefer. This book describes a number of such cases, primarily within the EU, but within the GATT has well.

At the same time, trade liberalization has also helped increase the leverage of NGOs and producers in greener countries over the regulatory policies of their trading partners. Thus the EU has significantly strengthened Germany's ability to shape the regulatory standards of Greece and Italy. A similar dynamic is likely to occur, albeit less dramatically, in North America. As a result of NAFTA, Mexican regulatory standards and their enforcement will be increasingly shaped by the preferences and influence of American producers and NGOs. Indeed, this has already occurred: American environmental organizations forced Mexico to strengthen both its environmental regulations and their enforcement as a condition for supporting trade liberalization.

Trade liberalization is most likely to *strengthen* consumer and environmental protection when a group of nations has agreed to reduce the role of regulations as trade barriers and the most powerful among them has influential domestic constituencies that support stronger regulatory standards. Thus, the stronger the commitment of nations to coordinate their regulatory policies, the more powerful is the California effect. Likewise, the weaker the institutions created by regional or international trade agreements or treaties, the weaker the California effect. Accordingly, the California effect has been most important within the EU and much less important within the GATT, with NAFTA falling in between.

Explaining Increased Interdependence

Trade and regulatory linkages are not new. As long as protective regulations have existed, they have affected trade, either indirectly by influencing the composition of imports and exports, or directly by determining the standards that imported products must meet. Moreover, the use of regulations as trade barriers has a long history. For example, through the 1920s the United States had enacted about a dozen federal laws that used trade restrictions to advance environmental objectives.[4] An 1897 statute prohibited the importation of wild animals or birds except under permit, while 1905 legislation forbade the importation of pests injurious to crops, forests, or "shade trees." The following year, the United States banned the import of sponges from the Gulf of Mexico that had been gathered by methods which harmed the sponge beds. The Underwood Tariff of 1913 prohibited the importation of plumes and feathers from specified wild birds, while the Alaska Fisheries Act of 1926 made it unlawful to import salmon caught in ways that violated American fishing regulations.

Food production and processing standards have also long restricted international trade. For example, in the late nineteenth century, American meats were banned from Italy, France, and Germany because of inadequate American sanitary standards for meat processing. During the 1930s the United States, anxious to protect the American cattle industry, banned all imports of Argentine beef following an outbreak of hoof and mouth disease in that country. The country-wide ban remained in place even after the disease had been confined to a few local areas. Notwithstanding the trade liberalization of the postwar period, the use of regulatory standards as trade barriers has persisted. Innumerable Japanese product, certification, and inspection standards have restricted access to the Japanese market. Likewise, European standards for products ranging from household appliances to bread, beer, and pasta long functioned as import barriers within western Europe as well as internationally.

Yet it is only relatively recently that consumer and environmental regulations have emerged as an important and continuing focus of trade conflicts, negotiations, and agreements. Why? The increasingly important contemporary linkages between trade and protective regulation reflect the convergence of three developments: the increase in regional and international efforts to promote economic integration, the growth in the number of health, safety, and environmental regulations, and the expansion of international trade itself.

The seven rounds of GATT negotiations prior to the Uruguay Round reduced tariffs by nearly 75 percent, while they have been eliminated within western Europe and are being phased out in North America. Accordingly, the relative importance of nontariff trade barriers (NTBs) such as health, safety, and environmental regulation has increased.

The greater the commitment to economic integration, the more trade agreements will intrude upon domestic policies. Efforts to limit the ability of protective regulations to restrict trade can thus be seen as part of a broader effort to address other NTBs such as public sector procurement, the protection of property rights, and restrictions on direct foreign investment—each of which extends the scope of trade policies and agreements to policy areas that were formally controlled exclusively by national governments. Not surprisingly, this chipping away of national sovereignty over environmental and consumer protection policies is most advanced in the EU, whose member states have also made the most extensive effort to create a single market. But both NAFTA and the Uruguay Round GATT agreement also seek to reduce the role of national regulations as NTBs in order to promote trade.

The second development is an increase in health, safety, and environmental regulations themselves. The last three decades have witnessed a significant expansion of government regulations which directly affect traded goods. These include regulations for automobile emissions; the content and disposal of packaging; chemical safety; the processing, composition, and labeling of food; and the protection of wildlife and natural resources. The growth of protective regulation has frequently forced exporters to cope with a diverse array of product standards, while many national regulations, such as those governing the shipment of hazardous waste or recycling, are inherently trade restrictive. While in general national regulatory standards have become stronger, especially in the developed nations among whom most world trade and investment occurs, nations continue to vary in their regulatory goals and in their specific means of achieving them. Since nations generally want to maintain their own standards in spite of— or sometimes because of—the burdens they impose on imports, the continual growth of national regulatory standards represents an ongoing source of trade conflict.

Not only has the amount of protective regulation steadily increased, but during the second half of the 1980s its scope broadened as well. A distinctive feature of many of the environmental issues that emerged during the 1980s was their global dimension. The protection of endangered species located in different countries or in international waters, the protection of the ozone layer, the reduction of environmental damage associated with the shipment and disposal of hazardous waste, and the preservation of tropical forests in less-developed nations all require nations to coordinate their regulatory policies. This coordination often includes restrictions on trade, either as a means of preventing "free-riding" or because the harm itself is trade-related. Nations have been making greater use of trade measures, whether formalized in international environmental agreements or imposed unilaterally, to influence the environmental polices of their trading partners.

The disparity in national regulatory standards, especially between rich and poor nations, has affected trade policies in another way: it has increased national differences in the cost of producing goods. Although these differences have had little measurable impact on patterns of international trade and investment, nonetheless many environmentalists worry that producers in nations with relatively strict standards will attempt to exploit these disparities in national regulatory standards by demanding that regulations be relaxed in order to enable them to remain competitive. Accordingly, they want international trade agreements to play a more active role in harmonizing national regulations, especially in the area of environmental protection. Not surprisingly, their proposals to "green the GATT" have been strongly opposed by less developed countries who fear the loss of export markets.

Third, the nearly sixty-fold expansion of international trade since 1950 has itself significantly affected public health, safety, and the physical environment. In a number of respects this expansion has improved environmental quality: it has promoted the dissemination of improved environmental technologies and encouraged the more efficient use of resources. Moreover, by increasing growth rates, it has made possible increased expenditures to improve environmental quality and expanded the market for greener products. Environmental quality in wealthier nations is measurably better than in poorer ones.[5]

But international trade has also exacerbated a number of environmental problems. In particular, the expansion of trade directly causes environmental damage; not only is the increased transportation of goods an important cause of pollution, but some goods shipped across national boundaries are inherently harmful, such as hazardous wastes. The expansion of international trade has also made it more difficult for governments to protect the health of their citizens, who are increasingly consuming goods produced in other countries. This is an especially serious problem with respect to agricultural products, always a politically sensitive area. The nearly ten-fold expansion of international trade in food between 1962 and 1993 has made the health of consumers much more dependent on the agricultural production and inspection practices of their nation's trading partners.

Moreover, as tariffs have declined and trade has increased, domestic regulatory policies are more likely to have international economic impacts. For example, in a relatively isolated domestic economy, a recycling regulation that encourages the use of bottles and discourages the use of cans makes domestic glass producers better off at the expense of domestic can manufacturers. But if both these commodities are freely traded, then this same regulation is also likely to affect the market share of producers in different nations. If foreign can producers have been disadvantaged, they will then complain to their governments, who in turn may challenge the recycling requirement as a trade barrier. The recycling requirement will, of course, be defended by both domestic bottle producers and environmentalists. Thus, the expansion of trade has itself made regulations into a more important source of trade conflicts.

The increasing importance of trade and regulatory linkages is reflected in the evolution of international treaties and trade agreements. Neither the original 1947 General Agreement on Tariffs and Trade nor the 1957 Treaty of Rome, which established the European Economic Community, mentions the word "environment." By contrast, the 1987 Single European Act explicitly addresses the relationship between the creation of the single market and European environmental standards, as does the 1993 Maastricht Treaty.

While the 1979 Tokyo Round GATT negotiations did address the role of technical standards as nontariff barriers through the Standards Code, the latter was not made part of the General Agreement itself; compliance remained voluntary. However, the Uruguay Round GATT agreement both expanded the scope of the Standards Code and incorporated it into the GATT itself, thus significantly expanding international scrutiny of domestic health and environmental standards.[6] Finally, the 1994 North American Free Trade Agreement among the United States, Mexico, and Canada, unlike the Free Trade Agreement between the United States and Canada which went into effect six years earlier, includes a Supplemental Agreement on the Environment.

The Internationalization of Regulation

Protective regulations are important for three reasons. Most obviously, they represent efforts to achieve a number of important public goals, such as protecting public health and improving environmental quality. Second, protective regulations have important macroeconomic consequences; they affect national rates of productivity growth, price and investment levels, and wage rates. Third, they politicize economic competition. Regulations rarely affect all firms equally; they usually make some better off and some worse off relative to their competitors. As Leone notes, "This simple fact is at the heart of the Iron Law of Public Policy: while government action may increase the costs of doing business, these cost increases are not the same for all competitors . . . differential costs of regulatory compliance can—and do—affect the competitiveness of individual firms."[7] Accordingly, firms often participate in the regulatory process in order to gain competitive advantages, or to resist the efforts of their competitors to do so.

Each of these three critical components of the regulatory process has an increasingly important international dimension. To begin with, many national regulatory policies also affect the health and welfare of other countries, or even the entire globe, thus blurring the distinction between domestic and international regulatory policies. Second, to the extent that national regulations affect the volume and composition of world trade, they influence the performance of the global as well as the domestic economy. Third, many national regulations, especially for traded goods, affect not only the competitive position of firms within a country, but between or among different countries. According to Luttwak, "Regulation is as much a tool of statecraft as military defenses ever were . . . the logic of state regulation is in part the logic of conflict."[8] Because national protective regulations often represent important sources of competitive advantage and disadvantage for firms competing in the global marketplace, national regulations also affect international competition and competitiveness.

For these reasons, the rules established by international institutions, treaties, and agreements that seek to govern the impact of national regulations on trade play a critical role in mediating between the domestic and international economy. They help determine the conditions under which both producers and nongovernmental organizations are able to influence both their own regulatory policies as well as those of their trading partners.

What Is a Nontariff Barrier?

Tariffs, by definition, distinguish between imported and domestic goods: a tariff is a product tax that only applies to imports. Many of the most economically important nontariff barriers also discriminate explicitly on the basis of the national origin of products or firms.

These include quotas, "voluntary" import and export controls, restrictions on foreign investment, and public procurement policies that favor domestic firms. By contrast, relatively few environmental and consumer regulations explicitly distinguish between producers or products on the basis of national origin. At least on the surface, most do not violate the key principle of free trade, which is nondiscrimination on the basis of country of origin, or "national treatment." However, many of these regulations do have the *effect* of creating barriers or obstacles to imports. But does this automatically make them nontariff barriers? How can trade agreements and treaties distinguish between necessary and unnecessary obstacles to trade? The answer to this question is essentially a political one.

An analogy can be made to the ongoing debate over the interpretation of American civil rights laws. Should only those laws or policies that explicitly distinguish among individuals on the basis of their race be considered discriminatory? Or should a law or policy also be defined as discriminatory if it has the *effect* of disadvantaging a particular group of people? Broadening the definition of a nontariff barrier represents an effort by supporters of trade liberalization to reduce the disadvantages currently experienced by many foreign producers in the same way that broadening the definition of discrimination represents an effort by civil rights activists to remedy the disadvantages experienced by various racial minorities.

And just as the definition of discrimination has important implications for the way American civil rights laws are enforced, so does the definition of a nontariff barrier have important consequences for both trade and regulatory policies. Proponents of trade liberalization tend to define NTBs relatively broadly, while proponents of stricter regulatory standards want them defined more narrowly. The former want to strengthen the ability of producers to challenge the regulatory policies of their trading partners, while the latter want to preserve the ability of nations with stricter standards to maintain them and, in some cases, impose them on their trading partners as well.

Consider the following extreme positions: If all regulations that disadvantaged importers were classified as nontariff barriers, then virtually all regulations could be considered protectionist. For example, the United States could not require that all product labels be printed in English, since this requirement clearly imposes additional costs upon foreign producers (or at least those from non-English speaking countries). Likewise, Singapore would be forced to rescind its ban on the sale of chewing gum, since this regulation clearly serves as a barrier to the import of Wrigley's products. In short, defining NTBs very broadly would have the effect of subjecting virtually all national regulatory standards to those of the least stringent exporting country. At the same time it would probably significantly expand international trade.

The consequences of defining nontariff barriers very narrowly are equally significant. A nation could demand that all imported products be produced according to the same standards to which domestic producers are required to adhere. Thus the United States could refuse to permit the imports of any cars, steel, or chemicals produced in facilities that violated American standards for factory emissions, land-use controls, or, for that matter, family-leave policies. If such a regulation was *not* considered a nontariff barrier, and was widely adopted, international trade would decline significantly. On the other hand, many nations might be to forced to upgrade their regulatory standards to match those prevailing in countries to whose markets they wanted access.

Few would consider the first group of regulations to be nontariff barriers, while most would consider the latter to be. However, none of these hypothetical examples explicitly discriminate between imported and domestic products; they hold both to identical standards. But where then should treaties and trade agreements draw the line? How should they distinguish between protective regulations that are actually disguised trade barriers and protective regulations which may have the same *effect* as disguised trade barriers but which nonetheless are necessary to protect the public's health, safety, and the physical environment? In other words, how can international institutions and trade agreements permit or promote environmental and consumer *protection* while limiting consumer and environmental *protectionism?*

The range of responses to these questions comprises much of the current debate over the impact of trade agreements and regulatory standards on one another. Different trade agreements answer these questions differently, and their answers have changed over time. Consider the following actual regulations, each of which led to a major trade dispute under one of the international agreements or treaties examined in this book:

- A German regulation bans the sale of liqueur with an alcoholic content of less than 25 percent. (Treaty of Rome)

- A regulation by the Canadian Province of Ontario imposes a 10 cent tax on beer sold in cans. (FTA)
- An American regulation prohibits the sale of tuna fish caught in ways that also kill large numbers of dolphins. (GATT)
- An EU regulation bans the sale of beef from cattle which have been fed growth hormones. (GATT Standards Code)

Each of these regulations has two things in common: they do *not* discriminate on the basis of national origin, and they *do* impose greater burdens on some importers. Specifically, these regulations disadvantaged producers of French liqueur, whose product had a low alcoholic content; American beer brewers, who shipped beer to Canada in cans because of transportation costs; Mexican tuna fishermen, whose fishing techniques and geography caused more dolphin deaths than those of American fishermen; and American cattlemen, who rely heavily on hormones to produce meat and meat products. Correspondingly, these regulations benefited German liquor producers, whose product contained a higher alcoholic content; Canadian brewers, who produced beer in bottles; American tuna fishermen, who had adopted fishing methods that reduced dolphin mortality; and European cattle farmers and beef producers, whose beef and beef products were produced without hormones.

In each case, the issue was not whether these regulations interfered with trade. It was rather whether the extent of their interference was *appropriate or necessary.* Thus, the Germans claimed that their high alcoholic content regulation helped prevent German consumers from developing an increased tolerance for alcohol; the Canadians argued that their tax promoted the use and reuse of glass containers, which both reduced littering and saved energy; the Americans contended that their restrictions on sales of "dolphin-unfriendly" tuna were necessary to protect the lives of intelligent marine mammals; and the EU justified its hormone ban on the grounds of consumer health and safety.

These and similar trade disputes have often led to a heated debate regarding the criteria for classifying regulations as nontariff barriers. This debate has revolved around a number of issues.

First, what standards of scientific proof should be required to justify a regulation that interferes with trade? In the case of the EU hormone ban, should the EU be obligated to prove that the consumption of meat from cattle which have been fed hormones is *unsafe,* or must the United States prove that meat from hormone-fed cattle is *safe?* In other words, what makes a regulation that restricts trade "necessary"? And on whom does the burden of proof of demonstrating that it necessary or unnecessary fall? Many protective regulations make no demonstrable contribution to either consumer or environmental protection, and they therefore can readily be rescinded or revised without adversely affecting public health or environmental quality. But in many other cases, there can be legitimate disagreement as to whether a regulation actually is necessary to protect public health or environmental quality.

Second, should the *intention* behind a regulation affect whether it is considered a nontariff barrier? While each of these regulations did benefit domestic producers, that was not necessarily the only or even the primary reason they were adopted. In the case of the American ban on imports of tuna from Mexico, American tuna fishermen neither asked for nor required import protection, since dolphin-safe tuna already commanded a substantial premium in the American market. The ban on tuna imports from Mexico came about as a result of a lawsuit filed by an American environmental organization. On the other hand, Ontario's beer-can tax was strongly backed by that province's beer bottlers as part of their long-standing effort to restrict imports of American beer, though it was supported by Canadian environmentalists as well.

In both the tuna and beer cases, the American position was that the purpose behind the regulation *did* matter. Based on this criterion, the Marine Mammal Protection Act *was not* a nontariff barrier because its primary objective was to protect dolphins, while the Ontario tax *was,* because its primary purpose was to protect the local beer bottling industry—as evidenced by the fact that the tax on cans did not extend to either soft drinks or food. Not surprisingly, their trading partners argued that the objectives of the regulations were not relevant for assessing their status as nontariff barriers. In addition, gauging intent is often difficult. While some regulations are simply disguised forms of protectionism, in many cases the motives behind a particular regulatory policy are complex. Thus, the EU's ban on the use of growth hormones was intended to protect small, inefficient farmers as well as European consumers.

Third, in enacting a regulation that affects trade, is a nation obligated to select the method of regulation that *least* restricts it? Thus if the United States could demonstrate that Ontario could accomplish the goals of its recycling program in a way that imposes fewer burdens on American beer exporters, does the tax on cans then constitute a nontariff barrier? Or is Ontario only obligated to demonstrate that its regulation is effective in achieving its goals? Similarly, if the United States could demonstrate that the health of European consumers could be adequately protected by a labeling requirement, does the EU ban then constitute an illegitimate interference with trade?

Fourth, should a nation be allowed to restrict the sale of a product on the basis of how it was produced outside its legal jurisdiction? Or is a nation only permitted to impose regulations on imports in order to protect its citizens or domestic environment? In other words, must a nation only hold imported *products* to the same standards as domestically produced ones, or can it also restrict or tax an imported product on the basis of how it was *produced,* that is, harvested, extracted, manufactured, or shipped by the citizens of another country?

This question was a central point of contention in the tuna-dolphin dispute between the United States and Mexico. On one hand, the tuna sold to American consumers that were caught by foreign fishing vessels using methods that also killed dolphins were identical in every respect to the tuna caught using dolphin-safe methods. On the other hand, the tuna differed in terms of the impact of their production methods on dolphin mortality. In its complaint against the United States, Mexico argued that the American regulation constituted an illegitimate interference with the domestic policies of a sovereign state; it claimed that the United States should not be permitted to restrict the imports of products from countries whose ways of producing them differed from its own. The United States in turn countered that its tuna processing standard was necessary to fulfill a legitimate conservation objective of the United States, namely dolphin protection. Accordingly, the nationality of the fishing vessels that injured dolphins was irrelevant.

Regulations and Trade Agreements

The concept of "proportionality" has frequently been employed to assess the legitimacy or legality of a regulation which restricts trade. This approach subjects national regulations that hamper the free movement of goods, but that do serve a legitimate public purpose, to a "balancing" or minimum-means test: it requires nations to select the means of achieving their regulatory objectives that do not "disproportionately" interfere with the free movement of goods. Accordingly, the benefits of a regulation must be weighed against the burdens it imposes on international commerce. This approach has been employed by the Supreme Court of the United States to interpret the interstate commerce clause of the Constitution, and by the European Court of Justice to interpret the Treaty of Rome and the Single European Act; variants of it have been incorporated into the texts of both the Uruguay Round GATT agreement, and NAFTA.

Proportionality can be regarded as the international application of cost-benefit analysis, which governments have frequently employed to assess the value or legality of domestic health, safety, and environmental laws. Both concepts seek to judge the value of a regulation by balancing its goals with its costs: cost-benefit analysis focuses on the costs of compliance to the domestic economy, proportionality on its costs to foreign producers and thus indirectly to domestic consumers as well.

Like cost-benefit analysis, however, the concept of proportionality is often difficult to apply in practice. For while the burdens imposed by a regulation on importers are readily apparent, assessing the value of a consumer or environmental regulation to the citizenry of the nation which enacted it often involves a more subjective judgment. How safe should processed beef be? How much recycling is necessary? How much protection should dolphins be accorded? And how much of a burden on commerce is each worth?

Since there is rarely a consensus on the answers to these questions within nations, it is not surprising that there has often been substantial disagreement among the governments, firms, and citizens of different countries. Many trade disputes reflect the different values nations attach to different policy objectives, as well as their willingness to interfere with markets to achieve them. As Martin Shapiro writes in connection with the EU: "There is simply no objective way of weighing the two pounds of reduced cancer risk to Frenchmen against the eight pounds of salami that Italy is blocked from selling to France. Proportionality is by its very nature in the eye of the beholder."[9]

These four cases also illustrate the kinds of consumer and environmental regulations that have frequently become the focus of trade disputes. Differences among national regulations for food labeling, processing, and composition represent a recurrent source of trade friction both within the EU and globally. National conservation policies in general and recycling requirements in particular are becoming an increasingly important source of trade conflicts within both the EU and North America. Finally, a number of trade disputes, such as the tuna-dolphin case, stem from the efforts of greener governments to make access to their domestic markets contingent upon changes in the environmental practices of their trading partners. Many, but by no means all, of these disputes pit developed against developing nations.

Baptists and Bootleggers

One important consequence of the growing linkages between trade and regulatory policies has been to create additional opportunities for alliances between producers and environmental and consumer organizations, or "Baptist–bootlegger" coalitions.[10] This phrase comes from study of the politics of prohibition in the United States: political support for keeping certain southern counties "dry" has come from both Baptists, who favor prohibition on moral grounds, and bootleggers, whose business depends on keeping alcohol sales illegal. Prohibition not only affects public morality but the market shares of legitimate and illegal alcoholic beverage producers and distributors. The battle over the rules governing the sale of alcoholic beverages thus has to do with both morality and markets.

Baptist–bootlegger alliances have long been a staple of domestic regulatory policy-making. For example, during the battle over the 1977 Clean Air Act Amendments, both environmentalists and eastern coal producers supported sulphur emission regulations that disadvantaged western coal companies. They have also, on occasion, affected regulatory and trade policies. The passage of the Federal Meat Inspection Act of 1906 was due to the combined efforts of American consumers, who were outraged by the meat processing practices they learned about from reading Sinclair's *The Jungle,* and large American meat processing firms, who wanted stricter federal meat inspection in order to convince the Europeans to reopen their markets—an early example of the role of international trade in strengthening product standards for traded goods.[11]

Some protective regulations disadvantage domestic producers vis-à-vis their international competitors who do not face the same regulations. This is most likely to occur in the case of production standards which may raise the relative costs of producing goods or harvesting crops and natural resources. These regulations present domestic producers with two political choices: they can either demand that the regulations be relaxed, or they can seek to impose them on their foreign competitors through international agreements or import restrictions.

If they choose the first strategy, environmental and consumer groups will oppose them; this is the classic pattern of much of domestic regulatory politics. But if they choose either of the second alternatives, they are likely to be supported by NGOs. The latter have tended to be sympathetic to the arguments of domestic producers that it is "unfair" for them to be forced to compete with foreign competitors who are subject to less stringent production standards. Moreover, environmental organizations often support the use of trade restrictions as a way of pressuring other countries to strengthen their regulatory standards.

However, many protective regulations make domestic producers *better off* vis-à-vis their foreign competitors to the extent that it is easier or less expensive to comply with them; this is most likely to occur in the case of product standards. In this case, domestic producers and NGOs also have similar interests. Both want to defend domestic product regulations that also serve as obstacles to importers. Consequently, many trade disputes over regulatory issues pit coalitions of NGOs and domestic producers against foreign producers.

For producers who wish to maintain or increase trade barriers, the convergence of trade and regulatory policies provides them with two significant political benefits. First, it furnishes them with an argument for trade restrictions that has relatively wide political appeal: consumer or environmental protection. They can argue against the removal of trade barriers on similar grounds. Second, it provides them with an important new source of political support, as consumer and environmental organizations enjoy considerable influence in a number of capitalist nations.

At the same time, the convergence of trade and regulatory policies also provides an important political benefit for environmental and consumer organizations: it provides them with allies from the business community in their effort to promote stricter regulatory standards. Domestic producers are more likely to support more stringent regulations if the costs of complying with them fall disproportionately on their international competitors, or if they can be imposed on foreign producers as well. In short, Baptist–bootlegger coalitions can not only increase bootleggers' profits, they can also help Baptists save souls. Such alliances appear frequently throughout this book, demonstrating the critical and complex role of domestic interests in affecting international conflicts over national regulatory standards.

The Organization of This Book

This book is organized around the most important regional and international treaties and agreements that govern trade. It evaluates each of them in terms of their impact on both shaping regulatory standards and reducing the role of protective regulations as nontariff barriers.

It begins by examining the relationship between trade and regulatory policies in the European Union. Not only does the EU has the longest and most extensive experience of any international institution in attempting to reconcile protective regulation and economic integration, but the means it has chosen for doing so have influenced other trade agreements as well. Chapter 2 examines EU regulatory policies in the critical area of food safety and processing, while Chapter 3 traces the relationship between the removal of internal trade barriers and environmental standards for traded goods. The experience of the EU demonstrates the critical role that powerful international institutions can play in both removing trade barriers *and* strengthening regulatory standards. At the same time, it demonstrates the endless difficulties of reconciling these two policy objectives.

The next two chapters turn to a much weaker international institution, the GATT. Chapter 4 focuses on the relationship between environmental regulation and the GATT. It begins with an extensive discussion of the tuna-dolphin case and its implications for both trade and regulatory policies, and then explores the increasing number of trade disputes stemming from divergent national environmental standards and preferences. In part due to the wide political and economic differences among its more than 120 signatory nations, the GATT has found it much more difficult to address the linkages between trade and regulation. Yet notwithstanding the furor of environmentalists over the outcome of the tuna-dolphin case, the GATT has not prevented its signatories from steadily strengthening their regulatory standards.

Chapter 5 examines another regulatory dimension of the GATT. It focuses on the role of the Standards Code established during the Tokyo Round in limiting the use of food safety and processing standards as trade barriers. It begins with the EU's beef hormone ban and then discusses several trade conflicts surrounding Japanese food safety and agricultural production standards. The chapter concludes with an analysis of the likely impact of the Uruguay Round's provisions to strengthen international discipline over national sanitary and phytosanitary (S&P) standards, such as quarantine procedures, food processing and production measures, inspection rules, and pesticide tolerances. It argues that these provisions have the potential to play a useful role in restricting national regulatory standards that contribute little or nothing to public health and safety, but that they are less likely to resolve trade conflicts stemming from significant differences in national regulatory preferences.

Chapter 6 examines the relationship between trade and regulatory policies from a different perspective: it describes the increasing importance of Baptist–bootlegger coalitions within American domestic politics and assesses their impact on both trade and regulatory policies. The growing involvement of American public interest groups in American trade policies has strengthened political opposition to trade liberalization in the United States, although it has not prevented the United States from continuing to enter into new trade agreements.

Chapter 7 focuses on the two agreements to promote trade liberalization within North America, the FTA and NAFTA. Both agreements were opposed by a number of environmental organizations who feared they would undermine national consumer and environmental standards. However, the FTA has not weakened either American or Canadian regulatory standards, and NAFTA is more likely to strengthen Mexican regulatory standards than undermine American ones.

The concluding chapter explores the conditions under which liberal trade policies and stronger regulatory standards are likely to reinforce one another.

-2-

Protectionism versus Consumer Protection in Europe

As the most important and ambitious effort of the postwar period to reduce national trade barriers, the experience of the European Community and its successor, the Union, illustrates the close relationship between regulatory and trade policies. In order to create a single market, the EU has had to limit the ability of its member states to enforce regulations that restrict the import of products produced elsewhere in the Union. At the same time, it has also found itself under considerable political pressure to prevent the creation of the single market from undermining consumer protection. To manage the complex and often conflicting relationship between these policy objectives, the Union has come to play an increasingly important role in the shaping of consumer regulation—an area of public policy that was formerly the responsibility of national governments.

This chapter details several case studies of the Union's efforts to reconcile economic integration and consumer protection in the food sector, which includes food products, beverages, and agricultural products. The food sector is the biggest contributor of jobs and value-added of all EU industries, accounting for slightly more than 4 percent of the EU's GNP.[1] It is also closely linked to a number of other significant components of the economy of the EU's member states, including agriculture, transportation, and retail distribution. Public policies toward this sector thus directly and indirectly affect the competitive position of large numbers of producers and merchants throughout the Union.

At the same time, the food sector has long been closely regulated by national governments. All EU member states have had long-standing and extensive rules and regulations governing the labeling, packaging, composition, and processing of food products. These regulations reflect not only distinctive national customs and traditions but the need to protect consumer health and safety as well. Many, though, also serve to protect domestic producers.

Because the food sector is both extensively regulated by national governments and important economically, creating a single market for food, beverages, and agricultural products has long been an important priority and challenge for the Community. Indeed, as Paul Gray notes, "The food sector has always been the trailblazer of policy making in creating the internal market."[2] The EC's very first directive, issued in 1962, specified the colorings permitted in foodstuffs. The key decision of the European Court which established the principle of mutual recognition in 1979 involved a food product, Cassis de Dijon. Through 1988, more than half of the cases brought before the European Court which alleged violations of the Treaty of Rome's restrictions on "quantitative barriers to imports" had to do with national food and beverage regulations. Of the 300 regulations listed in Lord Cockfield's 1985 White Paper as requiring action by the European Council of Ministers in order to complete the creation of an internal market by 1992, nearly one-third involved the elimination of restrictions on trade in food, beverages, animals, and plants.

The Legal Framework of EU Regulation

A central purpose of the establishment of the European Community in 1957 was to permit the free movement of goods among its six member states. Article 30 of the Treaty of Rome states that "Quantitative restrictions on imports and all other measures having equivalent effect shall . . . be prohibited between Member States."[3] These restrictions have been defined by the European Court as encompassing "all trading rules enacted by Member States which are capable of hindering, directly or indirectly, actually or potentially, intra-Community trade," or what economists term "cost-increasing barriers."[4] Article 100 empowers the Council of the European Community to "issue directives for the approximation of such provisions laid down by law, regulation or administrative action in member states as directly affect the establishment or functioning of the common market."[5] These two articles pursue different objectives, but are essentially complementary: the purpose of the former is to remove national tariff and nontariff barriers while the latter seeks to reduce "obstacles of whatever kind arising from disparities between [nations]."[6]

However, the Rome treaty also includes a provision that explicitly limits the purview of Article 30. Article 36 permits member states to restrict or even ban imports, exports, or goods in transit if such restrictions are necessary for reasons of "public morality, public policy or public security" or for "the protection of health and life of humans, animals or plants."[7] But these restrictions or bans cannot "constitute a means of arbitrary discrimination or a disguised restriction on trade between member states."[8] Thus these two articles implicitly create an EC free trade balancing test.[9] They permit a member state to maintain regulations that restrict trade, provided it can justify them.

As a response to increased public demands for additional health, safety, and environmental regulation in western Europe during the 1970s, the EC subsequently expanded its interpretation of Article 100. Rather than restricting its directives to rules and regulations that were necessary to promote intracommunity trade, the Community issued an increasing number of directives whose purpose was to improve the health, safety, and welfare of its citizens.[10] This change in emphasis was made official by the Single European Act (SEA), which came into effect on July 1, 1987. This amendment to the Treaty of Rome explicitly acknowledged the Community's commitment both to improve the quality of the physical environment and to enhance consumer protection—as well as to pursue the EC's original purpose of promoting economic integration.

The Community thus moved from "negative" harmonization, whose purpose is to remove national obstacles to trade, to "positive" harmonization, whose objective is to make the legal systems of the member states consistent with the broader political and social goals of the Community. In a sense, the EC employed Article 100 in much the same manner that the United States has interpreted the interstate commerce clause of the Constitution. Originally intended to provide Congress with the authority to prevent the states from restricting commerce among themselves—as they had done under the Articles of Confederation—it has subsequently been employed to justify a wide variety of "positive" federal regulations, ranging from nondiscrimination in employment to air and water quality standards.

Early Harmonization

By the middle of the 1960s, tariffs among the member states of the Community had been virtually eliminated. Accordingly, in May 1969 the EC's Council of Ministers began to turn its attention to the removal of nontariff or "technical" barriers to trade. The EC decided to rely on its powers under Article 100 to harmonize national regulations. As a Community document stated: "A national legal act in principle calls for a Community legal act."[11] The Council established a detailed schedule for the adoption of forty-two directives designed to ensure free trade in foodstuffs.

The Community's initial efforts to harmonize food regulations met with some success. For example, the EC's first directive in 1962 reduced the number of food colors permitted in the (then six) member states by 60 percent. At the time the directive was heralded as much as a triumph for diplomacy as for consumer protection.[12] However, subsequent progress was extremely slow, in part because of the provision of the Treaty of Rome that all Council legislation had to be approved unanimously. Between 1962 and 1979 the Commission managed to adopt only nine directives. It took fourteen years of negotiations to adopt a directive specifying the composition of fruit jams, jellies, marmalades, and chestnut puree, while it spent eleven years working on a directive on mineral water.

One important reason for the difficulty in harmonizing food standards was the wide divergence in national customs, traditions, and regulations, which were often the product of centuries of distinctive patterns of food production and consumption. For example, in the case of bread, some nations permitted the long shelf-life "Anglo-Saxon" loaf designed for use in the English sandwich, while in other countries bread was purchased on a daily basis. Developing a standard that could be applied to both proved extremely difficult. Each nation's bread producers wanted a standard that conformed to its current practices; none wanted a standard that would open up their market to bread produced in other member states. As one observer put it, the concept of "Eurobread" was like "trying to cross a baguette with a loaf of pumpernickel."[13]

Similarly, the German beer law, *Reinheitsgebot*, reflected standards that embodied the "state of the art" for beer production in one region of Germany in 1516 and which had been modified only slightly since.

Other nations brewed beer very differently; most included various additives that were prohibited by German law. One pundit observed that "the Belgians throw into their beers apples, wheat, anything that's not tied down."[14] Not surprisingly, it proved impossible for German and Belgian brewers to agree on the appropriate composition of "Eurobeer." The same was true of jam: the Dutch preferred smooth jam, the French, chunky jam, while the British liked marmalade. In many cases, distinctive national labeling requirements continued to restrict the sale of products made according to "foreign" standards.

Moreover, the EC's effort to standardize such products as bread, beer, and biscuits throughout Europe made it into an object of derision. The Community was accused of trying to force everyone to eat "Eurobland" food made with "Eurorecipes." In addition, the rigidity of those compositional standards on which the Community was able to agree threatened to undermine technical progress in what was a highly dynamic and innovative industry. One industry observer wrote in 1979 that "the result of [the] EEC food law harmonization program seems merely to burden us with regulations of unnecessary complexity, without benefiting consumers or manufacturers or helping trade."[15] The publication Eurofood added: "At its worst harmonization can damage companies, forcing them to give up long standing and harmless production systems and ingredients. At best harmonization . . . can be restrictive to new developments in the food industry."[16]

The Community also faced another obstacle: the wide divergence of national food safety standards. For example, while British poultry producers traditionally used arsenic in chicken-feed, French law prohibited the sale of eggs from arsenic-fed chickens, even though eggs produced in Britain contained no arsenic residues. In the case of food additives, some nations employed a positive list (only specifically approved additives were permitted), while others employed a negative list (any additive could be used unless specifically prohibited).[17] These differences were compounded by the divergence of national eating habits and recipes. For example, the British, whose citizens consumed relatively large amounts of processed food, permitted the extensive use of food additives, while the French, who purchase more fresh food, had more restrictive laws.[18]

Moreover, while the Community was making relatively little progress in harmonizing existing national food regulations, the number of such regulations was increasing. Some were inspired by producers seeking to insulate themselves from competition from foodstuffs and agricultural products produced in other member states.[19] For example, the French banned drinks with sugar substitutes in order to protect their domestic sugar-beet industry, thus preventing the emergence of a European diet soft-drink industry.[20] Other regulations were a response to the public's heightened demand for health and safety regulations—a development that was also occurring in the United States at about the same time.[21]

The result was that the Community's tariff-free internal market was becoming increasingly fragmented by a proliferation of nontariff barriers. By the end of the 1970s it was apparent that not only had the effort to create a common market in food and beverages lost much of its earlier momentum, but on a number of dimensions it appeared to have reversed course. Nor was this sector unique. Thanks in part to the economic recession of the late 1970s, "there were more nontariff barriers resulting from divergences in national regulations in the early 1980s than when the harmonization policy of the EC was initiated in the 1960s."[22]

In 1980, the EC's administrative body, the European Commission, conceded that the goals established in its 1969 General Program of eliminating technical barriers to trade had been unrealistic. It specifically noted that "in the foodstuffs sector progress has been less spectacular [than in industrial products] largely because of the structure of the food industry."[23] The Commission's food directives still covered only a relatively small portion of the food products consumed within the Community. The result was that "new products had to be adapted to pass a complex maze of different safety and technical standards for each European country."[24] This outcome, of course, was precisely the opposite of that intended by the Community's proponents: the European food market had become even more fragmented, the profit margins of European food processors had decreased, and consumers were confronted with higher costs.[25] Notwithstanding all of the EC's efforts, "foodstuffs constitute[d] the area most hampered by nontariff barriers to trade."[26]

Mutual Recognition

An important step in breaking this logjam was provided by the European Court in its 1979 decision in *Rewe-Zentral AG v. Bundesmonopolverwaltung für Branntwein* or, as the case is commonly known, *Cassis de Dijon*. Cassis de Dijon is a low alcohol (15–20 percent) black-currant liqueur produced in France that is commonly used in the mixing of kir. A German firm wanted to import this liqueur into Germany, but was refused a license to do so on the grounds that in 1922 German law required that all beverages defined as "liqueurs" have a minimum alcohol content of 25 percent. The German government justified this regulation on public health grounds: it argued that Cassis de Dijon threatened the health of German consumers because alcoholic drinks with low alcoholic content induced excessive consumption, thereby creating an increased tolerance for alcohol.

The Court acknowledged that under Article 36, "obstacles to movement within the Community resulting from disparities between national laws . . . must be accepted insofar as . . . [they are] necessary in order to satisfy mandatory requirements relating in particular to . . . the protection of public health . . . and the defense of the consumer."[27] The question before the Court was whether the German regulation was in fact necessary to satisfy one of these "mandatory requirements."

The Court concluded that the German minimum alcoholic content requirement served no legitimate public or national interest. Not only was the German regulation not essential to protect consumers—since other, less trade-restrictive measures, such as a labeling requirement, were available—but, as the Court noted, German consumers often added water to their liqueur to dilute it. Accordingly, since the German regulation had the "equivalent effect" of a "quantitative restriction on imports," and no legitimate health or safety rationale, it violated Article 30.[28]

It is important to note that the Court struck down the German product regulation even though it did not discriminate on the basis of national origin: it applied equally to imported and domestically produced goods. The Court thus interpreted the standard of "equivalent effect" rather broadly, defining it as "any national measure capable of hindering, directly or indirectly, actually or potentially, intra-community trade."[29] In other words, "the test of 'equivalent effect,' is not whether a measure discriminates against imports, but whether it restricts them."[30] This represented an important change in EC policy, since five years earlier the Commission had stated that nondiscriminatory measures were *not* to be considered violations of Article 30. By broadening the definition of a nontariff barrier, *Cassis* marked a significant tightening of the Community's scrutiny of national regulatory policies.

The Court did recognize that in the absence of "common rules" (harmonization), all member states had the right "to regulate all matters relating to . . . production and marketing . . . in their own territory."[31] Thus, Germany was free to require that liquor produced in Germany have any minimum alcohol content it wanted. But what it could not do was impose that requirement on liquor lawfully produced in another member nation. In other words, *Cassis* did not require that any nation change its domestic laws; it only restricted their scope to domestic producers.

This decision made explicit the concept of "mutual recognition": while nations remained free to maintain and enforce their own regulations for products produced within their jurisdiction, they could not prevent their citizens from consuming products that met the legal standards of another member state. In the words of the Court: "There is therefore no valid reason why, provided that they have been lawfully produced and marketed in one of the Member States, alcoholic beverages should not be introduced in any other state."[32] Following *Cassis,* a member state seeking to justify a regulation that hinders intra-Community trade on health and safety grounds has the burden of demonstrating both that its regulation achieves a legitimate public purpose and that it has employed the least trade restrictive means of doing so. Otherwise, mutual recognition applies.

The principles articulated in *Cassis* exposed a wide variety of national regulatory standards to judicial scrutiny. The following year the court ruled that an Italian regulation prohibiting the sale of all products labeled "vinegar" other than wine vinegar violated Article 30. It concluded that the purpose of Italy's regulation was to favor a national product, namely, wine vinegar. By not allowing vinegars made from apple cider or malt to be sold under the same product designation, Italy had placed products produced in other member states at an unfair disadvantage. Also in 1980, in *Kelderman,* the Court struck down a Dutch ban on imports of French "brioches" which had been justified on the grounds that their dry matter content did not conform to Holland's "Bread Order" or *Broodbesluit.* The Court reasoned that consumers could easily be informed of the bread's composition by means which were less trade-restrictive, "such as requiring labelling showing, for example, the weight and specific composition of an

imported product."[33] In *Sandoz,* the Court extended the *Cassis* principle to products which were lawfully sold in another member state,
even though they were not originally produced there.[34]

The Impact of Cassis

The *Cassis de Dijon* decision proved to be extremely significant because it provided those Community officials and European producers
who favored integration with an administratively viable strategy for
achieving it: national trade barriers could be reduced without going
through the time-consuming and cumbersome process of harmonizing
all national regulations. In contrast to harmonization, mutual recognition minimized the scope of national regulatory powers that had to
be transferred to the Community. Nor did it require extensive negotiations among national regulatory officials. Rather, all it required was
that the scope of national regulation over imports be limited to those
standards that met the Court's tests. Mutual recognition thus made
economic integration possible without replacing national regulations
with Community ones. In this sense it represented a form of "negative
integration." Indeed, it was the Commission's appreciation of the
deregulatory implications of *Cassis* that helped lay the groundwork
for the amendments to the Treaty of Rome contained in the Single
European Act of 1987.

The response to *Cassis* reflected the significant impact of mutual
recognition on the competitive position of European food producers.
It was greeted with enthusiasm by large producers, who perceived the
economic benefits of meeting one rather than twelve regulatory standards, as well as by some smaller producers, such as the French exporters of Cassis, who wanted access to the markets of other member
states. By contrast, producers who enjoyed a dominant position in
their domestic markets by virtue of distinctive national product standards strongly opposed *Cassis.* Among the decision's most vigorous
critics were Italian pasta producers and German beer companies. They
unsuccessfully lobbied their national governments to challenge the
Commission's support for the principle of mutual recognition.

The opposition of protectionist producers to *Cassis* was echoed by
the Bureau of European Consumer Unions (BEUC), though for different reasons. It expressed concern that the Commission would use
Cassis as a way of resolving the harmonization impasse in national

health and safety standards.[35] The BEUC feared that mutual recognition would lead to massive deregulation: EC consumers would find themselves exposed to products produced according to the standards of the least stringent national authority. The result would be a regulatory race to the bottom, with bad products driving out good ones.

In principle, this downward spiral could have been avoided by permitting nations to invoke the "exceptions clause" of Article 36. After all, *Cassis* only restricted the use of this article; it did not prohibit it. And in fact, following *Cassis,* the Court did uphold a number of national consumer protection laws that restricted imports. For example, in *Eyssen* (1980), the Court upheld a Dutch ban on the use of nisin in processed cheese on the grounds that since clear health risks had not yet been established for the maximum permissible daily intake of this preservative, the Dutch were entitled to restrict its use.

But relying on mutual recognition subject to judicial review was not a viable solution for several reasons. Politically, the Commission considered it important to assure consumers that progress toward the creation of a single European market would not result in any relaxation of consumer protection standards; it wanted consumers to perceive the creation of a common market as benefiting them by giving them wider choices and lower prices, not as making them worse off by possibly subjecting them to laxer health and safety standards. Moreover, from an economic point of view, allowing divergent national health and safety regulations—even if justified on public health grounds— would undermine many of the efficiency gains that the Commission hoped to achieve from the creation of the single market.

Thus mutual recognition, far from being a substitute for harmonization, had made it even more urgent.[36] At the same time, it also made harmonization considerably easier by limiting its scope to those consumer regulations that actually *did* affect the public's health and safety. As a Commission official noted in 1981, "There remains a need for harmonization programs but that harmonization will now apply over a narrower but better defined field."[37] In short, "harmonization would begin where liberalization left off."[38] This approach was strongly endorsed by Europe's export-oriented producers, who strongly favored uniform health and safety standards. As the British Food and Drink Industries Council put it, "There are still those national laws to which *Cassis de Dijon* principles cannot apply and for which harmonization will remain the only way forward."[39]

The White Paper

In 1985, still frustrated by the slow rate at which nontariff trade barriers were being removed in a variety of sectors—food being one of the more important—the Commission decided that a new approach was called for. The EC's Commissioner for Trade and Industry, Lord Cockfield, produced a White Paper on Completing the Internal Market.[40] It observed that national technical standards had recently increased, due to both technical developments and increasing concern for environmental, health, safety, and consumer protection regulations. Whatever their intentions, one of their results was to "protect domestic products against international competition . . . Barriers created by different national product regulations and standards have a double-edged effect: they not only add extra costs, but they also distort production patterns, increase unit costs, increase stockholding costs, discourage business cooperation, and fundamentally frustrate the creation of a common market for industrial products."[41]

The White Paper explicitly noted that one form of regulatory competition was inappropriate: nations should not compete over standards that might adversely affect the public's health and safety or environmental quality. In these "essential" areas, harmonization was necessary. In addition, harmonization was required to remove fiscal barriers consisting of differences in value-added tax (VAT) and excise duties, physical barriers caused by border controls, as well as national procurement policies. The White Paper listed almost 300 separate measures that the EC needed to harmonize to eliminate nontariff barriers to trade in goods, services, people, and capital. More than one-third of these measures covered veterinary and plant controls and food safety, composition, and processing standards. The report also specified a timetable for the Community to legislate on each measure; all were to be completed by the end of 1992.

The New Approach

A more detailed document than the White Paper entitled "Completion of the Internal Market: Community Legislation on Foodstuffs," was released the same year. Its main purpose was to distinguish between those regulations that required Community legislation and those that could be left to mutual recognition by the member states. As a senior

EC official subsequently noted, "It is not a case of applying the minimum rule but of applying the necessary rules, and applying them more strictly than in the past."[42] In practice this meant that the Commission would now officially abandon its clearly fruitless effort to specify the composition of foodstuffs; there would be no more attempts to create Eurobread or Eurobeer. Following *Cassis,* compositional standards would primarily be addressed by mutual recognition, thus respecting Europe's culinary diversity. Future Community legislation in the area of foodstuffs would be limited to those rules and regulations that were "essential" or "genuinely necessary" to protect health, provide consumers with adequate information, ensure fair trading, and provide for necessary public controls.[43] Based on these criteria, the Commission specified six areas that required Community legislation: food additives, materials and articles in contact with foodstuffs, foodstuffs for particular nutrition uses, labeling, some manufacturing processes, and official inspection. In each of these areas, the Council planned to preempt national rules and regulations.

Equally importantly, the Commission outlined a new approach that it hoped would expedite the approval of directives in these "essential" areas. Instead of issuing detailed regulations that in the past had become the subject of interminable negotiations by national officials, the Council would promulgate directives that established a "framework" or "general reference to standards." These would cover "essential requirements" such as health and safety standards, but would not encompass product specifications. (A precedent for this approach had been established by the Low Voltage Directive of 1973, which had defined EC safety requirements, but then left it up to a private standards-setting body, the European Committee for Standardization, to draw up detailed specifications.) The specific task of implementing these framework directives would then be left to the Commission, working in cooperation with national regulatory officials and scientific experts, or in some cases would be delegated to private standards-setting bodies.[44]

In 1986 the Council required the Commission to consult with the Scientific Committee on Food, composed of fifteen scientific and technical experts, before making decisions that affected the public's health; previously, the SCF's role had been advisory. One important purpose of this consultation requirement was to help implement a critical provision of the Single European Act, adopted the following year, namely, that in developing proposals in the area of consumer and environmental protection, the Commission should "take as a base a high level of protection."[45] The mandatory system of consultation was intended to assure consumers that appropriate scientific criteria were being applied by an independent body, and that harmonization would therefore *not* lead to a reduction in food quality.[46] This requirement further brought EC regulatory policy-making in line with those of its member states, most of whose regulatory authorities relied on the advice of similar independent or quasi-governmental committees. The Commission subsequently developed a set of cooperative arrangements with several national scientific institutes in order to exchange relevant scientific information and avoid duplication of effort among national regulatory authorities.

The SEA further simplified the Community's regulatory decision-making processes by abandoning the unanimity rule for legislation whose purpose was to remove obstacles to intra-EC trade. Now, only a "qualified majority," defined as fifty-four of seventy-six votes from at least eight member states (there were now twelve), was required to approve Council directives taken under Article 100A.* Equally important, by defining the Community's legal objective as the creation of "an area without internal frontiers in which the free movement of goods, persons, services and capital is ensured," the Single European Act created a "Blueprint for 1992," the symbolic date for the creation of a single European market.[47]

To reinforce the significance of this deadline, the SEA granted the Council the option of declaring, by qualified majority, that all national laws, regulations, and administrative practices that had not been harmonized by the end of 1992 "must be recognized as equivalent," thus potentially significantly expanding the scope of *Cassis*.[48] It also specifically authorized the Commission to challenge in the European Court all national regulations that fell short of the permissible exceptions to the single market outlined in Article 36. Both the White Paper and the SEA thus represented an important political triumph for those segments of the European business community that favored the removal of internal trade barriers.

At the same time, the SEA also sought to soften both the deregula-

---

*Under the SEA, the votes of each member state in the Council of Ministers vary, in part based on their population.

tory implications of mutual recognition and the centralizing implications of harmonization. Thus, Article 100A provided that harmonization measures approved by the Council may include clauses specifically authorizing national exceptions to Community-wide standards. It also repeated the exceptions outlined in Article 36 of the Treaty of Rome, which permitted member states to maintain national regulations needed to protect the health and life of humans. More importantly, Article 100a(4) went a step beyond Article 36 by permitting member states to "write new exceptions even after harmonization occurs," although these would be subject to Community scrutiny.[49]

To create additional political momentum for the creation of a single market, in 1988 the Commission released a report describing the economic benefits that would flow from the removal of all trade barriers.[50] The Cecchini Report, named after the EC commissioner who prepared it, cited the foodstuffs sector as one that was especially likely to benefit from the removal of trade barriers.[51] The report estimated that the removal of national trade barriers would reduce industry's costs by between 2 and 3 percent, or approximately 500–1000 million Ecu (approximately 550 to 1100 million dollars) per year. It specifically identified 218 NTBs that were preventing the creation of a single European market in food and beverages. Most took one of four forms: specific import restrictions, packaging and labeling laws, specific ingredient restrictions, and content and denomination regulations.

Among the most significant trade barriers cited in the Cecchini Report were national regulations that restricted the vegetable fat content of ice cream and chocolate, and a variety of national beef and pasta purity laws. Two of these barriers alone—restrictions on vegetable fat in chocolate and ice-cream—accounted for 40 percent of nontariff barriers in the food sector. A background study for the Cecchini Report characterized the Italian Pasta Purity Law, which reserved the generic name "pasta" for products made wholly from hard durum wheat grown only in the south of Italy, as a "technical barrier to intra-EC trade masquerading as an innocent product recipe."[52] It predicted that its abolition would save Italian consumers between 20–60 million Ecu (approximately 22 to 66 million dollars) between 1987 and 1992. The Report stated that the benefits to consumers that would result from the creation of a genuine common market in food and beverages included less expensive pasta products in Italy and

France, a wider range of imported beers in Germany, lighter beers in Italy and Spain, and the availability of diet soft drinks in France and Spain.[53]

Progress toward Harmonization

The Community's new approach to the removal of nontariff barriers significantly increased the rate at which directives were approved by the Council. Between 1985 and 1989, more than forty-five food-related directives were approved. By December 1992 the Council had completed action on 92 percent of the measures listed in the White Paper as essential for the creation of the single market. Seventy-five of eighty-one measures to remove veterinary and food processing standards had been adopted, as had eighteen out of nineteen proposals in the area of food law harmonization. Of the directives approved by the Council, 79 percent had been implemented into national legislation.

One of the most important framework directives approved by the Council regulated the use of food additives within the EC. This directive instructed the Commission to propose a "comprehensive directive" that would specify a list of approved additives as well as the conditions for their use. Approved additives were to be granted an "E" label. Once the Commission had completed its list, only additives included on it were to be permitted in the EC. Firms seeking approval of additional additives could then apply either to a member state or directly to the Commission. At the same time, no nation could prohibit the use of an additive that was included on the Commission's list. As of December 1992, the EC's Scientific Office, working with the SCF, had approved a total of 412 additives: all member states were required to permit their use, though EC rules also limit how much and in which foods they can be used.[54]

The Council also approved a directive establishing maximum levels for pesticide residues in cereals, fruit, and vegetables. Accordingly, no agricultural product can be kept out of a member state if it has less pesticide residue than the EC maximum.[55] The EC also approved directives designed to promote trade in meat, eggs, and milk; since 1989, heat-treated milk must satisfy various conditions before it can be sold in another EC state, while since in January 1992, the production of EC-traded eggs has had to conform to Community-wide standards. In 1985 the Council of Ministers voted to ban the use of all growth-promoting hormones in beef; previously the use of at least some of these hormones had been permitted by half the member states. This latter decision, which was enacted as a response to strong pressures from consumers and consumer organizations but which was also supported by small European beef farmers, embroiled the Community in a major trade dispute with the United States (see Chapter 5). The EC also prohibited throughout the Community the sale of milk from cows which had been fed growth hormones.

In order to prevent nations from enacting new nontariff barriers, in 1989 the EC issued a directive requiring member states to submit drafts of new technical regulations to the Commission, thus bringing the food sector in line with industry, whose introduction of new rules and technical standards had been subject to a similar restriction since 1983. The Commission was also given the authority to require member states to refrain from enacting national legislation while Community measures were being prepared or pending an assessment of their compatibility with Community law. Through 1991, the Commission had received 100 such requests, about one-third of which related to "recipe law." In most of these cases, the Commission has encouraged national governments either to use voluntary standards or to insert a "Cassis de Dijon" clause in national law, thus preserving the common market.[56]

The European Court

The European Court of Justice, which has become the world's most powerful judicial body after the American Supreme Court, has continued to play a critical role in reducing trade barriers in foods and beverages by enforcing the doctrine of mutual recognition. The most controversial and important case on national regulation of foodstuffs decided during the 1980s concerned the legality of the *Reinheitsgebot,* a German statute that prohibited the sale of any product labeled "bier" in the Federal Republic made with any ingredient other than malted barley, hops, yeast, and water. The oldest hygienic law in the world, the *Reinheitsgebot* had been originally enacted by the Bavarian Parliament in 1516; it was reissued in slightly modified form by the Federal Republic of Germany in 1952.

Regardless of its original purposes, the law now served to protect an extremely important German industry from international competition. In 1986 German per capita beer consumption was 148 liters (38.3 gallons) per year, the highest in the world. Yet less than 1 percent was imported, even though a number of other member states were large beer producers. In 1981 a French brewer complained to the European Commission that Germany was unfairly blocking the import of his product because it contained various additives which were permitted in France but not in Germany. The Commission agreed, and the following year it declared that the German regulation violated Article 30. Many Germans were furious: there were large public protests. Former Bavarian Minister-President Franz Josef Strauss characterized the Commission's "unacceptable attack on one of the world's oldest food legislation [as] a menace leading to the second loss of paradise."[57] The president of the German Brewers Association presented a petition signed by over two and a half million citizens in favor of maintaining the purity decree. The Commission was unmoved and, after Germany ignored a two-month deadline to comply, filed suit with the European Court.

In its decision issued six years later, on March 12, 1987, the Court acknowledged that as the Council had not yet completed its task of harmonizing additive regulations, member states maintained responsibility for determining which additives they wished to permit: they could chose to ban an additive entirely or limit its use for specific products. However, if a member state limited the import of a product containing an additive approved for use in another member state, it had to meet two tests: it had to prove that the additive was dangerous and that its restrictions on its use were "proportionate."

The Court concluded that the *Reinheitsgebot* fell short on both counts. German authorities had failed to present persuasive scientific evidence that the additives contained in imported beer were harmful. (All EC member states other than Germany and Greece permit brewers to use as many as twenty additives.) Indeed, some of the same additives authorized for beer in other member states were permitted in other German beverages—including German beer produced for export. The German rule also failed the proportionality test, since German law provided no mechanism by which importers could petition to allow specific additives to be permitted in beer sold in Germany. The Court, applying the principle of *Cassis,* observed that "while it is legitimate to seek to enable consumers who attribute specific qualities to beer manufactured from particular raw materials to make their choice in light of that consideration," this objective did not require restricting the designation "beer" to products made in a specific way; it could be achieved equally well by mandatory labeling requirements.[58]

Since *Reinheitsgebot,* the European Court has struck down a number of other long-standing national foodstuffs regulations. In 1988 the Court threw out Italy's restrictive pasta law, thus permitting imports of German pasta made with soft wheat.[59] The Italians responded by forming an alliance with Spain and Greece to lobby for a hard-wheat only directive, but their effort was unsuccessful. In 1989 the Court ruled that Germany could not protect the integrity of its *wursts* by banning the sale of foreign sausages made from nonmeat products such as milk, eggs, or soybeans; instead, it could only require that the ingredients of all *wurst* sold in Germany be clearly labeled.[60] The Court also ruled that France could not forbid the sale of nondairy imitation cream for desserts.[61]

National Cuisine

Few aspects of the EC's efforts to create a single market for food and beverages have been as controversial as its efforts to undermine long-standing national culinary standards. Notwithstanding the EC's decision to abandon its effort to impose "Eurorecipes," many Europeans remain convinced that the creation of the single market in foodstuffs threatens national culinary traditions. This anxiety was dramatically expressed in an article published in the French publication *Le Point* in February 1989. Entitled "Our Good Food in Danger," it described in graphic detail the threat posed by mutual recognition to the quality of French food: "What could happen on our plates within four years? . . . All that is needed is to look at the astonishing menus our neighbors are preparing for us: Spanish foie gras, made with pork fat; mock snails (from West Germany), ice cream made with vegetable fat (from Holland), chocolate made with animal fats (from Britain), minced meat mixed with soya (from Belgium), sausages made with flour (from Britain, a nation with no culinary traditions) and chocolate made with cocoa butter (from Britain)."[62]

Doubtless many Germans, who have seen the European Court strike down regulations for two of their most cherished national products, namely *bier* and *wurst,* would offer a similar appraisal of recent developments in European food law. Indeed, the EC's sweetener directive, approved after the *Reinheitsgebot* ruling, permits German beer manufacturers to put sweeteners into low-alcohol beer. The *Economist* noted that "this could, some Germans believe, be the beginning of the end . . . the great German beer row has, it is generally thought, done more for Euro-skepticism in Germany than any incident since the creation of the Community."[63]

In November of 1991 a major political outburst took place in France over a Community proposal to harmonize food safety standards by restricting the amount of bacteria allowed in cheese on the grounds of consumer safety. About one-quarter of the 400 different kinds of cheese produced in France are made with unpasteurized or raw milk, including Camembert, Brie, and Pont l'Evêque.[64] These cheeses are allowed to ripen with their naturally produced bacteria, some of which the Commission had determined to be harmful.

The French Ministry of Agriculture accused the Commission of being "obsessed with hygiene" and promised that everything would be done to "protect our cheeses." Claire Marcellin of the Normandy Milk Union claimed that the EC restriction would "mean the loss of a whole wealth of very French flavors."[65] The residents of Camembert (population 185) observed that "no one has ever fallen ill from eating raw-milk camembert." They accused Brussels of trying "to ruin the product which has made them famous."[66] *Le Figaro* editorialized: "Are we to be condemned to eat standardized, aseptic, industrialized cheese?"[67]

Even Prince Charles joined the debate. On a visit to Paris in March 1992, he publicly defended both French cheese and European diversity against "the kind of pettifogging, if well-meaning, bureaucratic interference which seems to be spreading like uncontrollable bacteria though so much of the single market."[68] In response, the Commission claimed that it had been misunderstood: it stated that it never intended to ban any kind of French cheese, only to ensure that it was labeled properly. The Commission subsequently issued a separate set of rules for raw-milk products, which were incorporated in a new directive on milk products approved by the Council in June 1992. Nonetheless, the political fallout was considerable. According to a French official in Brussels, "The French cheese story was probably responsible for five out of six French votes against Maastricht."[69]

The British also have been upset with EC regulations. When German-influenced sausage standards proposed by the EC prohibited the use of gristle, cheekmeat, and sinew, each of which was used to make sausages (bangers) in Britain, the British press promised "blood, sweat, and tears in defense of their peculiar breakfast delicacy." After EC officials pointed out that the EC standards would make British sausages healthier and better, the *Daily Telegraph* responded with the headline: "Hands Off Our Bangers, We Like Them Lousy."[70] Once again, the Commission retreated.

Those who live on the Continent are equally alarmed about the prospect of British food being sold in their countries. Commission officials are fond of repeating the story of an English sausage manufacturer who lay dying. "He gathered his family around him and said, 'my children, I must pass on to you a secret that has been in our family for many years. You can make sausages using meat.'"[71]

In 1991 another ruling from Brussels aroused the ire of the British public. A draft directive seeking to harmonize the use of sweeteners in specific foods prohibited the use of additives in snack food. This would have banned the sale of British crisps (potato chips) made with sweet flavors, such as prawn cocktail. Headlines in the British tabloid press denounced Martin Bangemann, the EC's internal market commissioner, as "The Sour Kraut Who Wants To Ban Our Crisps."[72] The EC's omission was in fact inadvertent: the British government had forgotten to include crisps on the lists of foods containing sweeteners that it had submitted to Brussels. Following strong protests from Britain's Snack, Nut and Crisp Manufacturers Association, the list was amended, thus saving the British crisp industry. Nevertheless, the cumulative effects of these and similar initiatives have become symbolic of Brussels' "bossy tendencies."[73]

The Politics of Hygiene and Inspection

Tensions between national regulations and the creation of a single market persist in other areas as well. Indeed, in recent years, a new focus of contention has emerged—one significant enough to be described by the head of the Commission's Foodstuffs Division as a "fourth level of protectionism."[74] It is rooted in the divergence of national control and inspection standards. For even as national standards were being harmonized—and other nontariff barriers rendered moot by the principle of mutual recognition—both national and local governments continued to vary in both their ability and their willingness to enforce safety standards for the production of foods and beverages.

Indeed, it is precisely the success of the EC in promoting intra-Community trade in food that has brought this issue to the fore: a growing proportion of the products consumed by Europeans are now produced outside their own country, thus making the health of all consumers increasingly dependent on the competence of inspectors in other nations. (This applies equally to food imported by a member state from outside the EC and then distributed throughout the Community.) At the same time, the steady growth in the consumption of processed food, combined with new technologies of food production, have increased the vulnerability of all European consumers to foodborne diseases which cannot be detected by a vigilant shopper.

According to a study conducted during the late 1980s, each year 16.5 million people, or roughly 5 percent of the Community's population, become ill as a result of food poisoning.[75] In 1989 large-scale outbreaks of foodborne disease took place in the United Kingdom, France, and the Netherlands. In recent years European consumers were exposed to botulism in nut-flavored yogurt, methanol in wine, salmonella in chickens, eggs, and powdered milk, lead in milk powder, harmful bacteria in soft cheeses, benzene in bottled water, and illegal growth hormones in beef cattle. In 1990 EC consumers became highly alarmed by the outbreak of "mad-cow" disease in Britain.

Consequently, food hygiene and food inspection emerged as important and highly contentious issues in Europe. Public concerns about the adequacy of national control and inspection systems not only pose an important challenge to intra-Community trade; in many cases they represented an important economic threat to both farmers and food processors. Not only does the lack of common principles of food controls undermine public trust in the quality of imports, but it requires that importing countries duplicate the inspections carried out in the country of production, thus creating additional obstacles to economic integration.

For more than a decade, the Commission has operated a rapid-alert system for dangerous foodstuffs. Upon becoming aware of a problem, it notifies appropriate national authorities and coordinates appropriate national or Community-wide restrictions, in effect establishing a system of mutual recognition in reverse. This system has worked reasonably well on a number of occasions. For example, following Chernobyl, it was employed on an almost continuous basis to communicate to national officials the state of contamination of foods both within and outside the EC.[76] Yet the Community's system for monitoring and recalling dangerous products already on the market has several shortcomings. In particular, the Commission's effectiveness has been limited by the fact that legal responsibility for inspecting foods at the points of production and sale remains solely in the hands of national authorities; the Commission has no police powers.

But member states vary widely in both their scale and their method of reporting outbreaks of illness. In some nations, reporting threats to public health from food contamination is centralized, while in others it is the responsibility of more than one agency. National reporting patterns are also affected by economic and cultural factors: all Community residents are not equally likely to resort to a doctor in cases of gastrointestinal illness of short duration, thus preventing a coordinated EC response to various unsafe foods.

Historically, the European Commission paid relatively little attention to questions of food hygiene, instead focusing its efforts on food composition and labeling. In 1987 the Commission polled officials of member states about the adequacy of their systems for food inspection. Not surprisingly, all member states reported that their inspection systems were good. In fact, however, this rosy picture is highly deceptive as the administration of inspection systems, the training of inspectors, and enforcement policies vary significantly among the member states. As a result, "in many cases what looks splendid on paper turns out to have little basis in reality."[77] A directive establishing common standards for food inspection officially went into effect in June 1992, but for it to accomplish its objective of creating a single market in foodstuffs, nations must have a degree of trust in one another's controls, which is still lacking.[78]

The creation of a common market in animals and plants has met with similar difficulties. Many nations are wary of allowing animals to freely enter their country because of the diseases that they may carry. The lack of mutual trust in each nation's system of animal inspections, and its potential as a obstacle to the creation of a single European market in animals as well as processed beef, was dramatically revealed in the winter of 1989–90, when widespread outbreaks of mad-cow disease occurred among cattle in Great Britain. Within months, more than 9,500 British cows were "spongy-brained, mad and dead."[79]

Britain's Ministry of Agriculture claimed that the disease (bovine spongiform encephalopathy, BSE) posed no danger to humans, although the British government did ban the feeding of diseased cows to other animals in order to prevent the spread of the disease among their livestock. However, British consumers were unpersuaded. Coming shortly after widely publicized outbreaks of salmonella, listeria, and botulism, the government's assurances—especially coming from a ministry widely regarded as "the farmer's mouthpiece"[80]—had little impact: sales of domestic beef in the United Kingdom fell between 20 and 30 percent.[81]

The outbreak of mad-cow disease in Britain also created tensions between Britain and other member states. In January 1990 Germany, which traditionally has had relatively strict consumer safety regulations, officially banned British beef, and it was soon joined by a number of other countries, including France and Italy. Although a veterinary committee established by the European Commission determined that the risk of human contagion was "remote," the panel did not declare the infected beef to be completely safe. Nevertheless, the EC commissioner responsible for the operation of the Common Agricultural Policy formally criticized the ban.[82]

The French initially refused to rescind their ban until a team of French veterinary experts had the opportunity to meet with their British counterparts. The French Minister of Agriculture stated that "we have taken these severe measures against the UK so that French people can eat meat in safety."[83] The British were furious. The *Times* labeled France's rejection of the EC's request that it lift its ban "an act of naked protectionism," adding that the "French Agricultural Minister . . . has sided with his farming lobby [which] fear[s] competition from cheap British imports." Its editorial concluded: "Protecting home markets under the guise of protecting public health defies the spirit as well as the letter of Community law."[84]

The British threatened to retaliate; both France and Britain have a long history of using health and safety concerns to protect domestic agricultural producers from their competitors across the Channel. This particular fracas threatened to provoke a trade war similar to the one that had been narrowly avoided the previous year when the British had threatened to ban sales of French soft cheeses on the grounds that they contained bacteria that caused listeria. In that case, the French in turn had threatened a retaliatory ban on British eggs on the grounds that they contained salmonella. Now the British once again threatened to ban sales of French soft cheeses. The dispute was eventually settled by the Agricultural Council in June 1990. After the British agreed to major new controls to prevent the export of affected meat, France, West Germany, and Italy agreed to lift their ban. However, the controversy left a residue of mutual suspicion and distrust, and caused considerable economic harm to British producers.

In an attempt to prevent similar incidents, the Commission has advanced a number of proposals to eradicate or control animal diseases such as swine fever, foot and mouth disease, brucellosis, and tuberculosis. It has also announced plans to issue directives regulating trade in and the transportation of pedigree cattle, pigs, and sheep, as well as their embryos and semen. However, agreement on the lifting of border controls on the transit of live animals—especially livestock—proved difficult, largely because Britain and Ireland remain worried about importing rabies from the continent. (So great is the British fear of rabies that they have installed special barriers in the tunnel under the English Channel to prevent wild animals from entering Britain.) In June 1990 the Council voted to remove border controls on the transit of live animals between member states by the end of 1992. (A parallel agreement for animal products had been approved the previous year.) Health checks will continue on animals at the points of departure and arrival, and the British will be allowed to continue to inspect incoming animals for rabies.

Radiation

The aftermath of the nuclear accident at Chernobyl in 1986 provides another illustration of the Community's continuing difficulties in preventing the use of health and safety standards as trade barriers, particularly when important economic interests are at stake. Following the accident in the USSR, France, Italy, and Germany unilaterally banned imports of fresh fruits and vegetables from Eastern Europe. However, Britain and Spain did not.[85] The EC's foreign ministers were initially unable to agree on common radioactivity levels for food sold within the EC. While Germany insisted on maintaining very strict standards, Italy, fearful of losing its market for early-season produce, insisted on more flexible ones. At the same time, Italy, which had previously been embarrassed by the methyl alcohol contamination in some of its red wines, demanded health certificates for all imported produce. This in turn threatened the export of French fruits and vegetables to Italy.

The result was a serious disruption of the free movement of agricultural products within the EC, as each nation established its own standards. In frustration, Carlo Ripa di Meana, the Italian commissioner responsible for a "Citizens' Europe," declared that the EC "does not exist as a political and scientific entity capable of reacting speedily to the problems created by the nuclear emergency."[86] It took several weeks of negotiations before the EC was finally able to agree on temporary safety levels for both imported and domestic food.[87] A report subsequently released by a European consumer group was highly critical of the way a number of European states had responded to the dangers of imported radioactive food, concluding that "those countries with the highest dependence on nuclear power tend[ed] to do the least."[88] Thus, while Germany, where antinuclear forces are politically powerful, tore up and destroyed the watercress growing along its bank of the Rhine river, the same plant on the French side of the river was harvested and sold—some of it to Germany.[89]

Due to both the scientific uncertainty surrounding the effects of radiation and the variations in national policies with respect to nuclear power, the Community has been unable to establish permanent maximum radiation levels for food. In May 1987 the Commission proposed stricter radiation limits for food and drinking water than those recommended by its own scientists, on the grounds that it was important to leave a safety margin, in the event of another nuclear accident. The Commission also contended that EC food exports could be badly affected if the Community's standards were below those of its major trading partners. This initiative was strongly opposed by those nations committed to nuclear power (namely, France, Britain, and Belgium) but was in turn supported by countries with strong antinuclear movements (most notably Germany and Denmark).[90]

As a compromise, a qualified majority of member states agreed to continue the temporary standards imposed after the Chernobyl accident for an additional two years; Germany, Luxembourg, and Denmark supported tougher standards but were outvoted.[91] However, in a special meeting held in November 1987, the EC's foreign ministers were unable to agree on permanent standards. The Community remained deadlocked between France, Britain, Spain, and Greece, which favored a relaxation of post-Chernobyl standards, and Germany, the Netherlands, and Denmark, which supported stricter ones. Stanley Clinton-Davis, the EC Environment Commissioner who proposed the new safety standards, described the EC's failure to reach a decision as "totally unacceptable and disastrous for the Community."[92]

Not surprisingly, one of the EC's most conspicuous failures has been its inability to harmonize standards for food irradiation. Six EC-member nations permit irradiation for the treatment of certain foods, while two—Great Britain and Germany—ban it. The others neither formally permit nor ban it. While irradiation has been endorsed by both the World Health Organization and the EC's own scientific advisors, an internal EC report notes that the idea is "one which public opinion doesn't appreciate."[93] Faced with strong opposition from Germany and Luxembourg, the EC has abandoned its effort to legalize the sale of irradiated herbs, spices, and teas, though it has resisted the demands of Green Party members of the European Parliament for an immediate ban on the irradiation of all foodstuffs in the Community.[94]

Impact on Trade Liberalization

The creation of a single European market for food, beverages, and agricultural products remains incomplete. In some cases, such as radiation standards, member states still maintain the ability to set their own regulations, and the resulting divergence of national standards continues to interfere with the single market. Differences in national inspection standards also continue to handicap intra-Union trade, as do the periodic efforts of France and Germany to ban imports of British beef because of the alleged dangers of mad-cow disease.

Nonetheless, over the last decade substantial progress has been made in creating a common market for food and beverages within the EU. At a 1989 conference, "Food Law and 1992," the Director for EEC and International Policy of the Food and Drink Federation, while noting that the "concept of the Internal Market [was] a gradually evolving phenomenon," concluded that "the Internal Market is already open for business." He added: "Do not wait for 1992."[95]

In 1989, after taking note of directives in progress, the *Times* concluded that "the internal market for foodstuffs, excluding labeling, is . . . all but complete."[96] In the fall of 1991, according to a representative of the Confederation of the Food and Drink Industries of the EEC, "while a few important issues remained to be resolved prior to 1992, virtually all economically significant obstacles to free trade in foodstuffs within the EC have either been removed or are in the process of being removed."[97]

The substantial progress the Council and the Commission have made in reducing the role of national food regulations as obstacles to intra-Union trade reflects both the political commitment of its member states to trade liberalization as well as the political strength of those producers who stand to benefit from the creation of the single market. The White Paper reflected and reenforced the preferences of both. By establishing December 31, 1992, as a "target date" for the completion of the single market, the White Paper put substantial pressure on European industry to reach agreement; indeed, a kind of informal rivalry has emerged among different sectors, with each seeking to make more progress than the others in removing obstacles to intra-European trade. In the case of the food processing sector, its noticeable lack of success in reducing trade barriers through the mid-1980s had become a source of embarrassment. This placed additional pressure on it to redouble its efforts following the issuance of the White Paper.

The Single European Act also has played a critical role, not only by introducing a system of weighted voting for legislation aimed at completing the internal market, but also by giving the Council the option of declaring that all national regulations not harmonized by the end of 1992 would be considered equivalent. The uncertainty created by this latter provision placed substantial pressure on both producers and national governments to harmonize as many regulations as possible by this deadline, since after that date nations might find themselves forced to accept the importation of goods produced according to the rules and regulations of any other member state.

Health and Safety

What has been the EU's impact on European health and safety standards? The Union's most important effort to reduce the role of consumer regulations as trade barriers, namely the doctrine of mutual recognition, has not adversely affected national food safety standards. It would be hard to argue that the Court's decision in *Cassis* or *Reinheitsgebot* has undermined the health of the German people. To be sure, mutual recognition may have threatened the culinary traditions of some European nations. But not only do these traditions have nothing to do with the protection of public health, but European consumers remain free to purchase the same products they always have; all that has changed is that they now have the option of purchasing those made according to the traditions of other member states as well.

In fact, there is little disagreement that virtually all national regulations that have been subject to mutual recognition were not needed to protect consumers. The Union's experience with mutual recognition reveals the extent to which numerous national consumer "protection" standards provide consumers with few or no benefits. Rather, their real purpose is to protect the market share of producers. They therefore can be subject to extranational scrutiny without comprising public health or safety. Indeed, by expanding the range of goods European consumers can purchase and by lowering their price, the deregulatory consequences of mutual recognition have made European consumers better off.

What about those cases in which there has been a lack of scientific consensus? In some cases, the Union has chosen to permit nations to maintain their own distinctive standards, even though the resulting lack of uniform regulations has hampered intra-Union trade. Thus, a number of food safety regulations have neither been harmonized nor subject to mutual recognition. Both radiation standards for food and water as well as regulations for irradiated foods fall into this category—two areas of regulatory policy that have been especially controversial and in which consensus has therefore proved elusive. In these cases, the Union has had no effect on national regulatory standards.

In other cases, the Union has established relatively strict harmonized standards, thus strengthening the regulatory standards of a number of member states. The banning of growth hormones for both beef and dairy cattle fall into this category. Indeed, in these two cases, the Council overruled the recommendations of its own scientific advisors and adopted the most restrictive standard of any member state, thus handing the European consumer movement a major political victory. In both cases, the Union's commitment to harmonization strengthened the influence of consumer organizations over EU regulatory policies.

However, in a few cases the Union has harmonized standards at a level laxer than that of some member states. The most important example of downward harmonization is the EU's regulation of food additives, which has significantly increased the number of food additives permitted throughout the EU.[98] The EU has approved a total of 412 additives: by contrast, German law had previously permitted the use of only 150, while Greece was even more restrictive, allowing only 120. Even Britain, whose food law was the most permissive on this score, had previously permitted only 300. This decision was strongly criticized by Melanie Miller, of the International Organization of Consumers' Unions, who argued that "the interests of food and chemical manufacturers were given preference over public health."[99] While admitting that some of the additives were harmless, Erik Millstone of the British consumer lobby Food Additives Campaign Team charged that "it has been a political rather than a scientific process. The negotiations have been between industry and government, and communication with consumers has been excluded."[100] However, virtually all the additives approved for use throughout the EU had been previously permitted in at least one member state. Moreover most of the differences in national regulatory policies reflected different traditions of food preparation rather than differences among health and safety standards. For example, the fact that Italy had Europe's tightest restriction on additives in bubblegum, permitting a maximum of 20, while other member states allowed up to 67, does not make Italian chewing gum safer.[101]

As the furor over the EU's proposed standards for bacteria in cheese and the content of British bangers suggests, the Union has been criticized as frequently for overregulation as for underregulation. On balance, integration has not come about at the price of consumer safety. Few EU food safety standards are laxer than those of the "average" member-state: in most cases they are comparable, and in a few cases they are stricter.

Conclusion

The European Union's more than three decades of effort to remove nontariff barriers to trade in food, beverages, and agricultural products demonstrates both their importance and the difficulty of removing them. NTBs in this sector stemmed from a wide variety of sources, including economic interests, cultural traditions, and health and safety concerns. Their cumulative impact was substantial: had the EU not been able to make significant progress in dismantling them, the Union's effort to create a single market in foodstuffs would have remained stillborn. At the same time, these regulations could not simply be abolished, since many of them did in fact serve a legitimate public purpose.

The challenge for the Union was to distinguish those regulations which were "essential" or "legitimate" from those which were protectionist or unnecessary. The Union in fact faced two challenges. The first was to construct a set of rules and procedures to determine which regulations were necessary to protect consumers. This was primarily accomplished through a judicial mechanism: the European Court established a set of criteria to determine when a regulation "unreasonably" restricted trade. The second was to determine the level of protection that was appropriate for those regulations that did serve a legitimate public purpose, and therefore needed to be harmonized. This decision was assigned to the Union's most important decision-making body, namely the Council of Ministers, which in turn worked closely with the EU's bureaucracy, the European Commission.

The Union could have erred in either one of two directions. It could have promoted integration at the expense of consumer protection, or maintained consumer protection at the expense of integration. Yet for the most part the EU has managed to avoid either extreme. The accomplishment of the Union has been an impressive one: it has made significant progress toward creating a single market for foodstuffs while for the most part maintaining—and in a some cases even strengthening—national food safety standards.

The key to the Union's ability to accomplish both these objectives lies in the degree of authority it has been able to exercise over both the trade and regulatory policies of its member states. The European Union not only has the authority to strike down national regulations that interfere with trade; all international trade agreements, by definition, subject some national laws to international review. What distinguishes the EU from other international institutions is that it also has the power to impose regulations on its member states. Thus, unlike the GATT, which only has the authority to engage in negative harmonization (that is, to instruct governments *not* to enforce laws which conflict with their obligations under the General Agreement), the EU also has the legal and political capacity to engage in positive harmonization—to enact regulations that governments *must* enforce.

It is precisely the balance between the scope of the EU's authority in the areas of both trade *and* regulation that has enabled it to reduce trade barriers without undermining the health and safety of European consumers. On one hand, the EU's definition of a nontariff barrier is considerably broader than that of any other international treaty. Specifically, it goes far beyond the traditional GATT principle of national treatment. Indeed, the assumption at the core of the "1992" project is that nondiscrimination was not sufficient to create economic integration. Thus, EU jurisprudence considers any regulation that has the *effect* of "restricting" imports as a "quantitative restriction" on trade. Such regulations are permitted, but only if the nation imposing them can demonstrate that they are both necessary to achieve a legitimate public policy objective and that the means chosen interfere with the free movement of goods as little as possible. No other group of nations has subjected their national rules and regulations to such extensive extranational oversight in order to promote trade.

On the other hand, the EU's authority to engage in negative harmonization is counter-balanced by its ability to engage in positive harmonization. No other international body exercises so much authority over such a wide array of national regulatory policies. The authority of the Union is problematic in a number of areas, but protective regulation is not among them. Indeed, in few other areas of public policy has the EU come to play such an active role; there may not be a European welfare state, but there certainly is a European regulatory state.[102] Regulatory policy-making in Europe has been effectively regionalized.

As Majone writes, "Each successive revision of the Treaty of Rome has expanded and strengthened the competencies of the Community in social regulation."[103] While the Treaty of Rome legitimated the Community's regulatory responsibilities primarily in terms of their impact on trade, the Single European Act states that directives which address quality of life issues need not be justified by reference to the completion of the internal market. Thus, the SEA expanded the scope of the Community's authority to make regulatory policies. The SEA also instructs the Commission to take as the basis of its proposals relating to health, safety, and environmental and consumer protection "a high level of protection." The Maastricht Treaty in turn includes a special section on consumer protection which explicitly confirms the Union's power to act "to protect the health, safety, and economic interests of consumers and provide them with adequate information."[104]

This continual expansion of the Union's role and competence in regulatory policy-making has played a critical role in preventing the completion of the internal market from undermining national consumer protection standards. The judicial doctrine of mutual recognition, reenforced by the Commission, helped make the creation of the single market possible. Mutual recognition, however, is essentially an integrative mechanism, not a regulatory one. It is the harmonization of national regulations by the Council of Ministers and the Commission that has made the removal of trade barriers compatible with protecting the health and safety of consumers. Harmonization without mutual recognition would have been administratively impossible, while mutual recognition without harmonization was politically infeasible.

In sum, the key to the EU's ability to balance consumer protection and economic integration lies in its ability to centralize decision-making in both areas. *The removal of nontariff barriers and the maintenance or strengthening of health and safety regulations requires a strong international authority.* In this sense, *Cassis* and the SEA complemented one another: the former decision expedited the removal of national regulations, while the latter, by changing the Council's voting procedures for legislation for all issues relating to the single market, facilitated the establishment of Union-wide regulatory standards. One promoted deregulation; the other regulation. Tensions between national regulatory standards and the single market continue, as do disagreements regarding the stringency of EU standards. But the Union has succeeded in creating a set of political, legal, and administrative mechanisms with the capacity to both reduce trade barriers and to protect public health and safety.

-3-

Environmental Regulation
and the Single European Market

As in the case of food and beverages, divergent national environmental standards, especially for products, have presented important obstacles to intra-European trade. However, in contrast to food standards, the most important of which long predated the establishment of the Union, environmental regulations are relatively new and their scope has been continually expanding. No sooner has the Union succeeded in reducing trade barriers in one area of environmental policy than one or more member states introduce new regulations, thus forcing the Union to begin the process of reconciling the goals of economic integration and environmental protection all over again. As a result, the common market has been continually threatened by the ever-expanding scope of the environmental agenda.

There is a second important distinction between food safety and environmental regulation in the EU. While the regulatory standards for food and related products varied considerably among the member states, the degree of public support for food safety standards did not. Moreover, consumer organizations were relatively weak in virtually all member states. By contrast, both the extent of public support for environmental regulation and the strength of environmental organizations and political parties have varied considerably among the Union's twelve member states. Environmental movements have been especially influential in Germany, Denmark, and the Netherlands. Consequently, the regulatory standards and policy preferences of these northern European countries have been consistently and considerably "greener" than those of the rest of the Union. This has often made it difficult to harmonize environmental standards.

There is a third important difference between food safety and environmental regulation in the EU. Many food safety regulations were clearly not necessary to protect the health or safety of consumers: they therefore could be subject to mutual recognition under the criteria established in *Cassis*. However, national environmental regulations generally do improve environmental quality. While they still may constitute "disguised barriers to trade," it is easier to justify them under Article 36 and more difficult to subject them to mutual recognition. Consequently, the Union has been often faced with the difficult choice of either harmonizing national environmental regulations or permitting member states to maintain their own stricter regulatory standards. But while the former may often result in the weakening of some regulatory standards, the latter threatens the single market.

As a result, the significant expansion of environmental regulation over the last quarter-century has continually forced the EU to confront the relationship between strong regulatory standards and economic integration. And in fact the priority the Union has given to each of these frequently conflicting policy objectives has varied. Through the mid-1980s governments were often forbidden from enacting stricter environmental regulations than those of other member states in order to preserve the common market. The passage of the Single European Act in 1987 brought a more equal balance between the two: Brussels attempted simultaneously to promote integration and to strengthen regulatory standards. Since the late 1980s, the scope of EU environmental policy has expanded significantly and its standards have become increasingly stringent. Moreover, the EU on occasion has permitted member states to maintain stricter national environmental standards for traded goods in spite of their interference with the single market.

The Treaty of Rome

The word "environment" does not appear in the 1957 Treaty of Rome which established the European Community. Nonetheless, in spite of the absence of explicit powers in the original treaty, the Community did develop an environmental policy. Between the early 1970s and the mid 1980s, the EC issued more than 100 environmental regulations and directives. They covered a wide range of areas, including air, water, and noise pollution, waste disposal, accident prevention, chemical safety, environmental impact, and wildlife protection. By the mid 1980s, virtually all aspects of environmental policy had been addressed, in one form or other, at the Community level.[1]

The significant growth of EC environmental regulation during the 1970s was due to several factors. First, the issue of environmental quality had become more politically salient. EC environmental policy was in part a response to the increase in public concern about environmental issues that took place throughout the industrialized world during the late 1960s and early 1970s. A 1973 survey taken in the (then) nine EC member states reported that "pollution was cited as the most important problem, ahead of inflation, poverty and unemployment."[2] At the same time, environmental organizations had become more politically active in a number of European countries, and most national governments significantly expanded and strengthened the scope of their own regulatory controls over industry.

In order to preserve their legitimacy, EC institutions attempted to respond to these new political forces and public pressures by enacting environmental regulations of their own. EC environmental policy represented a way for Community officials to address the "democratic deficit"—the gap between the Community's power over and accountability to the electorate of its member states. Environmental regulation also provided an opportunity for officials in Brussels to assert their competence in a new, rapidly growing and highly visible area of public policy while at the same time preserving the momentum of European integration, which in other respects had stagnated during the 1970s.[3]

The second factor contributing to the expansion of environmental regulation in Europe was the Community's commitment to the common market itself, to which the expansion of national environmental regulation posed a serious threat. If nations were allowed to adopt their own product standards, such as for chemical safety or automobile emissions, the free flow of goods within the EC would be impaired, since producers would be required to meet different standards in different countries. Moreover, these standards could also be used to protect domestic producers.

In the case of production standards, nations that had adopted more stringent pollution controls than other member states might find the goods produced by their industries placed at a competitive disadvantage. They might therefore be forced to choose between excluding goods produced by member states with weaker regulatory requirements or lowering their own standards to those of their competitors. The former threatened economic integration; the latter made national regulatory policies hostage to those of the least strict member state.

A third motivation for the expansion of EC environmental policy was geographic. The (then) twelve nations* of the EC comprised a large land area—roughly 1.6 million square kilometers—and encompassed a considerable diversity of climate and topography. However, a number of member states are physically close to one another; the quality of their physical environment, as well as the health of their population, is significantly affected by the environmental policies of their neighbors. For example, the Rhine flows west through Germany, France, and the Netherlands; accordingly the quality of Dutch water is strongly influenced by German and French pollution controls. On the other hand, because winds in Europe travel from west to east, air quality in northern Europe is affected by industrial emissions from Britain. As one journalist observed, "Environmental regulations are among the world's toughest in . . . West Germany and the Netherlands. But that does little good when winds waft Britain's loosely regulated power-plant fumes and their product, acid rain, eastward."[4] Moreover, industrial accidents do not respect national boundaries.

For all these reasons—political, economic, and geographic—the Community attempted to harmonize a wide range of national environmental regulations. Not surprisingly, this effort led to considerable conflict between those nations that favored stricter environmental standards and those that did not. Equally important, the Treaty of Rome, by not explicitly mentioning environmental protection, provided EC policy-makers with no framework for balancing environmental protection with other goals, the most important of which was obviously the creation of the common market itself. For virtually any level of environmental regulation was compatible with economic integration, provided that national standards for traded products were relatively uniform or did not otherwise discriminate against imported

*On January 1, 1995, three additional nations joined the European Union: Austria, Finland, and Sweden.

products. The Community's critics argued that since many EC environmental directives tended to reflect the lowest common denominator of national regulations, the Community had, in effect, subordinated environmental goals to economic ones.

The Single European Act

On July 1, 1987, the Treaty of Rome was amended by the Single European Act (SEA). In addition to facilitating the creation of a single European market, the SEA also introduced a number of important changes in Community environmental policy and policy-making. The two developments were related: in exchange for reducing their controls over access to their domestic markets, the EC's "greener" member states were assured that protective regulations would either be maintained or strengthened. The SEA thus committed the Community to both increase integration *and* improve European environmental quality.

Most importantly, Article 100A of the SEA explicitly recognized the improvement of environmental quality as a legitimate Community objective in its own right. This meant that EC environmental policies no longer had to be justified in terms of their contribution to economic integration. The EC now had a firm constitutional basis for regulating any and all aspects of the environment. Even more important was the SEA's statement that in harmonizing national regulations, "the Commission . . . will take as a base a high level of [environmental] protection." This statement associated harmonization with the improvement of environmental quality, rather than simply the removal of trade barriers, as under the Treaty of Rome.

Article 130R further declared that "environmental protection requirements shall be a component of the Community's other policies."[5] This provision accorded environmental protection an unusual priority among the Community's objectives, since no other EC goal was granted a commensurate provision. In practical terms, this Article strengthened the hands of the Commission's Environmental Directorate (DG XI) in its conflicts with those Directorates whose focus was essentially economic. To reassure those member states which feared that harmonization would require them to relax existing national regulations, member states were granted the right, under certain circumstances, to maintain or introduce national environmental standards stricter than those approved by Brussels, provided they did not constitute a form of "hidden protectionism" and were otherwise compatible with the Treaty of Rome.[6]

The SEA also facilitated the adoption of environmental regulations by the Council of Ministers. While legislation approved under Article 130 (the SEA's environmental article) still required unanimity, the SEA permitted directives approved under Article 100A—which provides for the approximation of laws concerned with the functioning of the common market—to be approved by a "qualified majority." This change made it substantially easier for the Council to reach agreement on the terms of environmental legislation.

The SEA also expanded the role of the European Parliament,* which has generally been more supportive of stricter environmental standards than the Council, in shaping Community legislation. For ten articles of the EC Treaty, the SEA established a "cooperation procedure" under which Parliament has the right to propose amendments to legislation approved by the Council of Ministers. If the Commission chooses to retain these amendments, then the Council must then either reject them unanimously or adopt them by a qualified majority.

The SEA also contributed to the strengthening of environmental policy in another, less direct, way. A primary purpose of amending the Treaty of Rome was to accelerate the move toward the creation of a single internal market—a goal which had been formally outlined in a Commission White Paper issued a few years earlier. However, Community officials recognized that the removal of all barriers to intra-Community trade by the end of 1992 was also likely to exacerbate Europe's environmental problems. A 1989 report entitled *"1992": The Environmental Dimension* noted a number of the adverse environmental consequences of the completion of the internal market.[7] The most important of these was a dramatic increase in transportation, which would significantly increase emissions of both sulphur dioxide and nitrogen oxides. In addition, the expansion of intra-Community trade also threatened to increase the exposure of member

---

*The European Parliament, which is responsible for advising the European Commission, is directly elected by the citizens of each member state. Members of Parliament are elected for five year terms. The first election took place in 1979.

states to imports of toxic and hazardous wastes. Thus, the Community's renewed commitment to economic integration made the strengthening of environmental standards even more urgent.

The strengthening of environmental protection within the Community's Constitution both reflected and reinforced the increased public concern with environmental issues that took place throughout much of Europe during the latter part of the 1980s. Stimulated in part by the Soviets' Chernobyl disaster and a massive chemical spill of toxins into the Rhine River which destroyed a half million fish in four countries—both of which occurred in 1986—environmental issues moved rapidly to a prominent position on the European political agenda. A survey published by the EC in 1989 reported "strong support for a common EC-wide approach to environmental protection."[8] The following year, an official EC publication observed: "Major disasters [and] global problems like ozone depletion and the greenhouse effect, and quality of life issues such as drinking water and air pollution have all contributed in recent years to a 'greening' of European public opinion, to a widening consensus in favor of cleaner and more sustainable economic growth."[9]

Following passage of the SEA, the momentum for Community environmental regulation accelerated significantly.[10] Between 1989 and 1991 the EC enacted more environmental legislation than it had in the previous twenty years. As of 1992, it had issued over 450 regulations and it is adding new ones at a rate of about 100 a year.[11] By the early 1990s the EC had succeeded in harmonizing standards for virtually every important aspect of environmental policy, including air and water quality, noise pollution, and wildlife and conservation. While the enforcement of many EC standards that do not directly affect traded products has been uneven, on balance the EC has made a significant contribution to strengthening environmental regulation standards throughout the community. Indeed, for those member states with relatively weak domestic environmental movements, the EC has been the single most important factor in improving their environmental quality.[12]

Finally, the Maastricht Treaty, which was ratified in 1993, further strengthened the European Union's competence in and commitment to environmental regulation. It defines one of the EU's basic tasks as the promotion of "sustainable and non-inflationary growth respecting the environment" and both clarifies and extends the SEA's requirements that environmental protection should be integrated into other EU policies and that Union environmental policy should "aim at a high level of protection."[13] It also extends qualified majority voting to all environmental policies, not just those affecting the single market. In addition, the principle of subsidiarity that informs Maastricht expands the rights of member states to enact environmental standards that are both stricter and laxer than those of the Union, though the precise significance of this change is as yet unclear.

Environmental regulations have affected economic integration within the EU both indirectly, through production standards which alter the relative costs of production among EU member states, or directly, though product standards, which may function as nontariff barriers. The remainder of this chapter describes the development of EU environmental policies in three areas, each of which has directly affected intra-Union trade: automobile emissions, chemical safety, and recycling.

Automobile Emissions

The setting of automobile emission standards has been one of the most important and contentious areas of EU environmental policy. Automobiles are among the EU's most widely traded goods, and significant automobile manufacturing takes place in seven of the Union's twelve member states. Germany, France, and Italy are home to major car producers, while a number of European, American, and Japanese multinationals have production facilities in Britain, the Netherlands, Spain, and Belgium. In addition, automobiles are an important source of pollution: restricting emissions from mobile sources has been an important component of the environmental policies of all industrialized nations.

Early Regulatory Efforts

In 1970 the European Community, like the United States, established emission levels for carbon monoxide and unburnt hydrocarbons. Four years later the EC also adopted restrictions on emissions of nitrogen oxides. Each of these standards was tightened in 1977, 1978, and again in 1983. However, unlike the United States, which had imposed uniform national standards (with the exception of California, which was permitted to exceed them by an amount specified by statute), the EC opted for "optional harmonization by setting maximum requirements and leaving member states the power to allow operation of vehicles on their territory that do not meet the EEC emission standards."[14]

Accordingly, while member states were not required to impose the EC's standards on cars sold within their borders, they were permitted to do so. At the same time, they were not permitted to restrict the sale of any cars that did meet the EC's standards. The EC's standards thus functioned as a ceiling rather than a floor: no member nation was permitted to impose stricter standards on imports than those specified in the directives. Nevertheless, because much of European car production is exported to other member states, auto producers had a strong incentive to comply with Community standards. Thus, in fact, the agreement approximated a system of total harmonization. Moreover, as the standards became progressively stricter, nations which sought to place stronger controls on vehicular emissions were gradually permitted to do so.

Through 1983 the establishment of EC emission standards had a relatively low political profile within the Community. In fact, the Community's standards for automotive exhausts were not even developed by the EC, but rather the EC essentially adopted the standards established by the UN Economic Commission for Europe, a regional organization headquartered in Geneva. These standards applied equally to EC member states as well as to members of the European Free Trade Association (EFTA), a free trade organization founded in 1960 as an alternative to the EC. (In 1985 the EFTA was comprised of Austria, Finland, Iceland, Norway, Portugal, Sweden, and Switzerland.)

By contrast, the EC's initial efforts to regulate the content of motor fuel created considerable conflict. By the late 1960s there was growing evidence that airborne lead—a significant proportion of which came from motor vehicles—threatened children's cognitive development. As a result, a number of member states began to restrict the lead content of gasoline sold within their borders. The most severe restrictions were imposed by Germany, which in 1972 announced a two-stage reduction: it set the maximum lead content for gasoline at .4 grams per liter for 1972 and .15 for 1976. The latter level was chosen because it represented the lowest amount of lead content that did not require changes in engine design. The British also established limits on the lead content of petrol, though not as severe as Germany's: in 1972 Britain's Parliament limited lead to .84 grams per liter. However, no other member states imposed restrictions on the lead content of fuel.

The resulting disparity in national rules and regulations represented an obstacle to the free movement of both fuel and motor vehicles within the Community.[15] Not only did these divergent national product regulations limit intra-EC trade in gasoline, but, even more importantly, since different car engines were designed to run on fuels containing different amounts of lead, they created a barrier to intra-Community trade in motor vehicles themselves.

In December 1973 the Commission forwarded to the Council a directive to establish a uniform standard for the lead content of gasoline sold anywhere in the Community. The Commission was motivated not only by the need to prevent technical barriers to trade, but also by an internal committee report that had concluded that "although there was no immediate danger for public health, it was desirable to prevent an increase in air pollution by lead and hence to limit lead because of the increase in car use."[16]

The debate over the lead directive was dominated by Germany, which was reluctant to weaken its standard in the interests of economic integration. As the debate proceeded, other nations tightened their standards; for example, in 1978 Britain adopted a phased reduction to .45 grams. Eventually, after prolonged negotiations,the Community approved a directive establishing both minimum and maximum standards. The former was set at .4; the latter at .15 grams per liter to "accommodate the decision the Germans had already made."[17]

The inclusion of a lower limit for the lead content of gasoline was added as a result of pressure from the British government, which wanted to ensure that "no barriers to trade in motor cars would be created by any one Member State insisting on lead free petrol."[18] Thus, the final form of this directive had as much to do with preventing trade barriers as with reducing lead emissions. Nevertheless, it did contribute to emission reduction as well by establishing an EC-wide ceiling of .4 grams per liter. At the time of the directive's adoption, the Commission stated that it intended to propose further restrictions on the lead content of gasoline, but to do so in a way that would not create additional trade barriers.

As the visibility of environmental issues increased in Europe during the first half of the 1980s, the EC found itself under growing pressure to enact new restrictions on automobile emissions. In 1984 the Commission presented to the Council two new, related directives on automobile emissions. One proposed the total elimination of lead from gasoline, while the second required a further 70 percent reduction in carbon monoxide, hydrocarbons, and nitrogen oxide automobile emissions. The two were linked, since the EC's proposed emissions standards required that all new cars be equipped with catalytic converters, and vehicles equipped with converters can use only unleaded gasoline.

The Council's proposal on emissions marked a significant departure in EC environmental policy-making. For the first time, the EC was attempting to formulate its own regulations for automobile emissions, rather than, as in the past, adopting European-wide standards. Equally important, the EC's proposed new emission standards were as strict as those of the United States. (Significantly, several EFTA countries had recently broken from the EEC and adopted standards modeled on those of the United States.) Subsequently, the American standards of 1983—widely referred to as "US '83"—became an important reference point for the debate over EC automobile emission standards.

The adoption of a new directive on the lead content of gasoline proved relatively straightforward; only six months elapsed between the Commission's proposal and its approval by the Council. The Council's 1985 directive on lead in gasoline maintained the maximum and minimum standards enacted seven years earlier. However, it contained two additional provisions. First, it urged each member state to achieve the .15 level as soon as possible. Second, the directive required that all member states offer at least some unleaded gasoline for sale beginning in October 1989. The delay was intended to give the petroleum and automobile industries sufficient time to make the necessary design changes, although the voluntary introduction of lead-free gasoline was permitted prior to the October 1 deadline.

The EC's endorsement of the goal of unleaded gasoline reflected both the increasing influence of European environmental organizations as well as a shift in producer preferences. European environmentalists had become increasingly critical of the EC's prohibition of national legislation requiring lead content below 0.15 g/l. In June 1983 the European Parliament approved a resolution urging that this restriction be ended. While not legally binding on the Commission, it exerted considerable pressure. In addition, following the recommendation of the Royal Commission on Environmental Pollution in June 1983, the British government reversed its opposition to lead-free petrol. Persuaded by the arguments of CLEAR, the Campaign for Lead-Free Air—a coalition of environmental, public health, and social welfare organizations which had been campaigning for the abolition of lead in gasoline since 1981—it now urged the Council to permit member states to require the removal of all lead from gasoline.

Finally, the British position coincided with that of Germany, which favored lead-free gasoline, though for a rather different reason. The emission requirements that Germany eventually wanted the Community to adopt, and which some of its manufacturers were already employing, required the use of catalytic converters. Accordingly, the German government wanted to make unleaded gasoline more widely available throughout the EC, since otherwise the owners of new German automobiles would not be able to drive their vehicles outside of Germany. In sum, the significant strengthening of European environmental standards reflected a convergence of interests between European environmentalists and German car producers.

The Luxembourg Compromise

However, reaching an agreement on new automotive emission standards proved much more difficult than in the case of lead-free gasoline. The Council's proposed emissions guidelines were designed so that their effect on the evironment would be the same as that produced by U.S. standards.[19] But meeting the strict U.S. guidelines required the installation of three-way catalysts and electronic fuel injection control systems on all vehicles. These technical considerations in turn became the focus of considerable controversy.

Those nations with strong environmental movements—Germany, the Netherlands, and Denmark—supported full conformity with U.S. regulations, now the world's strictest. German environmentalists, increasingly alarmed about the death of Germany's forests ("Waldsterben") owing to pollution, strongly supported the EC's adoption of American standards, while Dutch environmentalist Lucas Rêijnders went so far as to urge that EC standards be "replaced" by U.S. standards.[20] On the other hand, nations with weaker environmental movements—namely, France, Italy, and Great Britain—strongly opposed the EC's adoption of the American requirements.

Underlying, and for the most part reinforcing, the differing strengths of environmentalism within Europe were the conflicting interests of European automobile producers. The dispute over EC automobile pollution controls essentially pitted countries whose motor vehicle manufacturers produced larger, more expensive cars against those nations whose automotive firms specialized in smaller, less expensive vehicles. In practice, this primarily amounted to a battle between Germany—home to Mercedes-Benz, BMW, and Audi—and France and Italy, home to Fiat, Peugeot, and Renault. Only one-third of German automobile production consisted of small cars, as contrasted to three-quarters of Italian automobile production. Britain, although it had no important domestic automobile firms, was home to a number of foreign producers who primarily produced medium-size cars. Their interests tended to be similar to those of the manufacturers of smaller cars.

There was virtually no dispute over whether converters should be required on all new, large cars. Both the German and non-German manufacturers of larger vehicles supported this requirement. Rather, the dispute centered on whether they should be mandatory for all new small and medium-size vehicles as well.[21] The debate over this issue reveals the critical role of regulatory standards in affecting the terms of international competition.

First, the installation of expensive, technically complex pollution-abatement technologies raised the price of large cars proportionately less than that of smaller vehicles. Moreover, many large vehicles were already equipped with fuel injection systems in order to improve their engine performance. Since the major cost of the technology required to meet "US '83" standards was the fuel injection system rather than the converter itself, the installation of this abatement technology not only was relatively less expensive for the manufacturers of large cars; it also was less expensive in absolute terms. Further, since consumers who purchase smaller vehicles tend to be more sensitive to costs, the mandatory installation of converters on all vehicles threatened to disproportionately depress the sales of smaller ones.

Second, in contrast to most French and Italian car producers, whose markets were primarily domestic, most German car manufacturers were already producing large numbers of cars for sale in the United States and Japan, where catalytic converters were already mandatory.[22] (This was also true of the relatively small British and French producers of luxury vehicles.) For these firms, the adoption of American regulations by the EC would actually reduce their production costs, since they would no longer need separate production lines for cars produced for European and export markets.

Third, as has already been noted, vehicles equipped with catalytic convertors require the use of unleaded gasoline. But the availability of unleaded gasoline varied widely within the EC: the portion of stations carrying unleaded gasoline ranged from 98 percent in Germany and nearly 100 percent in the Netherlands, to only 3.5 percent in Britain and less than 2 percent in France, Italy, and Spain.[23] These differences largely reflected the different stances of each member state toward tighter vehicle emission standards. They also made it more difficult for the owners of vehicles equipped with converters to purchase gasoline in Britain, France, Italy, and Spain.

Finally, the market demand for vehicles equipped with advanced pollution control technology varied considerably within Europe. In July 1985 Germany began to provide tax incentives to increase the sale of less polluting cars. Thanks in part to these incentives, in 1985 both BMW and Daimler-Benz reported increased demand for cars equipped with catalytic convertors; even 20 percent of all Volkswagens sold in Germany were being ordered with some form of emission control. By contrast, the national markets in France, Britain, and Italy were considerably less "green"; there was much less consumer demand, and no tax incentives, for the purchase of "clean" vehicles.

The UK government favored the "lean-burn engines," which were designed to decrease engine pollutants. Ford UK had invested substantial sums in this technology, which the catalytic converter threatened to make obsolete. Indeed, the British argued that the catalytic converter was an antiquated 1960s technology. One British official stated: "We are not supporters of the outdated idea of bolting bits on the back of autos. There is no way that the British government is going to change its mind on this point."[24] Underlying the British position was Ford UK's inexperience in converter production and design. In addition, reflecting the relatively limited political influence of Britain's environmental movement, British Prime Minister Thatcher told German Chancellor Kohl that she thought U.S. standards were too high.[25]

Not surprisingly, Germany was the leader in the drive for emissions standards that made catalytic converters mandatory for all cars sold in Europe; the interests of their powerful automobile industry and their influential environmental movement complimented one another. For the French and the Italians, the interests of domestic automobile producers and relatively weak domestic environmental movements also reinforced one another. The French Trade Association of Automakers contended that "catalytic converters on automobiles would be costly and unnecessary" and that "the usefulness of catalytic converters remains to be demonstrated."[26] In a statement directed against Germany, which had no speed limits on its autobahns, French Prime Minister Laurent Fabius suggested that "governments should consider lowering speed limits rather than introducing catalytic converters as an immediate means of reducing pollution from automobile exhausts."[27] Pierre Perrin-Pelletier of the French Auto Makers Commission added that the United States is a "good example" of how strict regulations "do not necessarily lead to correspondingly low levels of air pollution."[28]

The German government first threatened to impose its own emission standards, which would have required all cars sold in Germany to be equipped with converters. This would have made it very difficult for French and Italian producers to sell their cars in Germany, thus wrecking havoc on intra-Community trade in motor vehicles. While this initiative pleased Germany's green constituencies, which had become increasingly impatient with the slow pace of Community environmental policy, the possibility of an intra-EC trade war frightened Germany's export-oriented car makers. They persuaded Bonn to back off on its threat to establish unilaterally its own automobile emission standards.

Although Germany did enact legislation requiring that all new cars be fitted with catalytic converters, it subsequently agreed to delay the law's implementation from 1986 until 1988 for cars above 2.0 liters and to 1989 for all other cars, in order to give the Community more time to act. However, the German automobile industry agreed to conform to the EC's 1983 standards as soon as possible and to offer vehicles equipped with catalytic converters for sale immediately.

To accommodate the interests of France, Italy, and Great Britain, the Council altered its guidelines on pollutants so that medium-sized cars could meet them by employing "lean-burn" engines or comparable cost-effective measures. Still looser standards were set for smaller cars. In addition, the manufacturers of both were given additional time to comply with the new standards. In effect, the German government traded off lower standards for vehicles produced outside of Germany in exchange for the ability to impose stricter standards on its domestic manufacturers.

In July 1985 nine members of the Council finally reached an agreement. The Luxembourg Compromise classified motor vehicles into three categories, based on their cylinder capacity. Different emission limits, along with different deadlines for meeting them, were established for cars in each category. In addition, stricter compliance deadlines were set for new models than for new vehicles since it was more difficult to change the specifications of a model already in production than to change the design of a new model. Like previous EC emissions directives, the 1987 legislation set a ceiling rather than a floor: member states were still allowed to set lower emission levels than those specified in the directive, but they could not exclude any cars that complied with its emission standards.

The Luxembourg compromise also addressed another important source of tension between national environmental regulations and European economic integration, namely, tax incentives. The incentives for the purchase of cleaner vehicles offered by Germany and the Netherlands had been strongly criticized by the French, Italians, and British, and the Commission had begun proceedings to determine their legality. Some Commission officials concluded these measures were "'compatible' with Community regulations because they provide for tax derogations to the final consumer on a 'non-discriminatory basis.'"[29] Others maintained that the incentives would lead to the distortion of free trade, arguing that they worked "in favor of German automobile and catalytic converter manufacturers."[30] The manufacturers of small vehicles feared that the incentives would hurt their sales in favor of German and Japanese producers. The Luxembourg compromise allowed nations to offer fiscal incentives for the purchase of cleaner vehicles, but restricted the terms under which they were allowed to do so.

The Luxembourg agreement represented a considerable departure from the EC's original objective of matching American emission standards. Acknowledging that its emission limits remained weaker than those of the United States, the Community now argued that their "ultimate effect on the environment" was comparable to that of the United States. Accordingly, the EC would be matching American standards in the sense that the overall amount of pollution generated by European autos would be the same as in the United States. Individual cars in Europe would, however, continue to emit more pollutants than their American counterparts.

European environmentalists were very disappointed with the Luxembourg Compromise: once again the Community appeared to have sacrificed significantly stricter pollution control requirements in order to prevent the emergence of new nontariff barriers. Although European emission standards were tightened, in the final analysis the interests of small-car manufacturers had carried greater weight than those of Europe's environmentalists. However, the latter did secure one important concession: the Luxembourg agreement included a provision requiring the EC to adopt new, stricter emissions requirements for small and medium-size vehicles in 1987. These would go into effect in 1992 and 1993.

Although France, Italy, and the UK remained unenthusiastic about the proposed compromise, all three countries were prepared to go along with the proposed directive, largely to head off the possibility of unilateral action by Germany. However, the Commission's proposal was vetoed by Denmark, on the grounds that it was too lenient. Thus, it was not until after the passage of the SEA, when Denmark lost its veto power over EC legislation, that the Luxembourg Compromise was finally adopted by the Council. Approved in July 1987, it was the first directive adopted under the EC's new "qualified majority" voting procedures.

The directive still had one more hurdle to pass, namely, the European Parliament, which, under the provisions of the SEA, had the right to review Council directives. In view of the political strength of environmentalists within the EP, debate was heated. Many members strongly criticized the Council for ignoring a (nonbinding) resolution the Parliament had adopted in 1984 calling for much stricter emission standards for all vehicles. One Member of Parliament accused the Council and the Commission of "deliberately spurning" the Parliament, adding that "it is high time the strictest limits should be defined, and they must be mandatory. It seems that even in this Year of the Environment, the interests of industry are placed higher than those of the environment. One can only speak of scandal."[31] Another stated, "This situation is intolerable . . . If we maintain the dates in this compromise, we will wait nine years. A child will have walked nine years ingesting all the dirt that escapes from our cars, with our complicity and connivance."[32]

A defender of the Council agreement countered that "all that is excessive is derisory . . . 1992 requires the Europeans to preserve the unity of their market . . . This objective is as important for the German as for the French auto makers."[33] At the end of the debate, the EC's Environment Commissioner, Clinton-Davis, pleaded with the Parliament not to undermine a hard-fought, and fragile, compromise. He warned that the Commission would reject any amendments approved by the Parliament, and argued that "some progress is better than none at all."[34] On November 18, 1987, with many MEPs abstaining, an amendment to tighten the proposed emission standards was defeated and the following month the Luxembourg Compromise became law.

The Small Car Directive

Shortly after passage of the Luxembourg Compromise in 1987, the Commission began work on a directive to establish stricter emission standards for smaller vehicles. However, both the political and economic context for the making of emission standards had changed considerably since the mid 1980s. First, the European environmental movement had gained considerable strength in a number of European countries, including Britain. Its influence in the European Parliament had also grown, which in turn placed considerable pressure on both the Council and the Commission to enact stricter standards than they might otherwise have supported.

Equally important, with the approach of 1992, the EC was under growing pressure to harmonize its environmental regulations—particularly those that directly affected free trade. The device of optimal harmonization, which the Council had used in the past to reconcile divergent national environmental and economic interests with respect to automotive emissions, was no longer viable. The Community thus found itself under increasing pressure to enact automobile emission standards that were both uniform *and* strict.

Nonetheless, at the outset familiar divisions reappeared. The British, French, and Italian governments attempted to maintain the spirit of the Luxembourg Compromise: they urged that smaller vehicles be allowed to meet laxer standards. The Dutch, Germans, and Danes countered by proposing standards for smaller vehicles that were stricter than the 1987 standards for medium-sized ones, thus effectively abandoning the basis of the Luxembourg Compromise. In February 1988 the Commission struck a compromise between the two positions; it proposed to subject small vehicles to the same standards as medium-size ones, but to maintain lower standards for both.

In June 1988 the Council tentatively approved the Commission's compromise, with Denmark, the Netherlands, and Greece dissenting. It also agreed to propose a further reduction in emissions by the end of 1991. Equally important, the Council agreed to forbid member states from offering financial incentives for the purchase of cleaner vehicles. However, the following month, after the Dutch announced that they planned to offer fiscal incentives for consumers to purchase cleaner small cars, the French government abruptly withdrew its support for the small car plan. German auto leaders immediately criticized the French for putting "financial interests before environmental aspects."[35]

But the French government's opposition to the mandatory use of converters for small vehicles no longer reflected the position of its domestic industry, because the opposition of Europe's small and medium-size car producers to catalytic converters had diminished since 1987. Not only had they acquired more experience with this technology, but the demand for cleaner vehicles on the part of European consumers had grown considerably; in a number of European markets, the "cleanliness" of a car had become a quality symbol. Significantly, both Renault and Fiat had begun to manufacture vehicles equipped with three-way catalysts for sale in the Netherlands.

Faced with Renault's change of position, and concerned that their opposition to the Small Car Directive had created the impression that, in the words of France's Environment Minister, "cleanliness was a German vice and dirtiness a French virtue," the French government now decided to support the Council resolution.[36] The UK also initially expressed reservations about the Small Car Directive, hoping to buy time for its industry to perfect a cheaper lean-burn engine technology. However, by 1989 Britain had given up on such hopes and was prepared to abandon its opposition to catalytic converters.[37]

The focus of debate now switched to the European Parliament. The European Environmental Bureau, a lobbying group representing 100 European environmental organizations, criticized the Council's position as a "revealing example of the inadequate character of the European strategy for environmental protection."[38] It demanded that the EC require emission standards as strict as those of the United States, beginning in January 1993. One MEP argued, "It is not with limits like these that we can end the defoliation of our forests." Another stated: "Trees are dying, walls are cracking, and people are falling ill. We in Denmark don't want to wear oxygen masks, like they do in Tokyo."[39]

Recognizing that the Parliament, faced with upcoming European elections, was likely to insist on standards which might prevent the enactment of any directive at all, the Commission and the Council were forced to compromise. They also were spurred to propose stricter standards by the decision of the Netherlands to require catalytic converters on all vehicles sold in that country. While the EC could have challenged the Dutch requirement in the European Court, such a move would have proven politically unpopular and would clearly have undermined the Commission's green credentials.[40] Accordingly, on April 5th, one week before the EP was to vote, the Commission announced that it would shortly propose much stricter emission standards for small cars.

However, a new proposal by the Council was delayed by two disagreements. One concerned timing. The Dutch, Germans, and Danes wanted new standards for small automobiles to be implemented as quickly as possible. However, the British, French, and Italians, anxious to give their domestic manufacturers as much time as possible to adjust, pressed for a later date. The Council compromised by setting a deadline of July 1, 1992, for all new models, and six months later for vehicles then in production.

A second issue concerned whether or not governments could offer financial incentives for the purchase of cleaner vehicles—an issue which the EC had addressed a few years earlier. The Dutch had already done so, and the Germans and Danes indicated that they planned to follow suit. The issue of fiscal incentives was particularly important because without a Community-wide policy, competition among car sellers in different countries could become distorted.[41] Once again, the Council compromised: member states were allowed to offer fiscal incentives to new car purchasers until July 1992, providing the amount did not exceed 85 percent of the cost of the catalytic converter.

In July 1989 a second version of the Small Car Directive was approved by the Council of Ministers by a qualified majority, opposed only by Denmark and Greece. Its passage marked a significant step forward in both the tightening and harmonization of pollution control standards within the Community. Strict new limits on emissions were established for *all* small cars sold in the EC. To meet these standards, small cars would be required to be fitted with catalytic converters—and thus run on unleaded gasoline. In fact, the new limits, which aimed to cut existing emissions levels by 73 percent, were even lower than the 1987 standards for medium and large cars, thus standing the Luxembourg Compromise on its head.

Thus, after nearly two decades of wrangling, the EC had finally managed to harmonize emission standards for the majority of vehicles sold in Europe. Of equal importance, it had set these standards at a relatively high level. The directive was hailed by environmentalists as a major victory. EP Environment Committee chair Ken Collins boasted: "We forced the catalytic converter on a reluctant Britain and France."[42] EC Environment Commissioner Carlo Ripa di Meana described the agreement on the Small Car Directive as "a milestone for Europe," and announced that the Commission planned to put forward new proposals to impose stricter emission standards on medium and large cars that would bring them into line with American norms.[43]

Nonetheless, despite this substantial progress toward both the harmonization and strengthening of European auto emission standards, tensions among the member states has persisted. For example, in September 1990 the issue of German speed limits (or to be more precise, the lack thereof) was again raised by the French government. In a newspaper interview, French Environment Minister Brice Lalonde threatened that "Paris [would] ban imports of West German BMWs, Mercedes and other fast cars if Bonn did not introduce speed limits to help the environment."[44] Lalonde added, "I want talks on speed limits and carbon monoxide gas emissions. A West German commitment on this point is indispensable."[45]

A somewhat more substantive disagreement emerged in 1990, when Denmark enacted legislation establishing automobile emission standards considerably stricter than those mandated by the Community. It based its action on Article 100A, paragraph 4, of the SEA, which permits member states to exceed Community standards if doing so is necessary to improve environmental quality. The Commission in turn expressed the fear that the extensive use of this provision would create "islands" within the single market; it further argued that this "escape clause" applied only to national laws enacted prior to the SEA, not subsequent to it.[46] However, the Commission decided not to take Denmark to court, since the Council was about to approve the first draft of a new directive on car emissions that set standards comparable to those enacted by Denmark.

In July 1991 the EC gave its final approval to a directive which significantly tightened emission standards for all vehicles, thus obviating the Danish challenge. Two years later, emission standards were tightened still further. A 1993 directive required new cars to reduce carbon dioxide emissions by an additional 30 percent, hydrocarbons by 55 percent, and nitrogen oxides by 38 percent. Stricter emission standards were also established for diesel engines.[47]

Chemical Safety

The European Union's prolonged difficulties in harmonizing automobile emission standards stand in marked contrast to its relative ease in establishing a uniform system for the regulation of chemical safety. Nonetheless, negotiations for the Sixth Amendment, which both strengthened and harmonized a system of notification and testing for the marketing of new chemicals, took six years. Moreover, agreement was finally made possible only as a response to developments in the United States.

The Union's basic legislation for regulating chemicals is the 1967 Framework Directive on Dangerous Substances, which provided for a uniform system of listing, classification, packaging, and labeling of these substances.[48] Member states were required to classify dangerous substances according to the nature of the hazard they presented and to ensure that they would not be marketed unless they were appropriately packaged and labeled. More than 1,000 substances subsequently received EC labels, containing their chemical identity, a warning symbol, and standardized risk and safety phrases.[49]

However, this directive only established a framework for labeling, packaging, and classifying dangerous substances. It did not impose any restrictions on their use. Any chemical could be produced and marketed throughout the Community, provided it was appropriately labeled and packaged. Furthermore, the actual implementation of the directive proved rather difficult.[50] As of 1969, not one member state had notified the Commission that it was in compliance. Following two successive one-year extensions, the Council ultimately established a compliance deadline of January 1, 1972, more than four years after the directive had been adopted.

In 1973 the EC adopted a directive applying the same system of packaging and labeling for solvents. This extension highlighted the EC's broadening interpretation of products that required more uniform regulatory standards. It required member states to prevent any solvent from being placed on the market unless it complied with the directive's requirements. However, the Council rejected a Commission recommendation for total harmonization which would have made compliance with EC requirements both a necessary and sufficient condition for dangerous substances to be introduced into the market of any member state.[51] Instead, the directive allowed the member states substantial discretion in implementing its provisions. It thus represented an approximation, rather than a harmonization of the laws of the member states.

That same year, the EC adopted a directive establishing a simplified procedure for adopting technical standards to control all aspects of dangerous substances. A technical committee was formed to review existing standards for both dangerous substances and preparations and to modify them in light of continued technical advances. Two years later, in 1975, the Council adopted the Fifth Amendment to the 1967 directive. Its primary aim was not to strengthen EC standards but to reduce the ability of member states to use national chemical regulations to restrict intra-EC trade. Member states were forbidden from banning a dangerous substance from their national markets if the substance met EC standards. Even if a member state could demonstrate that a substance was unsafe despite its compliance with Community standards, it could only prohibit its marketing on a provisional, temporary basis. The Commission then had six weeks in which to assess and, if it so chose, to overrule the national restriction.

In July 1974 the Commission noted that its existing restrictions on labeling and packaging toxic substances were still inadequate to protect public health and safety. It also expressed concern about the wide variety of national regulatory standards, and the likelihood that they would become stricter due to the public's increasing concerns about the impact of chemicals on both people and the environment. In order to tighten controls over chemicals throughout the Community and at the same time prevent new national regulations from restricting intra-Community trade, the Commission proposed that the EC establish a new system for the testing and notification of new chemicals.

Two years later, following a review by the Public Health Committee of the European Parliament, the Commission submitted to the Council a slightly revised version of its original proposal on the marketing of dangerous substances. This proposal, which represented the Sixth Amendment to the 1967 directive, established an entirely new system for regulating the safety of chemicals sold within the Community. Reflecting the EC's heightened concern with environmental quality, it established a new classification: "dangerous for the environment." It was also preventive: new substances had to be tested for potential hazards before they could be marketed. At the same time, the proposal sought to create a common market for chemicals. New chemicals would no longer be tested by each nation in which they were marketed, but rather only by the EC member state in which the substance was first sold. Provided these tests were conducted according to standards outlined in the directive, all member states would be required to recognize their results.

However, agreement on the Commission's proposal proved difficult, primarily because of differences between Europe's two major chemical producers, namely Great Britain and Germany. Each nation had a long-standing and distinctive approach to regulating chemicals. They were reluctant to surrender national authority over the regulation of this important and politically powerful industry. The British regarded the German approach as too rigid, while the Germans feared that adopting the more flexible British style of regulation would lead to lax enforcement in other member states, thus placing German firms at a competitive disadvantage. They also disagreed over such matters as the extent to which chemicals sold in small volumes would be exempt from testing requirements and the degree of flexibility national authorities would be allowed in determining specific testing requirements.

This deadlock was broken by the 1976 passage of the Toxic Substances Control Act (TSCA) by the United States, which established requirements for the manufacture of all new and existing chemicals in the United States. This legislation was strongly opposed by many European industrialists, who regarded it as a major threat to their continued ability to export to the United States.[52] In 1977 the United States entered into negotiations with other developed nations under the auspices of the Organization for Economic Cooperation and Development (OECD) to harmonize test procedures and provide for the mutual recognition of test data and laboratory procedures. But these negotiations were hampered by the uncertainty surrounding the adoption of the EC's regulatory policies and procedures. However, as they proceeded, all participants came to recognize the importance of establishing common regulations for the marketing of chemicals on both sides of the Atlantic.

Equally important, European officials realized that their bargaining power over the United States would be strengthened if they were able to reach an agreement among themselves. They urgently needed to develop a European-wide system for new chemical screening which they could then use as the basis for negotiating an agreement with the United States that would standardize requirements in both chemical markets. In the spring of 1978, the European Commission asked the Council for a formal mandate to negotiate with the United States and to develop "parallel" legislation. A year later, with the French about to implement their own Chemical Control Law, and the United States about to implement TSCA, a compromise formula was adopted by the Council.

The Sixth Amendment established a system for the premarket notification of new chemicals, based on a modified system of mutual recognition. It required manufacturers to register each chemical with the appropriate regulatory authorities in any member state in which they planned to market it. (This provision applies to chemicals both produced in and imported into the EC.) Registration requires a standardized "base set" of data, along with a risk assessment. The competent national authority then has a maximum of forty-five days to review the data accompanying the request for registration. If the registration of a chemical has been approved, the member state is required to submit a summary of its findings to the Commission. The Commission then forwards this information to all other member states. Upon the receipt of this data, regulatory officials may confer with and make suggestions to their counterparts in the member state that initially received the notification. Should the latter fail to follow a suggestion of another state as to additional testing or requests for additional data, or fail to respond to the satisfaction of the other state, either may ask the Commission to resolve the conflict.[53]

Since the failure of one member state to evaluate adequately the data contained in a notification dossier can be challenged by any of the other eleven, mutual recognition has been supplemented by a system of checks and balances. Moreover, each member state agreed to adopt similar testing methods and to exchange information on a regular basis. As the initial regulatory hurdles faced by the manufacturer of a new chemical are now, in principle, identical throughout the EU, a manufacturer has no incentive to apply for approval in a nation whose regulatory officials appear to be somewhat more permissive. At the same time, once a chemical has been registered in one country, all other EU members are required to accept it in their markets, thus eliminating a potential barrier to trade. The EU has thus created "an international system of interlocking procedures and obligations in which each E.C. member country in effect acts as the agent of its partners in permitting a new chemical onto the E.C. market."[54]

The Sixth Amendment has substantially contributed to the free movement of chemicals within the EU. Indeed, no other environmental directive has ever been implemented so rapidly.[55] By the September 1981 deadline specified in the Amendment, two of Europe's three major chemical producers, namely, France and Germany, had passed national legislation implementing it, and they in turn worked with the Commission to pressure compliance by other member states. Britain, Belgium, and Italy soon followed. By early 1983 most member states had established the necessary institutional machinery to receive and review notification requests.

According to Louis Jordan, head of the Technical Division of the European Council of Chemical Industry Federation, "European industry has no real difficulties with the Sixth Amendment; it is a good balance between environmental protection and the administrative burden on industry and government."[56] Equally important, as a result of frequent meetings among national regulatory officials organized by the Commission, an informal consensus has emerged regarding appropriate criteria and standards. According to Brickman, Jasanoff, and Illgen, "the Sixth Amendment now stands as the EC's crowning achievement in the area of chemical control."[57]

Like the Small Car Directive, the Sixth Amendment both strengthened European regulatory standards and facilitated intra-European trade. At the same time, it also brought European standards closer to American ones. Following the passage of the Sixth Amendment, the EC and the United States, acting under the auspices of the OECD, agreed to establish common testing standards for the introduction and marketing of chemicals, thus further facilitating EC-USA trade.

What accounts for the EC's relatively rapid progress in harmonizing chemical safety standards, as contrasted with its prolonged difficulties in harmonizing automobile emission standards? Most obviously, not only were the costs of compliance relatively modest for the chemical industry—no costly changes in technology were required—but they were relatively evenly distributed. No chemical firm stood to gain a competitive advantage by the establishment of a particular standard: all wanted a level playing field. Unlike a number of European automobile manufacturers, who marketed their product primarily in a few nations, the European chemical industry was highly international. None of the major firms stood to benefit by the enactment of regulatory standards that protected their domestic market; since all depended heavily on exports to the other member states, all wished to avoid the difficulty of having to comply with divergent national regulations.[58] For this reason, both the German and British chemical industries strongly favored EC rather than national regulatory standards. Finally, as already noted, with the passage of regulatory legislation in the United States, the European Chemical industry needed to speak with one voice, for which the Community was the logical vehicle.

Solid Wastes

An increasingly important dimension of environmental regulation involves the promotion of recycling in order to conserve raw materials and reduce the volume of solid wastes. However, these regulations often interfere with trade by making it more difficult for exporters to design products that meet national packaging and recycling requirements. In fact, recycling requirements usually improve the competitive position of firms whose production facilities are located closer to the markets in which their products are sold, which is an important reason for its popularity among producers seeking to reduce foreign competition.

In 1981 Denmark enacted legislation requiring that manufacturers market all beer and soft drinks in reusable containers. Furthermore, all beverage retailers were required to take back all containers, regardless of where they had been purchased. These containers had to be approved in advance by the MiljOstrelsen, the Danish environmental protection agency, in order to assure that they were suitable for recycling and that a sufficient proportion of the returned containers would actually be reused. The Danish government subsequently restricted the number of different beer and soft drink containers that could enter the Danish market to about thirty; otherwise the handling costs for retailers taking part in the system would be too high, since they would be required to store too many different kinds of containers.[59]

A number of beverages produced in other member states did not meet Denmark's strict recycling requirements and the Danish government therefore prohibited their sale. The companies that produced these beverages complained to the European Commission, contending that the additional costs they were forced to incur in modifying their containers made it more difficult for them to sell their products in Denmark. The Commission agreed; it ruled that Danish regulations violated Article 30's prohibition against "quantitative restrictions on trade."

In response to the Commission's ruling, Denmark amended its statute in 1984. The new law permitted the marketing of containers not approved by the Danish government, but with the following restrictions: the quantity of the containers could not exceed 3,000 hectoliters, the containers could not be made of metal, and the manufacturer had to establish a system for collecting and recycling used products that was similar to that required for comparable authorized containers.

Not surprisingly, this legislation also failed to satisfy the Commission. It argued that while Denmark could maintain its mandatory recycling system, its restriction of the number of nonapproved containers had the "equivalent effect" of a "quantitative restriction on imports." On December 1, 1986, the Commission brought a complaint against Denmark to the European Court of Justice. The British government also intervened in support of the Commission.

The Commission's decision to take Denmark to the European Court "clearly signaled its fear that member states would take refuge behind the environmental banner to avoid opening their markets to imports."[60] Significantly, the Cecchini Report on the benefits of the single market, which was published two years later but which was in preparation about this time, had specifically singled out Denmark's recycling laws as a significant barrier to intra-Community trade in beverages. It stated that while Denmark's laws appear to be nondiscriminatory, "the transportation costs of two-way bottles makes them impractical over 300km—a distance easily exceeded when exporting to Denmark."[61] The report claimed that Denmark's recycling requirement was one reason why "Denmark has both the highest level of beer consumption per capita in Europe after Germany and a negligible level of imports as a percentage of consumption."[62] Indeed, Denmark's imports of foreign beer had fallen after the introduction of its recycling requirements. Thus, the Danish bottle law functioned as Denmark's equivalent of the German *Reinheitsgebot*.

In its brief, the Commission anticipated the analysis of the Cecchini Report. While noting that Denmark's requirements applied equally to domestic and imported products, the Commission argued that the Danish collection system put imported products at an unfair disadvantage due to the higher costs involved in the long distance transport of empty containers. Moreover, while approved containers could be returned to any store, nonapproved bottles had to be taken back to a retailer that sold that particular product. In addition, since all containers in excess of 3,000 hectoliters had to be reused rather than simply recycled, the producers of imported products incurred higher costs than those imposed on Danish manufacturers. Accordingly, the Commission claimed that "even though on the surface indiscriminately applicable to Danish and non-Danish manufacturers, the rules bear in practice more heavily on the latter."[63]

The briefs of both the British government and the Commission also questioned the "sincerity of the ecological worriers of Denmark."[64] They claimed that the real effect of the Danish rebottling requirement was to force foreign beverage firms to produce their drinks in Denmark and deliver them in Danish containers, since otherwise it would be extremely difficult for them to establish the necessary infrastructure for recycling, sorting, and transporting their containers. They also noted that the recycling requirement only applied to beer and soft drinks; it excluded products such as wine and spirits which were not threatened by imports. Moreover, the Danish regulation only applied to beer and soft drinks sold *within* Denmark: Danish beer producers continued to produce beer in metal cans for export.

Two European economists argued that, "although we may never be able to prove it (and this is one reason why environmental protectionism may be a very attractive policy to follow for some governments), the Danish regulation represents a textbook case of 'environmental protectionism': Why did Denmark ban the use of metal containers when the recovery of metal is a widespread and successful practice in Denmark? Why did Denmark use a regulatory approach . . . when it is one of the leading users of pollution taxation? It seems that Denmark may have been solely targeting the containers of beer and soft drinks because it knew it could get away with it and protect its own producers."[65]

While recognizing that national measures taken to protect the environment did constitute a legitimate exception to Article 30, the Commission claimed that since the Danish countryside would be equally free of litter if the unapproved bottles were recycled instead of reused, "the adverse impact of the collection system on trade was disproportionate to the objective of protecting the environment."[66] Advocate General Sir Gordon Slynn made a similar argument. He told the Court that "although the conservation of resources is an important objective, it does not seem to me that in the present state of Community legislation that an obligatory reutilization should be accepted if its effect is seriously to inhibit the free movement of goods."[67] He added: "Cassis . . . does not give Member States carte blanche—the level of protection required for one of the acceptable categories must not . . . be excessive or unreasonable and the measures taken to the achieve the requirements must be necessary and *proportional*."[68]

The Danish government replied that the sole purpose of its legislation was waste reduction and denied that its regulations were a disguised form of protectionism. It contended that its rebottling requirement had been highly effective, with 99 percent of approved bottles being returned and some being used up to thirty times. According to the Danish brief, "Some bottles which are not returned by the purchaser are returned by enterprising children, the deposit repaid forming a valuable source of pocket money. The result is a cleaner countryside and a saving of raw materials."[69] An official from the Danish Ministry of Foreign Affairs told the Court: "It seems the Commission has not followed the increasing ecological awareness which has arisen in recent years throughout Europe and which has led to the giving of priority to the protection of the environment over the free movement of goods, which while remaining a fundamental objective, is no longer seen as an aim which must be achieved at any price."[70]

Neither the Commission nor the British government questioned the efficiency of the Danish scheme. Rather, they argued that the objectives of environmental protection must be balanced against the need to assure the free movement of goods within the EC. They concluded that the Danish law failed this balancing test: it had established a level of protection at an "exaggeratedly high level . . . other solutions should be allowed, even if they guarantee a little less effectively the aim pursued."[71] Sir Gordon stated: "There has to be a balancing of interests between the free movement of goods and environmental protection, even if in achieving this balance the high standards of environmental protection sought must be reduced."[72]

No one, including Denmark, denied that the Danish bottling requirements restricted trade by imposing a more difficult burden on non-Danish beverage producers. The issue before the Court was whether these restrictions were permissible under Article 36 of the Treaty of Rome, which permitted member states to restrict imports if such restrictions are necessary to protect "the health and life of humans, animals or plants." Since *Cassis de Dijon*, (1979), which helped establish the principle of mutual recognition, the Court had oscillated between interpreting Article 36 broadly and narrowly. In general, it had held that there were three conditions under which recourse to Article 36 was justified. First, the harm to the health and life of humans which the national restriction addressed was not adequately dealt with at the Community level (it had not been harmonized); second, the regulation must not discriminate against importers; and third, it must be "proportionate": it must not only be necessary to achieve its ostensible objective, but it must do so in the way that least restricts the free movement of goods.

However, the previous cases brought before the Court seeking exemptions under Article 36 had to do with such issues as consumer protection, chemical product regulations, and so on. This was the first case to come before the Court in which a member state had sought to justify a limit to trade on *environmental* grounds.

On September 20, 1988, the Court issued its ruling. It found Denmark's requirements regarding the mandatory disposal and recycling of empty containers to be legal, since the Community had no recycling program and "a deposit and return system was . . . indispensable for recycling containers."[73] It rejected the Commission's criticism of Denmark for having established an overly ambitious environmental goal, challenging it to define what level of recycling was "adequate" and what was excessive. (The Commission was unable to come up with an alternative system that was as efficient and effective in protecting the environment as the one the Danes had devised.) The Court held that protecting the environment was "one of the Community's essential objectives" and that, accordingly, environmental protection constituted a "mandatory requirement capable of limiting the application of Article 30 of the Treaty of Rome"—a view which it found confirmed in the SEA, which was nearing passage at the time the bottle case was being heard.[74]

However, the Court did strike down one provision of Denmark's recycling statute. It held that Denmark's restriction on the marketing of nonapproved containers was "disproportionate to the aim of the legislation."[75] Since Denmark's environmental objectives could just as easily be achieved if nonapproved bottles were subject to a deposit and return scheme, there was no valid reason to require them to be rebottled. Accordingly, Denmark could not restrict foreign bottlers of beer and soft drinks from selling their products in Denmark in their original containers in whatever quantity they chose—provided the bottlers made arrangements to recycle the containers.

The Danish bottle case left a number of questions unanswered. Was any degree of interference with free trade—provided it was necessary to improve environmental quality—justified under Article 36? In other words, under what circumstances, if any, could a national environmental regulation that interfered with the creation of the single market be judged unnecessarily strict? What precisely was the line between disproportionate and proportionate measures? Another issue concerned the relationship between Community and national standards. If an environmental regulation were harmonized, could a member state still enact legislation that exceeded its standards on the grounds that its national regulations were more effective at protecting its domestic environment?

These ambiguities aside, the decision in the Danish bottles case was very significant. The Court had, for the first time, sanctioned an environmental regulation that clearly restricted trade. Moreover, in balancing economic integration with the commitment of some member states to stricter standards, the Court had favored the latter. Significantly, it had not chosen to second-guess the reasonableness of the goals of Denmark's recycling program, but only to inquire whether the means it had chosen to achieve them were essential.

The Court's decision outraged the British drinks and container industry. The UK Committee on Packaging and the Environment stated that the judgment had "absolutely enormous implications. If a can ban can be compatible with the Treaty of Rome, then anything less far reaching, like a mandatory deposit scheme, is not going to be challenged."[76] The Committee's concerns proved to be well-founded. The Court's decision opened the way for a rash of new national packaging regulations, many of which also had protectionist consequences and, in some cases, intentions as well. Shortly after the Danish bottles decision was announced, Germany, which had previously hesitated to enact a mandatory recycling program lest it breach EC law, enacted a mandatory plastic bottle deposit and return regulation in order to promote reusing and recycling and to reduce waste.[77] Since the deposit for plastic bottles was nearly double that for glass bottles, and the scheme relied exclusively on retailers for collections and returns, German beer and soft drink retailers switched from plastic to glass containers. The result was to force French and Belgium producers of mineral water to export their product to Germany in much heavier glass containers, thus significantly increasing their transportation costs. (EC rules required that mineral water be bottled at its source.) However, for their part, Danish brewers, who were major exporters to Germany, welcomed the German law, since given the strict nature of their own recycling system, they were relatively well positioned to comply with the new German requirements.

The Commission decided not to challenge the German scheme—although it did demand one relatively minor modification in it: the German government could not require that the deposits be collected only by retail stores.[78] In addition, following the Danish bottles decision, the Commission was forced to reconsider an earlier decision to take Italy to the European Court over a law restricting the use of plastic packaging, while Irish authorities were encouraged to proceed with a ban on nonrefillable containers for beer and soft drinks. A number of southern EC states promptly restricted the sale of beverages in plastic bottles in order to protect their environment and, not coincidentally, domestic glass producers as well.

In April 1991 the German government approved the world's strictest recycling law. Its objective was to reduce the amount of waste going into landfill and incineration. All companies were required to take back and recycle all packaging used during transport, or pay another firm to do so. Similar requirements were subsequently imposed on "secondary packaging," such as gift wrapping and boxes. On January 1, 1993, all packaging, including candy and butter wrappers, were included as well.

The *Economist* remarked that "the ferocity of the new obligation is extraordinary: when fully implemented, it will require a level of recycling that not even the most environmentally conscious middle-class community in any western nation has achieved."[79] It required 90 percent of all glass and metals as well as 80 percent of paper, board, and plastics to be recycled, while incineration, for whatever reason, was not permitted. The German Environmental Ministry subsequently announced that it planned to extend the recycling requirement to automobiles and electronic goods.

To recover and reuse packaging waste, nearly 3,000 German companies established the quasi-public Duales System Deutschland.[80] Packaging companies paid the DSD to put a green dot symbol on their products, indicating that they can be returned and reused. The collection and recycling system is, in part, financed by the money charged companies for the "green dot." A number of manufacturing firms established divisions responsible for environmental technology, and many firms, including automobile companies, began to develop new recycling techniques and technologies for their products. A leading department store chain asked suppliers to dispense with outer packaging.

Non-German firms complained vigorously to the EC. They argued that "the DSD scheme . . . puts one more barrier in the way of a foreign firm wanting to sell in Germany."[81] The European packaging industry was particularly irate. In their eyes, the German law had crossed "the indistinct line between national environmental protection and protection of a more reprehensible sort."[82] Britain's Industry Council for Packaging and the Environment contended that the rules "restrict the free movement of goods into Germany."[83] The representative of a packaging firm described the Germany plan as "absolute lunacy."[84] He noted that "more resources are being spent transporting waste packaging around Germany, sorting it, recycling it, warehousing it and dumping it on other markets, than are being saved."[85]

Importers specifically complained to the EC about a provision in the packaging law, inserted at the last minute, that permitted only 28 percent of beer and soft drinks to be sold in disposable containers. They claimed that this clause was inserted to protect small brewers in Bavaria, who would find it relatively easy to collect and refill empty containers.[86] By contrast, importers would incur considerable additional costs if they had to take their bottles back for refilling. Non-German firms also charged that the requirement that companies both collect and recycle their used packaging would discourage retailers from stocking imported goods. Eucofel, a European trade association representing fruit and vegetable shippers, complained that since they were unable to recycle the wooden crates in which most of the fruits and vegetables they exported to Germany were shipped, they were required to ship them in reusable plastic crates, thus raising their costs.

Moreover, the plan's very success in turn created a new source of tension between Germany and its trading partners. The amount of packaging materials collected by the DSD far exceeded that of the plan's designers. In 1992 the DSD collected 245,000 more tons of plastic than it was able to recycle.[87] Unable to find any commercial (re)use for the increasingly large quantities of packaging materials they were collecting, and finding their nation's recycling capacity overwhelmed by the unexpected large volume of collected materials, German producers began to export it. When German plastic containers turned up at French dumps and incinerators, it created a major scandal in the EC.[88] In 1993 a third of the plastic and paper packaging materials collected by the DSD were exported, mostly to Britain and France, though substantial portions were shipped to the third world as well.

The collection and export of German waste materials also had an unexpected competitive impact: it undercut the recycling programs of other EC member states. Britain, France, Ireland, Italy, Luxembourg, and the Netherlands all complained that their newly established recycling industries were being overwhelmed by "subsidized" German exports.[89] British commercial recycling firms found themselves swamped with offers of free material from German waste-paper merchants, thus undermining the British government's efforts to encourage its domestic packaging industry to recycle their materials. A British plastics recycling firm established by the plastics industry had been paying local governments for plastic bottles for which it was seeking a market. Now German firms were offering to *pay* the same amount for processors to take their waste. Largely as a result of Germany's packaging law, imports of plastic waste into the UK increased 45 percent between 1991 and 1992. French waste-paper merchants drove their trucks through the streets of Paris to protest against the collapse in the price of their product, and the French threatened to ban imports of waste from Germany.[90] On the other hand, many German industries were able to benefit from new supplies of cheap recycled materials.

The German government defended its waste exports, contending that the criticisms by foreign governments failed to take into account the country's substantial imports of raw materials. Clemens Stroetmann, state secretary in the Environment Ministry, argued that "it is almost impossible to ensure the environmentally-sound disposal of used paper levels in Germany using our national capacity alone."[91] He also denied that the exports of commercially valuable waste material were subsidized, claiming that the fees collected by the DSD essentially covered the costs of collection. Finally, the Germany government stated that the export of waste was a temporary problem, which would be resolved as soon as two new recycling plants in eastern Germany were completed.

The European Commission, fearful of being labeled "antigreen," hesitated to challenge the legality of the German recycling law; moreover, in view of the Court's decision in the Danish bottles case, it was unclear whether it would prevail, since the Germany recycling program was clearly effective. Instead, the Community attempted to write a directive on packaging waste.[92] But this proved rather difficult, largely because both public enthusiasm and the necessary infrastructure for recycling varied widely among the member states. For example, while the Dutch recycled over half of their paper, the Italians recycled just one-third. Likewise, while Germans recycled over half of their glass, the British recycled less than one-fifth.[93]

Moreover, the EC's poorer countries compounded the problem still further: many citizens in the south of Europe regarded the increased use of packaging as a sign of affluence. They were therefore unenthusiastic about regulations that sought to limit it. In addition, the British, French, and Italians wanted incineration in which the heat is reused to count as a form of recycling, a proposal to which European environmentalists strongly objected. For its part, the European packaging industry generally opposed strict European-wide packaging standards, contending that many packaging products, such as beverage cartons, are not easily recyclable. Finally, Germany expressed its strong opposition to any EC recycling standard that would require it to reduce its own ambitious recycling targets.

However, the continuing flood of German exports of used paper, board, and plastic to other member states placed increased pressure on the Community to establish European-wide recycling regulations. Not only was Germany's program disrupting the recycling efforts of its trading partners, but other member states, including the Netherlands, Denmark, France, and Italy, began to introduce their own comprehensive recycling schemes, thus threatening to compound still further the Community's difficulties.[94] These plans had little in common, save that they all undermined the single market by establishing distinctive national recycling requirements.

Finally, in December 1994, after nearly three years of wrangling, the EU approved a packaging directive. It requires member states to recover at least half their waste packaging and recycle a quarter of it, with a minimum of 15 percent for each material, within five years. Ireland, Greece, and Portugal were given slightly lower targets. Nations that wish to recycle more than 65 percent of their packaging may do so, but only if they have the facilities to use their recycled products.

The European packaging industry strongly supported the proposed directive. The director of the UK Industry Council on Packaging and the Environment stated, "This is good news for the industry. Everybody can plan for the future knowing what the targets are."[95] The Association of Plastic Manufacturers of Europe characterized it as well balanced because it does not discriminate between industries.[96]

Germany, Denmark, and the Netherlands voted against the directive. Klaus Topfer, Germany's environment minister and architect of its recycling program, protested that it would "set back progress on environmental protection in Europe and force Germany to produce more waste." Noting that Germany already exceeded the EU's recycling targets, he stated: "It is not supposed to be the EU's job to standardize the environmental tempo in all member states at any price or even to reverse it," adding that the directive violated the principle of free trade.[97] However, while the directive will restrict Germany's exports of waste, it will not prevent Germany from insisting that 72 percent of its bottles containing drinks be refillable. Nor will it affect

Denmark's ban on the sale of beverages in cans. Thus tension between some national packaging requirements and the single market will persist. At the same time the directive's minimum standards will significantly strengthen the recycling programs of the "grubbier majority" of EU member states.[98]

Ironically, notwithstanding the German government's strong defense of its recycling program within the EU, the program has been criticized in Germany. Some German producers contend that the DSD program places "an unfair burden on businesses struggling against recession and intense foreign competition."[99] Moveover, as much more material is being collected than can be reprocessed, the plan is proving much more expensive than had initially been predicted; in its first year of operation, it ran a deficit of between $180 and $300 million. The plan has also proven relatively expensive for German consumers, raising the prices of some packaged goods by as much as ten cents.[100]

Conclusion

The making of environmental policy in the European Union reveals the close links between environmental regulations and trade policies. Since the economies of the member states are relatively closely integrated, a wide range of national and EU environmental regulations affect intra-Union trade. These have included regulations governing the lead content of gasoline, the installation of catalytic convertors on small vehicles, tax incentives for the purchase of cleaner vehicles, the labeling and testing of chemicals, and recycling requirements for bottles and other kinds of packaging. The disputes over many of these regulations reflect not only different national preferences for environmental regulation, but also the distinctive ways in which these policies affect producers in different countries.

Yet, in the case of food safety standards, the Union has on balance made substantial progress in reducing the role of divergent national regulations as nontariff barriers. The progress it has made is due to two factors. One has to do with the role of internationally oriented producers. Thus the EU's success in harmonizing standards for the marketing of new chemicals reflected the interests and influence of major European chemical producers. Harmonizing regulatory standards was critical not only to their ability to market their products throughout the EU, but also to their ability to export to the United

States, which had previously tightened its own regulatory standards. Likewise, the push for more uniform automobile emissions standards was led by Germany, home to Europe's most internationally oriented car firms.

The second factor has to do with the role of the Union's institutions. By removing the ability of any one member state to veto Council proposals, the Single European Act significantly facilitated the EU's ability to harmonize regulatory standards. Indeed, the Small Car Directive was the first piece of legislation to approved under the system of weighted voting established by the SEA. The strengthening of Community institutions under the SEA was an important factor in increasing the rate at which environmental directives were enacted.

What has been the impact of the European Union on environmental standards? The experiences of the EU illustrate both dimensions of the California effect. One way trade liberalization can promote the strengthening of national regulatory standards is by encouraging producers in greener nations to support stricter environmental standards than those of their trading partners in order to gain a competitive advantage. The preferences of Germany for stricter automotive emission standards and of both Germany and Denmark for stricter recycling requirements reflected a convergence of interests between segments of their domestic industry (that is, bootleggers), and green pressure groups (that is, Baptists). Thus Denmark's recycling requirements for beverage containers both made the Danish countryside cleaner and kept Danish beer imports low. The same is true of the prohibitions of various member states on the sale of beverages in plastic bottles: they protected domestic glass bottlers and encouraged recycling or bottling. Similarly, Germany's packaging laws encouraged domestic recycling and made it more difficult for goods packaged or produced overseas to enter the German market. Likewise, had the EC permitted Germany to require all vehicles sold in that country to be equipped with catalytic convertors, German air quality would have been enhanced and the market share of automobile imports would have declined, thus pleasing both Germany greens and German automobile manufacturers.

Equally important, the preference for stricter standards on the part of the EU's richest and greenest member state also contributed to the strengthening of regulatory standards in its trading partners. Thus, in part because of the large size of Germany's domestic market for automobiles, the preferences of Italian and French producers changed as well; they too began to support stricter emission standards in order to be able to export to greener markets within the Community and internationally. Indeed, the German car industry supported stricter emission standards in the first place in part because of the experience they had gained in complying with American emission standards. Thus, both German environmentalists and German producers favored the adoption of "US 83" standards. Indeed, in this case, the California effect was a literal one, since half of all German automobile sales to the United States are in California, which has the world's strictest automobile emission standards.

In this context, it is also significant that the one country which supported Germany's strict repacking law was Denmark. Precisely because Denmark already had its own relatively strict recycling requirements, its domestic bottling industry was in a more favorable position to comply with Germany's. Moreover, thanks to their being forced to develop new recycling technologies, German firms will have a competitive advantage when similar legislation is adopted elsewhere.

The second dimension of the California effect has to do with the role of international institutions. The preferences of Germany, Denmark, and the Netherlands for stricter environmental standards for traded products have continually threatened European integration. They have forced the Union to choose between permitting stricter national standards and preserving the common market. What is important about this tension is not only its persistence, but its long-term impact on European regulatory standards.

To avoid having to choose between the reduction of national trade barriers and the strengthening of regulatory standards, the Union has usually attempted to fashion a compromise. As the history of EU automobile emission and packaging standards demonstrates, these standards have frequently been harmonized at a level somewhat laxer than that preferred by the Union's greenest states but stronger than that favored by less green members. This not only preserves the single market, but also improves environmental quality in the Union as a whole. For while some harmonized regulations for traded products have required that environmental standards in the greener states be lowered, they have also required that the environmental standards in other member states be strengthened: what is a "ceiling" for Germany, Denmark, or the Netherlands has frequently represented a "floor" for Italy, Britain, or Spain.

The role of the Union's greener members in setting its environmental agenda has been a critical one; it is primarily their political and economic importance, combined with the interests of the rest of the Union in preserving the single market, that have served to make EU standards progressively stricter. Were the EU's richest and most powerful nations not also among its greenest, it is highly unlikely that the Union's commitment to economic integration would have resulted in the steadily upward trend in environmental standards. Indeed, it might well have relaxed them.

Consequently, for the *majority* of member states and EU citizens, the increasingly important role of the EU in making environmental policies has resulted in a steady and significant strengthening of regulatory standards. The Union has driven the national regulations of the "average" EU member state steadily upward. Indeed, for a number of member states, the EU has been the single most important factor in strengthening national environmental regulations. Moreover, the SEA, by strengthening the role of the European Parliament, where green political constituencies are relatively influential, has increased the ability of European environmentalists to shape Union policies. Their influence will increase still further as a result of the continued strengthening of the EP's role in shaping Union legislation under the Maastricht Treaty.

This process has been dynamic: new issues, and new regulations, keep emerging. For no sooner has a compromise standard been agreed to than one or more of the member states invariably attempt to issue national regulations which go beyond it. The result is another series of prolonged negotiations, resulting in a new harmonized standard. And, as the history of automobile emissions reveals, these new standards are invariably stronger than those which preceded it. In this sense, the continual tension between national environmental regulations and the single market has contributed to the strengthening of environmental standards. Indeed, it is precisely the threat, and at times the ability, of one or more of the Union's greener states to "go it alone"—especially on the part of Germany, the largest market—that has served to prod the other member states into supporting a ratcheting upward of Union standards, lest the common market be undermined. In a sense, the EU has forced the green movements of Denmark, the Netherlands, and Germany to make a tradeoff: it has weakened their ability to influence the environmental standards of their own nations, while at the same time strengthening their ability to influence the environmental standards of those member states in which domestic environmental pressure groups are less powerful.

The entrance of Austria, Finland, and Sweden into the European Union in 1995 is likely to accelerate this dynamic.[101] All three nations have powerful environmental movements, and many of their environmental standards are stricter than those of the Union. For example, Austria has banned the use of leaded gasoline, while Finland's rules on the sulfur content of diesel oils are stricter than those of Brussels. An agreement reached in December 1993 permits each member state to maintain stricter national environmental standards for a transition period of four years, after which they will be required to accept the *acquis communautaire* (the existing body of EU law). In turn, the Union has agreed to try to raise its existing standards. Thus, while the EU will force some of the national standards of these new entrants to the EU to be lowered, on balance their entrance into the Union will contribute to further strengthening European environmental standards as they add their votes and voices to those of Germany, Denmark, and the Netherlands. Equally important, if and when the European Union expands to central Europe, these new member states too will be forced to accept existing EU regulations and directives, which will invariably be stricter than their current domestic environmental regulations. In sum, the European Union has become a vehicle for exporting the environmental standards of Europe's greener nations to the rest of the continent.

-4-

Greening the GATT

The relationship between trade and regulatory policies has an increasingly important global dimension. This chapter examines the relationship between the General Agreement on Tariffs and Trade (GATT)—the world's most important agreement to reduce trade barriers—and national and international environmental regulations. Compared with the European Union, the GATT is a much weaker and more narrowly focused international institution. Accordingly, its impact on national and international environmental standards has been much more limited. But like the EU, the GATT is finding itself under conflicting pressures to both reduce the role of environmental regulations as trade barriers and increase the ability of its signatories to enact regulatory standards that interfere with trade.

Just as the policy preferences of the EU's greener members have posed a continual threat to the single market, so have the environmental preferences of the world's greener countries and regions, namely the United States and the European Union, continually challenged global trade liberalization. Significantly, more than half of the complaints formally filed with the GATT alleging the illegal use of environmental or consumer regulations as technical barriers to trade have been brought against one country, the United States—a nation which has occupied a role in global environmental policy-making analogous to that of Germany and Denmark within the EU.

Originally established in 1947, the General Agreement currently has more than 120 signatories. The GATT essentially consists of a series of rules which govern the policies of signatory nations toward the treatment of domestic and imported goods and services. One of the most important of these rules has to do with national treatment: Article III limits the ability of governments to discriminate against products on the basis of their national origin. In addition, GATT signatories are required to treat imports from all other GATT members equally.

As in the case of the Treaty of Rome, the word "environment" does not appear in the original text of the GATT. However, the GATT does contain a clause analogous to Article 36 of the Treaty of Rome. Article XX, the GATT's General Exceptions clause, permits signatory nations to enact policies that restrict trade if they are "necessary to protect human, animal or plant life or health."[1] However, these policies cannot "be applied in a manner which would constitute a means of arbitrary or unjustifiable discrimination between countries where the same conditions prevail, or a disguised restriction on international trade."[2] Article XX also permits trade restrictions "relating to the conservation of exhaustible natural resources if such measures are made effective in conjunction with restrictions on domestic production or consumption."[3]

For the first four decades of the GATT's existence, there was relatively little interest in the impact of its rules on protective regulations. It is a measure of the low salience of environmental issues among the signatories to the General Agreement that a Working Group on Environmental Measures and International Trade, which was established in 1971, did not meet once during the next two decades. Nor was the role of environmental standards as nontariff barriers a prominent issue in the Tokyo Round which concluded in 1979. While the Agreement on Technical Barriers to Trade (the Standards Code) states that "no country should be prevented from taking measures necessary . . . for the protection . . . of the environment," it attracted little attention at the time of its enactment and no trade disputes emerged from it.[4]

However, largely as a response to the 1991 tuna-dolphin case, the impact of the GATT on both national and international environmental regulation has become much more visible—and controversial. Many environmentalists have criticized the GATT for placing too many restrictions on the efforts of governments to protect both their domestic environment and the global commons.[5] The GATT's defenders have expressed precisely the opposite concern, worrying about an increase in "eco-protectionism" that could undermine the gains of free trade.

Previous Disputes

Prior to the 1991 tuna-dolphin case, GATT dispute panels had issued decisions in only four cases involving national environmental and consumer regulations. Two of them involved disagreements between the United States and Canada over national conservation policies.[6] As part of a long-standing disagreement between the two countries regarding their respective jurisdiction over Pacific fisheries, in 1979 Canada seized nineteen American tuna boats caught fishing inside Canada's 200-mile fisheries zone. The United States, acting under the Fishery Conservation and Management Act of 1976, retaliated by prohibiting the entry of all tuna and tuna products from Canada. Although the embargo was subsequently lifted following the two nations' signing of a treaty on Pacific coast albacore tuna, Canada nevertheless insisted that a GATT dispute resolution panel address the GATT consistency of the American embargo.

The panel rendered its decision in 1982. It agreed with the United States that tuna stocks did constitute "an exhaustible natural resource" whose trade could be restricted under Article XX. However, it ruled that this article did not apply because the United States had not imposed identical or similar restrictions on domestic tuna consumption or production. Accordingly, the American action constituted an illegal "quantitative restriction" on trade.

Six years later, another dispute over conservation policies between the United States and Canada came before the GATT. Canada, as part of its effort to improve the conservation and management of its fisheries, had prohibited the exports of unprocessed herring and pink and sockeye salmon. It contended that these prohibitions were necessary to prevent the export of unprocessed herring and salmon that did not meet its quality standards for these fish. The United States complained to the GATT on the grounds that the Canadian export restriction was discriminatory: it treated fish caught for domestic consumption differently than fish intended for export.

The dispute panel ruled that Canada's export ban was inconsistent with its obligations under the GATT because it did not place similar limits on the domestic consumption of these fish. Its policy only limited the access of foreign producers and consumers to unprocessed fish. Moreover, Canada did not limit access to herring and salmon supplies in general, but only to certain unprocessed salmon and herring. Accordingly, "there was no link between conservation of these species and the export prohibition." The panel noted that "the purpose of including Article XX in the General Agreement was not to create a loophole for discriminatory or protectionist trade policy measures, but to insure that GATT rules would not hinder conservation policies."[7]

In 1987 the GATT adjudicated a case brought by Canada, the EC, and Mexico against the excise tax provisions of the Superfund Amendments and Reauthorization Act of 1986. In order to raise revenue to clean up hazardous waste sites, the American legislation had imposed an excise tax on certain imported substances produced or manufactured from various feedstock chemicals. The plaintiffs contended that these excise taxes violated the GATT requirement that imported and domestic products be treated alike and, furthermore, that they were not justified under Article XX since the production of chemicals in Europe did not adversely affect the American environment. This case marked the first time that a GATT dispute panel had addressed the legitimacy of a border tax adjustment scheme intended to raise revenue for environmental purposes.

In its decision, the dispute panel chose to ignore the environmental dimensions of the dispute. It held that the purpose of the tax was irrelevant; nations were free to raise revenue for whatever purposes they wished. The consistency of a tax with GATT rules only had to do with its form. On this basis, the panel upheld the position of the United States: it ruled that the tax did not discriminate against imported products because the imports subject to tax were produced from chemicals that were also subject to an excise tax in the United States. It also noted that the tax rate was based not on the total value of the imported substance—which would have violated the GATT—but only on the amount of the chemicals used in the imported substance. The panel stated that "if a charge is imposed on perfume because it contains alcohol, the charge to be imposed must take into consideration the value of the alcohol and not the value of the perfume, that is to say, the value of the content and not the value of the whole."[8]

The following year a GATT dispute panel heard its first case to address the GATT consistency of a consumer regulation. Under the terms of its 1966 Tobacco Act, Thailand prohibited imports of cigarettes without a license. Thailand had not granted such a license for a decade. In addition, Thailand imposed higher excise taxes on imported cigarettes than on domestic ones. The United States, whose domestic cigarette firms were seeking to expand into Asian markets, filed a complaint with the GATT.

Thailand defended its restrictions on cigarette imports on the basis of Article XX, arguing that they were "necessary" both to make effective its domestic program to reduce smoking, and to protect its citizens from American cigarettes, which contained harmful additives. However, the GATT panel ruled that the Thai restrictions were not necessary, because Thailand had alternative ways of protecting the life and health of its citizens which were not inconsistent with the GATT. For example, instead of seeking to limit cigarette imports, it could have imposed high excise taxes on both domestic and imported cigarettes, restricted all cigarette advertising, or banned the sale of all cigarettes containing harmful additives. While the panel decision was criticized by American antismoking groups, their anger was directed less at the GATT than against the Office of the United States Trade Representative for bringing the case on behalf of the American tobacco industry in the first place (see Chapter 6).

For its part, the government of Thailand had used the eighteen-month interval between the start of negotiations with the United States and the GATT dispute panel ruling to enact what one of their government officials characterized as "the most stringent regulations in the world."[9] It banned all cigarette advertising and promotion, the distribution of cigarette samples, the reduction of price as a promotional aid, and all cigarette displays in retail shops. None of these restrictions were affected by the GATT ruling; indeed, much to the disappointment of the American tobacco industry, the panel specifically upheld the GATT consistency of Thailand's advertising ban on the grounds that it applied equally to imported and domestic cigarettes.

Thus in all four of these disputes, the basis of the GATT dispute panel's rulings was similar: GATT signatories could impose whatever conservation, quality controls, taxes, or advertising restrictions, and so on, they wished, provided they applied *equally to imported (or exported) and domestic goods*. Each of these panel reports was formally adopted by the GATT Council. They attracted little attention from either the public or policy-makers. Indeed, prior to 1991 the relationship between environmental regulations and the GATT was virtually ignored in both the popular press and academic journals.

The tuna-dolphin dispute panel, however, addressed a much more difficult and complex set of issues. Its decision, and the controversy surrounding it, has raised a critical question: under what circumstances, if any, should a nation be permitted to restrict imports in order to protect the environment outside its legal jurisdiction? This now-celebrated clash between the rules governing international trade and a national environmental regulation has firmly placed the relationship between trade and regulatory policies on both the domestic and the international political agenda.

The Tuna-Dolphin Case

During the 1960s, American commercial fisherman abandoned traditional pole-and-line fishing and began to employ purse seines to catch tuna.[10] Purse seines are enormous nets approximately one mile long and 600 feet deep, which are placed under and around schools of tuna. They are then tightened, the water is gradually let out of them, and the tuna are brought on deck. The use of these nets significantly increased the size of the tuna catch: a single net can bring in up to 250 tons of tuna. By the early 1970s, the United States' purse seine fleet numbered over 100 vessels, each costing between six and ten million dollars and capable of holding more than 1,000 tons of tuna.

Because many dolphins drowned when the nets designed to trap the tuna swimming beneath them were tightened, the introduction of this new fishing technology had a catastrophic effect on dolphin mortality. By the end of the 1960s, tuna fishing boats—nearly all of which were American-owned—were killing close to a half million dolphins each year. These deaths all occurred in the eastern tropical Pacific (ETP)—a six to seven million square mile triangle of ocean extending from southern California to northern Chile—where dolphins tend to travel above schools of yellowfin tuna. Accordingly, dolphins were used by fishermen to guide the setting of their nets. Most of the ETP falls either in international waters or in the coastal waters of Central and South American nations. Approximately one-quarter of the global tuna fish catch comes from this region.

The Marine Mammal Protection Act

Public outcry over the increase in dolphin deaths helped prompt passage of the MMPA in 1972. This legislation sought to protect all warm-blooded animals which swim in the oceans—sea lions, seals, whales, porpoises, dolphins, sea otters, manatees, walruses, and polar bears—from hunters and fishermen. It established as a goal of American policy reducing the rate of dolphins killed or maimed to "insignificant levels."

Senator Earnest Hollings (D-S.C.) characterized the MMPA as "one of the most important pieces of wildlife legislation" ever approved by the Congress. He added that it "will make the United States the leader among nations in the conservation of its wildlife and of those marine mammals under its jurisdiction." While Representative George Goodling (R-Pa.) acknowledged that American legislation alone was unable to "ensure world-wide conservation and assistance to these important species," he expressed the hope that "our domestic legislation [would] serve as a model for other nations and the international community."[11]

The MMPA set a permanent moratorium on the killing of ocean mammals by American fishermen and in American territorial waters; it also prohibited imports of products made from these mammals. However, to protect the American tuna fishing industry from foreign competition, commercial tuna fishermen were exempted from the ban for two years to enable them to design new techniques to reduce the number of porpoises injured and killed in their tuna fishing nets. The Act also provided that once the secretary of commerce had issued rules limiting the incidental killing of dolphins by American tuna fleets, tuna caught by foreign nationals using fishing methods banned in the United States could no longer be sold in the United States.

In 1976 the National Marine Fisheries Service—the federal agency responsible for the MMPA's enforcement—established an initial quota of dolphin kills by American commercial tuna fishermen of 78,000 per year. As a result of improvements in fishing techniques and gear, as well as a mandatory observer program, the number of dolphins killed by American-registered fishing boats declined significantly—from 368,000 in 1972 to 166,000 in 1975, 25,000 in 1977, 20,000 in 1979, and 18,500 in 1980. When the law was reauthorized in 1981, the maximum number of dolphins American tuna fisherman were permitted to kill in the ETP was further reduced to 20,500—a level which the U.S. fleet had already met.

In 1984, when Congress reauthorized the MMPA for a second time, it established more precise standards for dolphin kills by non-American fishing fleets. The statute allowed tuna caught using purse seine nets in the ETP to be imported into the United States only if the government of the country of origin could demonstrate that it had implemented a dolphin protection program "comparable" to that of the American fishing fleet. Similar restrictions were placed on tuna imports from "intermediate" countries which had purchased tuna from nations whose fleets exceeded the MMPA's dolphin mortality standards.

However, the executive branch did not issue formal rules to require foreign fishermen to comply with the standards established by Congress in 1984. At congressional hearings on the reauthorization of the MMPA in 1988, a broad coalition of twenty-eight national environmental organizations urged Congress to legislate a four-year phase out of all purse seine fishing. While Congress refused to do so, the 1988 Amendments to the MMPA went a significant step further in regulating foreign fishing practices. They specifically limited the number of dolphins that could be killed in the ETP by foreign-registered tuna vessels to a rate not to exceed 1.25 times the average of the incidental killing rate of the U.S. fishing fleet. The Amendments also stated that, "unless the Secretary of Commerce issued a finding that foreign tuna imports met standards comparable to those of the United States, these imports must be banned."[12] In order to prevent "tuna laundering," similar import restrictions were placed on tuna from countries which had purchased the fish from noncomplying nations.

The increased focus on non-American fishing fleets in the 1984 and 1988 Amendments to the MMPA reflected the extent to which dolphin mortality had become an international rather than a domestic problem. By 1987 U.S. purse seine fishermen were responsible for less than 20 percent of the dolphins killed in the ETP. This was due not only to improvements in American fishing techniques but also to a significant decrease in the number of American-owned fishing boats in this region. Owing in part to the expense of complying with fishing regulations established by the MMPA, the proportion of U.S. registered fishing vessels in the ETP had declined from more than 90 percent in the early 1960s to 32 percent in 1988. Most relocated to the western Pacific, where tuna and dolphins did not have the same ecological relationship.

By contrast, between 1976 and 1985 the number of Mexican boats using purse seine techniques, primarily in the ETP, tripled. Mexican frozen tuna production increased threefold between 1979 and 1985—virtually all of it from the ETP. Approximately 10 percent of Mexico's total ETP tuna harvest was sold in the American market. In 1988 ships registered by Latin American countries bordering the Pacific Ocean accounted for half of all tuna caught in the region.

Labeling Legislation

Although total dolphin mortality had declined significantly, it was still high: approximately 130,000 dolphins were killed in 1986, and 100,000 in 1989. As America accounted for slightly more than half of the global tuna consumption, American consumers had considerable leverage over global fishing practices. In January 1988 a coalition of environmental groups launched a boycott of canned tuna in order to pressure the major American importers of canned tuna to halt their purchases of tuna caught with purse seine nets. In September the boycott was expanded to include pet food products. This effort was highly visible and effective. In April of 1990 three American companies, H. J. Heinz, Van Camp, and Bumble Bee, announced that they would no longer sell tuna which had been harvested by purse seine techniques.

However, environmentalists were concerned that food processors other than Heinz, Van Camp, and Bumble Bee were misleading consumers by also labeling their tuna "dolphin-safe," even though it was caught in ways that killed substantial numbers of dolphins. In 1990 Congress responded by enacting the Dolphin Protection Conservation Act. This law required companies selling "dolphin-safe" tuna to be able to demonstrate that their product was caught using methods that limited dolphin deaths. It also required all other tuna to be labeled "caught with technologies that are known to kill dolphins."[13] In supporting the statute, Senator Joseph Biden (D-Del.) argued that "it is . . . important that as dolphin-safe tuna enters the market we provide consumers with the strongest assurance possible that their good intentions in selecting dolphin-safe tuna are not being taken advantage of."[14] All three major tuna processors testified in support of the bill, leading Representative Barbara Boxer (D-Calif.) to describe the legislation as "a happy blending of support from environmentalists and tuna companies."[15]

The threat of import restrictions under the MMPA, combined with the labeling requirement and changes in American consumer preferences, led a number of other nations to modify their tuna fishing procedures. The governments of the Congo, New Zealand, Senegal, and Spain urged their fleets to follow the MMPA guidelines for dolphin release procedures. In addition, Bermuda, Canada, the Republic of Korea, and Nicaragua halted the use of purse seining in the ETP.

The Embargo against Mexico

Overall, total dolphin mortality in the ETP continued its steady decline: half as many dolphins were killed in 1990 as in 1989. The American proportion of dolphin deaths also continued to drop: it went from 15 percent in 1989 to less than 10 percent in 1990. The following year total dolphin mortality again decreased by nearly 50 percent: approximately 28,000 dolphins were killed by tuna fishermen in the ETP—only 800 of which were killed by American fishing vessels. The average dolphin kill per set by foreign-owned vessels dropped by more than two-thirds between 1989 and 1991.

In 1988 American officials had begun to express concern to the Mexican government about the number of dolphins killed by Mexican-owned fishing vessels. The Mexican government agreed to modify its tuna fishing regulations, and the number of dolphins killed by its fishing fleet declined from 49,000 in 1988 to 16,000 in 1991.[16] Between 1986 and 1992 the average number of dolphins killed by Mexican fishing vessels in each setting of the purse seine went from 15 to 1.85—a decline much more rapid than that of the foreign-owned fleet as a whole.

Nonetheless, Mexican fishing fleets were still killing dolphins at a higher rate than their American counterparts—in part because of the even more substantial reduction in dolphin fatalities on the part of American fishing vessels in the ETP. The number of the latter also continued to diminish: by 1991, only eleven American-registered boats were still fishing for tuna in the ETP. However, the secretary of commerce still did not issue the comparability findings mandated by Congress that would have permitted him to determine which nations would be allowed to export tuna to the United States, in part because of concern that the MMPA's import restrictions conflicted with GATT rules.

In the fall of 1990, the Earth Island Institute, a California nonprofit organization that had helped organize the tuna boycott, sued the Department of Commerce to demand the enforcement of the MMPA's restrictions on tuna imports. The suit was successful. In October 1990 a U.S. District Court ordered the secretary of commerce to ban the importation of canned, frozen, and fresh tuna from Mexico, Venezuela, and the Pacific islands of Vanuata because their methods of catching tuna violated the MMPA. This decision affected approximately $30 million worth of tuna imports per year.

In addition, tuna imports were also prohibited from Costa Rica, France, Italy, Japan, and Panama because they purchased tuna from the three nations subject to the direct embargo. This decision, along with a judicial ruling the following year that required the secretary of commerce to ban imports of tuna from twenty additional "intermediate" countries which imported tuna from Mexico, Venezuela, and Vanuata, affected roughly half of the 266,000 metric tons of tuna imported annually into the United States.

The Dispute Goes before the GATT

Mexico had entered the GATT in 1986 as part of its effort to become more closely integrated into the global economy. For Mexico, the American tuna embargo was symptomatic of the efforts of developed nations to protect themselves from growing competition from third world countries. In February 1991 Mexico requested the convening of a GATT dispute settlement panel on the grounds that the American enforcement of the embargo provision of the MMPA violated American obligations under the GATT. Its complaint was supported by Australia, the European Union, Indonesia, Japan, Korea, the Philippines, Senegal, Thailand, Venezuela, Canada, and Norway. Mexico also challenged the legality of the Dolphin Protection Conservation Act. The GATT Council convened a dispute resolution panel, made up of three individuals from Uruguay, Hungary, and Switzerland.

The case was unique in a number of respects.[17] First, it was the first time a GATT panel had been asked to rule on the legality of a trade restriction the purpose of which was to protect a global, rather than a national or regional, resource. While technically about conservation, this case was really about environmental protection, because the purpose of the MMPA was not to "conserve" dolphins but to protect them. In marked contrast to the two previous conservation disputes that had come before the GATT, the embargo imposed by the United States was not intended to conserve a resource that had commercial value; it was intended to protect a species for its own sake.

The case was unprecedented in a second respect: it marked the first time a GATT dispute panel had been requested to address the extrajurisdictional scope of a national environmental regulation, since the MMPA had extended American regulatory jurisdiction and standards to foreign-owned ships fishing in international waters who wanted to export tuna to the United States. Third, in marked contrast to the three previous trade disputes over national protective regulations, in this case the national regulation being challenged *was,* at least on its face, nondiscriminatory. Indeed, the United States had imposed even stricter restrictions on domestic producers.

Most important, this particular trade dispute involved an environmental issue that had aroused strong public emotions, since preventing dolphin slaughter on the high seas had been a major priority of American environmental organizations for nearly two decades. Thanks in part to the television program *Flipper* and the George C. Scott movie *Day of the Dolphin,* itself adapted from a best-selling novel about intelligent dolphins working with humans, dolphins had become a part of American popular culture. Substantial numbers of Americans, including millions of school children, cared about dolphins and had enthusiastically participated in the tuna boycott. Adding to its political significance, the case involved a conflict between the environmental policies of two nations which were in the midst of negotiating a trade agreement whose purpose was to *reduce* trade barriers.

The Mexican Case

Mexico claimed that the American trade embargo was inconsistent with three articles of the GATT: Article III (national treatment), Article XI (quantitative restrictions), and Article XIII (discretionary import rules). Mexico also contended that the American labeling requirement violated Article IX (marks of origin). The American position was that both laws were justified by the "exception clauses" of Article XX. Since the Mexican fleet was killing a higher number of dolphins per unit of tuna caught than the American fleet, the Americans contended that banning the import of tuna from Mexico was a legitimate conservation measure. Specifically, the United States argued that the MMPA's import restrictions fell within the scope of Article XX because they served the sole purpose of protecting dolphin lives and that "no alternative measures were reasonably available to the United States to protect dolphin health and lives outside of American jurisdiction."[18]

The Mexican government responded that the Article XX exception only applied to the protection of animals *within* the territory of the nation imposing the restriction. While admitting that a nation could impose trade restrictions to protect endangered species located outside its borders, it argued that it could do so only on a multilateral basis— for example, to enforce compliance with the Convention on Trade in Endangered Species (CITES) Treaty, an international agreement to protect endangered species. However, the CITES Treaty did not cover the species of dolphins that tuna fishermen were killing; thus, according to international law, they are not endangered. Mexico argued that if the Americans wished to protect dolphins caught by Mexican fishing fleets or in Mexican territorial waters, they should do so by negotiating an international agreement with Mexico or by adding the dolphin species being killed to CITES—not by acting unilaterally.

Moreover, Mexico contended, Article XX only permits trade restrictions which are "necessary" to protect health and life. The Mexicans argued that the import ban was not "necessary." For not only were dolphins in the ETP not endangered, but thanks in part to changes in Mexican fishing practices, the total number of dolphins that were currently being killed in this region was considerably lower than the number killed by the American fleet during the 1970s. Moreover, they noted that the average incidental killing rate of the Mexican fleet had significantly declined during the 1980s.

The Mexican government concluded that since the Article XX exception did not apply, the American tuna fish ban violated the GATT rules governing trade barriers. Specifically, it was inconsistent with the GATT's "national treatment" provision, which requires that all "like products" receive similar treatment, regardless of where or how they were produced. Since dolphin-friendly tuna fish were identical in every respect to those caught with purse seine nets, the United States had no legal right to restrict imports of the latter.

The Mexican government also claimed that the American ban was in fact discriminatory since it only applied to tuna caught in one region. Since the 1984 and 1988 Amendments to the MMPA, the American tuna fishing fleet had moved virtually all its operations to the western tropical Pacific, where dolphins and tuna do not swim near each another. However, Latin American fishermen were denied this option because they did not have the same access to ports in the western Pacific. Thus, the Mexicans argued, in practice the American regulation only applied to foreign suppliers; its real effect was not to protect dolphins, but to protect American tuna fishermen.

This view was echoed by Venezuela, which, like Mexico, had substantially reduced its dolphin kills in response to American pressures. Following their cut-off from America's tuna market in August 1990, Venezuela's tuna fleet had shrunk by nearly two-thirds. Laura Rojas, the Director General of Venezuela's Institute of Foreign Trade, stated that "environmental protection can't be had at the cost of another country."[19] Rojas claimed that the United States had set impossibly high standards for third world fleets in order to protect its own, and that unlike the Americans, Venezuelans were prisoners of geography since the western Pacific was too far for them to fish profitably.

The Mexicans also charged that the American embargo fell afoul of the national treatment provision of the GATT because of the way in which the Americans calculated the permissible kill-rate of dolphins. Foreign fishermen were only permitted to sell tuna in the United States if their *average* incidental kill rate was less than 1.25 times that of their American counterparts. But since this rate could only be measured at the end of each season, foreign fisherman were placed at a significant disadvantage; they could not know until the season was over if they would be permitted to export their tuna to the United States. On the other hand, American fisherman were not subject to a similar restraint; as long as they met a fixed dolphin protection standard, they were assured access to the American market.

Finally, the Mexican government challenged the American labeling requirement on the grounds that it was "unnecessarily costly" and that it violated the GATT provision on marks of origin. According to Article IX of the GATT, nations cannot require marks of country origin on products which materially reduce their value.

The Panel's Ruling

In August 1991 the GATT dispute panel reached its decision: it found that the American trade embargo violated the terms of the GATT, but that the American labeling regulation was GATT-consistent. Specifically, the panel held that the American dolphin protection legislation violated the national treatment provision of Article III. According to the panel, GATT rules do not permit signatory nations to restrict the imports of products on the basis of how they are produced. Imports can only be restricted on the basis of characteristics of the product itself—provided similar restrictions are imposed on domestically produced ones. In short, the GATT national treatment requirement "calls for a comparison of the treatment of imported tuna *as a product* with that of domestic tuna *as a product.*"[20]

Having decided that the American legislation was inconsistent with the GATT's national treatment provisions, the panel then went on to consider whether or not the American embargo qualified as an "exception" under Article XX. The panel concluded that Article XX only applies to activities within the jurisdiction of the country adopting the measure. It was intended to permit countries to enact policies "primarily aimed at rendering effective restrictions on production and consumption within their jurisdiction."[21] It could not be used to allow countries to regulate production or consumption outside their borders. Otherwise, the panel concluded, nations would only be assured of access to the markets of other nations if the regulations of both were identical. The result would be to create an enormous loophole that would undermine the central purpose of the General Agreement, namely, to *reduce* trade restrictions and barriers. The panel contended: "If the United States can dictate conservation measures to Mexico as a condition to Mexico's access to the U.S. market, the GATT will be eviscerated."[22]

Moreover, the panel held that even if Article XX allows for extrajurisdictional actions, the MMPA's direct embargo provisions did not qualify because they were not "necessary," according to the definition of this term employed in the Thai cigarette case. First, the United States had not demonstrated that it had exhausted all reasonable alternatives available to protect dolphins. Second, because the MMPA used a variable standard for determining Mexican compliance, its standards were too unpredictable to be necessary. Finally, the

United States had not presented scientific evidence that its restrictions on foreign fishing fleets were necessary to conserve dolphins.

The panel did, however, uphold the legality of the Dolphin Protection Consumer Information Act. It argued that the labeling provisions did not limit access to the American market, since any advantage accorded dolphin-safe tuna was simply due to American consumer preferences.

In its concluding remarks, the panel stated that its decision was not intended to reflect on the appropriateness of either Mexican or American conservation measures, only their consistency with the trade agreement that both nations had signed. It noted that nations remain entirely free to tax or regulate domestic production for environmental purposes. They can also impose whatever product standards on imports that they wish—provided the same regulations apply to domestically produced ones. But what the GATT does not permit its signatory nations to do is to "restrict imports of a product merely because [the product] originates from a country with environmental policies different from its own."[23]

If GATT members wished to restrict their trade with one another on environmental grounds, the appropriate course to follow was either to amend GATT rules or waive GATT obligations, not to attempt to distort the intent of the exception clause of Article XX. According to GATT panel chairman Andras Szepsi, pursuing either of these alternatives "would enable GATT members to limit the range of policy differences justifying trade sanctions and to devise safeguards to prevent abuse."[24] Last, the panel noted that its report was not intended to discourage nations from harmonizing their environmental policies or cooperate to solve global environmental problems.

The Political Reaction

The GATT dispute panel ruling was the most visible—and controversial—in the trade agreement's forty-four year history. GATT members—including the entire thirty-five member GATT Council—overwhelmingly endorsed the panel's decision; not a single country supported the United States. One Japanese official stated, "We have been telling the American officials that this regulation is GATT-illegal. And it's against international law that internal regulations are applied to foreign countries."[25] The European Union, whose annual exports of approximately $5 million of tuna to the United States had been threatened by the American secondary boycott, reiterated its long-standing objection to American unilateralism in general and the trade penalty provisions of the MMPA in particular.[26]

Not surprisingly, environmental groups, particularly in the United States, were outraged. The case immediately became a *cause célèbre* among environmental organizations, one of whom characterized it as a battle between "Carla Hills [the United States trade representative] and Flipper."[27] Other environmentalists referred to the case as "GATTzilla vs. Flipper." David Phillips, the executive director of the Earth Island Institute, stated that the Mexicans "are kidding themselves if they think that GATT can force the U.S. to abandon laws to protect the global environment. In the 1990s, free trade and efforts to protect the environment are on a collision course."[28] A spokesman for Congress Watch, a public interest lobbying group founded by Ralph Nader, characterized the GATT panel's decision as a "breathtaking attack on the progress made in the last 10 years."[29] Lori Wallach, the organization's staff attorney, stated, "This case is the smoking gun. We have seen GATT actually declaring that a U.S. environmental law must go. These [trade] agreements must be modified to allow for legitimate consumer and environmental protections."[30] A policy analyst for the World Wildlife Fund depicted the decision as "a major setback because it totally disregards legislation designed to provide environmental protection for common resources."[31]

Congressional reaction was equally hostile. At a congressional hearing on the GATT ruling, Congressman Henry Waxman (D-Calif.), chairman of the House Subcommittee on Health and the Environment, stated: "This is a worst-case scenario come true—repeal of a vital environmental law because of conflict with a trade agreement."[32] A group of Congress members wrote a letter to the President claiming that "this inhumane ruling would run roughshod not only over these hard-fought dolphin protection measures, but over our fundamental right to engage in worldwide conservation measures."[33] The House Committee on Merchant Marine and Fisheries showed its defiance of the GATT ruling by approving legislation imposing even harsher penalties than those in the MMPA on imports from nations that used driftnets. The committee also directed the U.S. trade representative to seek to "reform [the GATT] to take into consideration the national environmental laws of contracting parties and international environmental treaties."[34] Sixty-four senators and nearly a hundred representatives wrote to President Bush opposing the panel ruling. They stated that they would refuse to weaken the MMPA and demanded the GATT be changed to make it compatible with all American environmental laws.

What bewildered many Americans about the GATT decision was the lack of any apparent conflict between the purposes of the GATT and the intent of the MMPA. The GATT's objective is to promote international trade by restricting the ability of nations to favor domestic producers. The embargo provision of the MMPA obviously did injure foreign producers; otherwise Mexico would not have filed a complaint in the first place. But while it may have had protectionist *consequences,* it did not have protectionist *intentions.* No American producer supported the embargo. American tuna fishermen neither needed nor requested protection from tuna harvested by foreign fishing vessels in the ETP. Not only had they virtually ceased to fish in this area, but thanks in large measure to the impact of the consumer boycott organized by the Earth Island Institute, dolphin-safe tuna commanded a premium of roughly $400 per ton on the American market—more than enough to compensate for the additional costs of fishing in the western Pacific.[35] Nor had the domestic tuna industry urged that the MMPA's embargo provisions be enforced. They were being enforced only as a result of a lawsuit filed by an environmental organization.

The Dispute Is Partially Resolved

From the perspective of the Bush administration, both the timing and substance of the GATT panel could not have been worse. Domestic political reaction to the panel ruling threatened to undermine the administration's efforts to secure ratification of both a free trade agreement with Mexico and a new GATT agreement. Indeed, it was precisely because it had anticipated the likelihood of an adverse panel ruling that the administration had not enforced the embargo provisions of the MMPA in the first place. While the *Economist* reported that "word has it" that the Bush administration had encouraged Mexico to file its complaint with GATT, according to other accounts, "U.S. negotiators tried to discourage the Mexicans from taking their case to the GATT."[36]

In any event, the administration quickly moved to diffuse the political damage from the GATT panel ruling. Secretary of Commerce Robert Mosbacher and U.S. Trade Representative Carla Hills pressured the Mexican government not to request that the GATT General Council officially adopt the panel ruling. This would mean the United States would be under no legal obligation to comply with it. Recognizing, on one hand, that Congress was unwilling to amend the MMPA and, on the other, that its own political interest lay in quickly resolving the dispute—the United States began bilateral negotiations with Mexico.

For their part, the Mexicans, anxious not to endanger congressional approval of the North American Free Trade Agreement (NAFTA), also adopted a conciliatory stance. Mexico's President Carlos Salinas de Gortari suddenly got "animal religion."[37] He announced plans to open a Mexican turtle museum and agreed to help fund the as yet nonexistent Cousteau Society of Mexico. After confessing to "a deep love of dolphins," he flew to California to announce a ten-point plan to protect them.[38] Most important, in spite of considerable pressure from thirty-five nations that the panel report be submitted to the GATT Council for formal adoption, Mexico refused to do so.

In May 1992 the United States, Mexico, and eight other nations, which collectively accounted for 99 percent of the tuna catch in the ETP, signed the first major international accord to protect dolphins. Made under the auspices of the Inter-American Tropical Tuna Commission, its signatories agreed to phase out, by 1994, the setting of nets around schools of tuna that included dolphins. This agreement was endorsed by the Earth Island Institute and other American environmental organizations. In October 1992 Congress approved the International Dolphin Conservation Act, which authorizes the secretary of state to negotiate an international agreement to establish a global moratorium on the use of purse seine nets that encircle dolphins, and provides for an embargo of up to 40 percent of a nation's fish exports to enforce compliance. David Phillips, executive director of the Save the Dolphins Project at the Earth Island Institute, described the legislation as "a breakthrough proposal for dolphins."[39] The following month, the European Parliament called for a ban on imports of tuna caught by encircling dolphins. Although this measure was not adopted by the EU's Council of Ministers, who did not want a complaint to be filed against the EU, the Union did ban ships owned by its own members from using purse seine nets that killed dolphins. As a result of all these initiatives, less than 5,000 dolphin deaths were associated with tuna fishing in the ETP in 1993—a hundredfold decline in the space of two decades.

Nevertheless, the U.S. tuna embargo remained in effect because a 1993 amendment to the MMPA had reduced the U.S. quota of dolphin kills to 800 in 1993 and to zero after February 28, 1994. Thus, even though the fifty Mexican boats fishing in the ETP were only killing, on average, less than one dolphin for every shoal of tuna they netted, they were still in violation of the MMPA's 1.25 kill ratio because the four American boats still in the ETP had an average kill rate of near zero. Accordingly, even one dolphin death per shoal placed Mexico in violation of the MMPA. While American officials admitted that "there is no longer a viable environmental argument" for continuing to enforce the embargo, environmentalists and their allies in Congress appear "determined to enforce the law to the letter."[40]

The Debate over the Panel Decision

The GATT's tuna-dolphin decision prompted a wide-ranging discussion of the relationship between GATT rules and environmental protection. Criticisms of the panel's decision centered on four key issues: the extrajurisdictional scope of Article XX, the distinction between product and process, the meaning of the term "necessary," and the role of unilateralism in improving global environmental practices.

Criticisms of the Decision

Regarding the panel's distinction between domestic and extrajurisdictional environmental regulations, one student of environment and trade law commented, "The foreign domestic distinction is being rendered obsolete by a growing number of trans-border and global environmental problems. As it becomes more apparent that mankind shares one biosphere, the line between paternalism and domestic interests continues to fade away."[41] From this perspective, the conservation of dolphins swimming in international waters *did* affect America's environment, since America was a part of the world. Two environmental lawyers argued: "The Panel's domestic limitation is nonsensical, because it fails to take into account the fact that domestic environmental harms are now, increasingly, being traced to actions occurring beyond a nation's borders. Limiting the reach of a nation's environmental laws to domestic activities substantially undercuts its ability to protect itself from adverse extraterritorial activities."[42] Moreover, "if no country is permitted to take extrajurisdictional action, then much of our environment would be unreachable by environmental trade measures"[43]

The GATT panel's ruling on this point was also criticized on legal grounds. One critic claimed that the dispute panel had misinterpreted the intention behind Article XX(b): it was not "intended to disable nations from protecting global common resources through the use of green trade barriers."[44] Rather, "the drafters sought to ensure that Article XX(b) restrictions were not used to discriminate against imported products or protect domestic producers."[45] Moreover, nothing in the language or drafting history of Article XX limits its application to the jurisdiction of the contracting parties. Indeed, the phrase "extrajurisdictional" appears nowhere in the General Agreement; it was first introduced into GATT jurisprudence by the panel. Furthermore, the sheer volume of international agreements that use trade measures to protect human, animal, and plant life beyond a nation's borders, signed both before and since the GATT, clearly indicates that international law does recognize that nations can enforce extrajurisdictional regulations.[46]

A second criticism focused on the panel's distinction between product and process; the panel had held that the GATT permits countries to restrict imports on the basis of the former but not the latter. But environmentalists argued that this distinction was both artificial and inappropriate, since it was precisely the way that most products were made that constituted their primary environmental impact. Indeed, only a small portion of environmental regulations seek to regulate the physical quality of a product; most seek to improve or safeguard the environment precisely by regulating how, where, or whether it is produced.

It therefore made no sense to confine the extrajurisdictional reach of a nation's environmental laws to *product* characteristics. As British environmental economist David Peace argued, "From the point of view of the importing country, it should be irrelevant whether environmental losses arise during production or consumption."[47] An American environmental lawyer added: "The GATT's focus on 'products' makes it virtually incapable of capturing the environmental costs of externalities related to methods of production."[48] According to Roht-Arriaza, "Any move toward clean production requires an ability to distinguish between goods made in an environmentally sound manner and those which are destructive."[49] Moreover, the panel ruling would make it impossible for nations to adopt the "polluter pays" principle for goods produced outside their legal jurisdiction.

Steven Shrybman, counsel to the Canadian Environmental Law Association, argued that the "panel grossly misinterpreted the purpose of trade sanctions authorized by the MMPA and similar legislation."[50] He wrote: "Nothing in the statute entitles one country to dictate the internal regulations of another. It simply requires those who wish to sell in domestic markets to meet the same or similar obligations that domestic producers face . . . without the authority to restrict imports, countries may have to choose between their commitments to the environment and their commitments to their domestic producers."[51] He concluded: "The greater threat to the sovereign ability of nations to choose their own course to achieve environmental objectives is to be found not in measures such as those proscribed by the MMPA, but rather, in this GATT ruling."[52]

A third criticism focused on the panel's strict definition of the term "necessary." According to the panel, for an import restriction to pass muster under the Article XX exception, not only was a nation required to demonstrate that a particular regulation was "necessary" to ensure the protection of human, animal, or plant life; it also had to prove that it had also exhausted all other means of achieving this objective—including the negotiation of an international agreement.

But the panel's critics argued that both these hurdles were too demanding. The first limited "the ability of the contracting parties to take precautionary action in the face of the scientific uncertainty that often tempers early analyses of environment threats [which in turn] conflict[s] with the internationally recognized precautionary principles that have developed in the field of international environmental law."[53] The second was also unreasonable, since negotiating international agreements is invariably extremely time-consuming. In fact, the United States *had* been attempting to seek an international agreement to protect mammals threatened by commercial fishing since the mid 1970s. Indeed, only a week before it requested the GATT panel, Mexico had refused to endorse a new intergovernmental agreement to cut dolphin mortality—a fact which the GATT panel ignored.

Consequentially, and contrary to the GATT panel's ruling, there was a compelling environmental case for unilateralism, since the unilateral actions of one nation often play a critical role in bringing about an international environmental agreement.[54] According to Charnovitz, "for nearly 100 years, there has been a fruitful interplay between unilateral measures and international environmental treaties."[55] Moreover, extraterritorial regulation is often the most effective way to bring about international cooperation, especially to protect endangered species.[56]

Defending the GATT Panel Ruling

From the perspective of the GATT's supporters, the tuna-dolphin conflict was the "trade issue from hell—one almost guaranteed to advance the cause of those who care more about raising the price of chunk light than making the Pacific safe for Flipper."[57] They feared that the furor over the tuna dispute would undermine the efforts of the Uruguay Round to further liberalize global markets. Advocates of liberalized trade were particularly worried that the tuna decision would convince the public that free trade and environmental protection were incompatible—and that this belief would be seized upon by both producers and environmentalists opposed to further trade liberalization.

Abraham Katz, the president of the United States Council for International Business, observed, "The dolphin issue has really brought things to a boil. American environmentalists are not only attacking Mexico, but the whole system of world trade to support their concept of sustainable economic development."[58] In a paper prepared for the 1992 World Development Conference, Piritta Sorsa of the World Bank's Geneva office noted that "environmentally related trade friction is on the increase" and predicted that "the GATT may be headed for a major protectionist attack in the 1990s from . . . environmental policies."[59]

This view was echoed by GATT Director-General Arthur Dunkel, who warned that "the issue of the environment is being kidnapped by trade protectionist interests."[60] He added: "The danger of a proliferation of different environmental standards leading to trade policy friction is very real."[61] World Bank Chief Economist Lawrence Summers noted: "The last thing the world needs is a new argument to justify protectionism or managed trade policies."[62]

Shortly after the tuna-dolphin decision, both the GATT itself and the World Bank issued reports defending the GATT rules in particular and the environmental impact of trade liberalization in general. The GATT's 1992 annual report featured a special section on "Trade and the Environment," written primarily by Columbia economics professor Jagdish Bhagwati.[63] He noted that "to someone unfamiliar with or indifferent to the contribution of economic efficiency and the trading system to postwar economic growth, trade measures can too easily seem to be low-cost and readily available tools for pursuing environmental goals."[64] The report acknowledged that the resolution of many environmental problems required international cooperation. However, it argued that unilateral restrictions on trade were not an effective way to promote this cooperation.

Not only were they "never the most efficient instrument for dealing with an environmental problem . . . [but] protectionists would welcome such unilateralism," since they would then be able to propose national legislation that "unilaterally defines environmental agendas that other countries are likely to find unacceptable."[65] Moreover, to the extent that trade restrictions reduced underdeveloped country exports, environmental quality might well decline, since "incomes growth has been associated with reduced pollution over significant ranges of per capita income."[66] This latter view was echoed by a Tanzanian GATT official who argued that "freer and open trade policies . . . increase the capacity of countries to take nationally appropriate environmental measures and to co-operate at the international level in solutions to global environmental problems."[67]

The GATT report also vigorously argued against proposals to tamper with the key GATT principle of nondiscrimination. For it was this principle that "protects trade relations from degenerating into anarchy through unilateral actions in pursuit of unilaterally-defined objectives, however valid they may appear."[68] Undermining it threatened to lead the international trading system down the "slippery slope" of protectionism which would, in the name of environmental concerns, "risk an eventual descent into chaotic trade conditions similar to those that plagued the 1930s."[69]

What especially worried supporters of trade liberalization was the support expressed by environmentalists for expanding the grounds on which a nation could exclude imports. If nations could restrict imports from countries with weaker environmental laws, could they not use the same logic to keep out imports from countries with lower occupational health and safety standards, or even from countries whose industries paid lower wages? Such policies threatened the very logic of international trade, which was based in part on the *divergence* of national production costs. As expressed by the GATT report, "Countries are not clones of one another, and will not wish to become so—certainly not under the threat of unilateral trade restrictions."[70] The GATT report argued that if developed countries wished to encourage less developed ones to improve their environmental practices, particularly to the extent that the latter affected the global commons, they should offer them financial incentives, not restrict their exports.

The GATT report emphasized that the GATT's rules presented no obstacles to countries' efforts to protect their own environment, either by product or production standards. Nor did eschewing the use of unilateral trade sanctions mean that nations could not seek to affect the environmental policies of other nations. For example, their consumers could choose to purchase greener imports while nongovernmental organizations could attempt to persuade citizens in other countries of the need for stricter regulations. Most important, nations were free to negotiate international agreements that addressed common or similar environmental problems. And indeed, 127 such agreements had been negotiated to date. Moreover, while seventeen of these agreements either required or authorized trade restrictions, these too were compatible with the GATT, provided the restrictions were agreed to by the affected parties. Consequently, "GATT rules could never block the adoption of environmental policies which have broad support in the world community."[71]

Three months after the release of the GATT report, the World Bank issued a report entitled *International Trade and the Environment*.[72] Its conclusions essentially echoed those of the GATT report. In their keynote paper, "Trade Policy and Pollution," Bank policy analysts Patrick Low and Raed Safadi contended that the use of trade restrictions to improve environmental quality was almost always "either inappropriate, second best or a reflection of underlying policy failure."[73]

The World Bank publication also argued against requiring nations to harmonize their domestic environmental regulations on the grounds that it was entirely rational for different countries to value environmental protection differently, depending in part on their level of development. Accordingly, allowing countries to dictate how imported goods were produced would "work against the realization of comparative advantage . . . undermine the rule-based nature of the GATT and reduce the opportunities for gains from specialization through trade."[74] Nations should also not be permitted to impose tariffs on goods made in nations with laxer environmental regulations, for "protection because of higher costs . . . is precisely what the GATT attempts to limit. It is hard to see how . . . GATT could permit individual member governments to set imports charges in relation to the costs of production."[75]

Much of the tone of both the GATT and the World Bank publications on trade and environment was somewhat defensive; the international trade community clearly felt threatened by the growing chorus of criticism from the environmental community that followed the tuna-dolphin panel report. However, both institutions also sought to defend the environmental benefits of liberal trade policies. Thus, in a study of the relationship between the toxicity of industrial output and the openness to trade in Latin America, Nancy Birdsall and David Wheeler reported that the more closed the economy, the greater its development of "dirty" industries.[76] Another World Bank study, which examined the rates at which sixty different countries around the world had adopted a cleaner wood processing technology, concluded that the technology was adopted much more rapidly in countries that were more open to trade and investment.[77] The implication of both of these studies was that "pollution havens" were more likely to exist in protected economies than open ones. Not only were industries in the former less likely to purchase imported greener technologies, but protected industries also tended to use resources more inefficiently—observations which appear to have been borne out by the experiences of the former Soviet bloc.

Tuna: Round Two

Following the passage of the International Dolphin Conservation Act of 1992, the United States informed France, the United Kingdom, and several other countries that they had been removed from the list of nations subject to the intermediary embargo as they had certified that they were no longer importing yellowfin tuna from the nations still subject to the direct embargo. However, the American secondary embargo continued to be applied to tuna imports from Spain, Italy, Costa Rica, and Japan.

The EU had strongly criticized the refusal of Mexico to submit the tuna-dolphin disputes panel report to the GATT Council. It argued that "what had started as a dispute between two parties was now of interest to us all," and demanded that the GATT Council hold a full debate on the tuna report in order to correct the false "impression in some quarters that the report had placed environmental and trade issues on a collision course."[78] Frustrated by the fact that the panel report enjoyed no legal standing, in June 1992 the European Union, acting on behalf of the two member states (Spain and Italy) still affected by the American embargo, requested a second dispute resolution panel.

In its submission to the panel, the United States argued that its secondary embargo fell well within the terms of Article XX, since it was intended to protect an "exhaustible natural resource," whose physical presence on the high seas made "them more rather than less in need of conservation."[79] Furthermore, it had been imposed in conjunction with restrictions on domestic production and consumption; indeed, far from being protectionist, the United States had imposed even more stringent requirements on its own fishing fleets. The United States further argued that "there is nothing in the General Agreement that distinguishes between 'unilateral' measures and other types of measures." In fact, the term "unilateral" appears nowhere in the General Agreement. Moreover, "the vast majority of measures taken by sovereign nations in all fields of activity are 'unilateral.'"[80] According to the Americans, "at stake is the ability of a nation to take measures to protect global resources."[81]

The EU in turn stated that the American interpretation of Article XX would allow any nation to place environmental labels on discriminatory trade measures. The EU's position was that "while it agrees with the environment goal being pursued by the U.S., it objects to the U.S. imposing its laws on the rest of the world."[82] It also claimed that it had suffered substantial economic injury, because tuna fish that otherwise would have been sold in the United States was flooding the world market, thus lowering tuna prices outside the United States.

In June 1994 the GATT dispute panel issued a decision which found the secondary embargo to be GATT inconsistent. Like the earlier decision, it was strongly denounced by environmental organizations, though it attracted far less public attention.[83] However, in one important respect the panel's reasoning differed from that of the previous tuna-dolphin dispute panel. It explicitly recognized that there were circumstances under which a nation could employ trade restrictions to influence environmental policies outside its legal jurisdiction. Specifically, it could do so in order to protect a global resource pursuant to an international agreement. Accordingly, the primary reason that the American secondary embargo was GATT inconsistent had to do with the fact that it had been imposed unilaterally—a position that echoed that of the EU. The "tuna two" decision thus appeared to represent an attempt on the part of the GATT to diffuse at least some of the criticisms that followed the earlier tuna-dolphin panel report, but to do so in such a way that also limited environmentally related trade restrictions.

Other U.S. Environmental Trade Restrictions

The fact that the first visible political clash between trade rules and environment regulation involved the use of trade policy for conservation purposes by the United States was hardly coincidental. During the last two decades, the United States has made more extensive use of trade instruments to influence the conservation policies of other nations than any other country. Not only did the tuna-dolphin case mark the second time a GATT dispute panel had ruled against the United States in the case of an American boycott of tuna, but, as Indonesia noted in its statement to the GATT tuna-dolphin dispute panel, "the action against Mexico was the *twenty-third* time since 1975 that the United States has instituted an embargo on tuna imports."[84] Indeed, no other country has so frequently employed trade restrictions to achieve such a wide variety of noneconomic policy objectives, ranging from the protection of human rights to national security and now, increasingly, environmental protection. What makes the MMPA unusual was not that the United States authorized the use of trade instruments to influence environmental policies outside its legal jurisdiction, but that an action of the United States became the subject of a GATT dispute panel.

For example, the Pelly Amendment to the Fishermen's Protective Act, approved in 1971, authorized the United States to enforce sanctions against the fishing industries of other countries which violated the terms of internationally agreed marine conservation treaties or conventions—though it made the imposition of such restrictions contingent upon their compatibility with GATT. Originally intended to protect salmon, it was subsequently applied to all species of fish, and later to endangered or threatened species as well—provided they were covered by an international conservation program. The 1979 Packwood-Magnuson Amendment allowed the President to impose an embargo on all fish from any country that fails to live up to the International Whaling Convention.

In 1987 Congress passed legislation requiring the secretary of commerce to monitor international compliance of other nations with the South Pacific Drift Net Convention, which restricted the use of large-scale driftnet fishing in this region. A 1989 statute requires the U.S. President to ban shrimp imports from countries that have not made efforts to reduce their accidental catches of sea turtles comparable to those of the America shrimp fleet. Turtle protection devices had been required on all American fishing vessels since 1988—much to the displeasure of U.S. shrimpers, who contended that turtle mortality was not a significant problem, and that the devices cut deeply into their shrimp catch.[85] The objectives of this Amendment were similar to the 1984 and 1988 amendments to the MMPA. Its purpose was to reduce the number of turtles—estimated at more than 150,000 per year—that were drowned by foreign shrimping fleets when they were caught in the long nets shrimpers drag across the ocean floor.

In 1990 the MMPA was amended to permit the United States to prohibit the importation of all fish or fish products harvested using large-scale driftnets on the high seas. This essentially extends the scope of 1984 and 1988 amendments from tuna fish to all fish which are caught in ways that result in an incidental taking of marine mammals in excess of the American standard, which is essentially zero, since the United States has banned any use of large-scale driftnets by U.S. fishermen. Accordingly, nations which engage in high seas driftnet fishing and wish to export fish to the United States must first provide documentary evidence that their catch was not harvested using large-scale drift nets on the high seas.

The motives behind these statutes have been mixed. In some cases, they reflect an effort to protect American fishermen from foreign competitors that do not have to comply with stricter American environmental standards.[86] In other cases they stem from an American interest in promoting conservation in international fishing areas or enforcing international conservation agreements. More recently, they stem from the growing interest of many Americans in international wildlife conservation.

These statutes all work in much the same manner: they attempt to protect or conserve various species of mammals or fish not only by prohibiting the import of the endangered or protected species, but also by prohibiting the import of other fish or fish products from the offending nation. While many of these statutes state that their enforcement should be consistent with the GATT, that requirement appears to be very difficult, if not impossible, to meet. Based on the ruling of the tuna-dolphin dispute panel, it is highly likely that almost any attempt by the President to embargo fish imports under American legislation would violate the GATT, unless the embargo was authorized by an international agreement.

Why then have so few complaints been filed against the United States? The answer is very simple: with the notable exceptions of the Mexican and Canadian embargo, no embargo of any consequence has been enforced by the United States. (During the mid 1980s, the United States did deny Soviet fishing fleets access to American waters because the USSR continued to hunt whales. But this was not a trade sanction and, in any event, the Soviet Union was not a member of the GATT.) However, by threatening to use the embargo weapon, the United States has effectively pressured a number of countries to alter their conservation practices.

In the early 1980s the threat of Pelly and Packwood-Magnuson Amendment sanctions persuaded Spain, Peru, Korea, Taiwan, and Chile to bring their whaling practices into conformity with the International Whaling Commission (IWC).[87] In the 1980s the threat of Pelly Amendment sanctions played a critical role in securing Japanese approval of a bilateral agreement that removed the Japanese objection to the IWC moratorium on commercial whaling. In addition, following last-minute negotiations with the United States, Japan reached an agreement that enabled it to be certified under the Driftnet Control Act. A similar development took place in the cases of Korea and Taiwan.

In the case of the American statute to protect sea turtles, the U.S. State Department has hesitated to enforce the ban, on the grounds that to do so would reduce American shrimp imports from eighty countries totaling $1.8 billion—more than 75 percent of the value of all shrimp consumed in the United States. Secretary of State James Baker explained to Congress in November 1990: "The impact of the resulting embargoes would be unprecedented—both internationally and domestically."[88] In response, the Earth Island Institute filed suit in federal court. According to the Institute's attorney, "The facts are clear. The secretaries of commerce and state are willing to sacrifice these magnificent animals [sea turtles], in clear violation of the law, to protect big business."[89]

However, in May 1991 the State Department did ban shrimp from Surinam until that government committed itself to a program of turtle protection. The country complied several months later and the ban was lifted. The following year the United States banned shrimp imports from French Guyana for the same reason. And in April 1994 it imposed limited trade sanctions against Taiwan for refusing to halt the sale of tiger bones and rhinoceros horns. These sanctions banned all Taiwan wildlife exports to the United States, amounting to approximately 25 million dollars or 0.1 percent of Taiwan's exports to the United States.[90] However, the GATT consistency of the latter ban was irrelevant because Taiwan was not a member of the GATT at the time these sanctions were imposed.

Trade Restrictions of the European Union

The use of trade restrictions to enforce extrajurisdictional changes in environmental policies has not been confined to the United States. Ironically, notwithstanding its harsh criticism of American unilateralism, the EU has frequently engaged in similiar practices. For example, following a number of resolutions by the European Parliament that drew public attention to the hunting methods used to cull baby seals off the Canadian coast, in 1983 the European Council banned the import of skins of pup harp and hooded seals, as well as products derived from them.[91] The Council, hesitant to threaten directly Canada's economic interests, justified its restriction not on humanitarian grounds but on the need to preserve the common market, since a number of member states had previously enacted similar bans.

The Canadian government strongly protested the EU's action and filed a complaint with the GATT on the grounds that the General

Agreement does not permit a nation to unilaterally ban the import of a product which is only produced outside its borders unless its consumption harms its own citizens or environment. Canada subsequently withdrew its complaint and shortly thereafter announced an end, on conservation grounds, to all commercial hunting of seal pups. When the ban was extended in 1988, the European Commission noted that harp seal pup hunting in both Canada and Norway had significantly declined as a result of its 1983 Directive and the hunting restrictions both countries had adopted.

In 1991 the EU Council of Ministers again used a trade restriction to attempt to protect wild animals outside its legal jurisdiction.[92] The Council approved legislation that both banned the use of leghold traps to catch wild animals within the Union and, beginning in 1995, prohibited the importation of all fur-bearing mammals into the Union from nations that had not effectively banned the use of leghold traps. The purpose of this resolution was to persuade the United States, Canada, and the countries belonging to the former Soviet Union—the main suppliers of pelts of wild mammals to the EU's fur industry—to follow the Union's lead and outlaw the use of leghold traps because of the pain they inflict upon the wild animals caught in them.

This regulation raises issues strikingly similar to the tuna-dolphin case: it uses trade restrictions to regulate foreign production practices in order to advance a humanitarian objective. Therefore, under the reasoning of the tuna-dolphin panel, it is probably not consistent with GATT.[93] However, both the United and Canada subsequently indicated that they would take steps to conform to the Union's standards, thus avoiding a legal dispute, and once again demonstrating the leverage of greener states with large domestic markets over the regulatory policies of their trading partners.

Trade Restrictions to Protect Forests

Trade restrictions are also increasingly being both proposed and used to protect rainforests.[94] At the 1990 G-7 summit, a coalition of environmental groups urged the nations in attendance to agree to import tropical timber made only from "sustainable" forests. Two years later Austria became the first country to impose a mandatory tropical timber labeling requirement. Beginning in September 1992, it required all wood products sold in Austria to contain labels indicating whether they contained tropical timber. Austria also announced plans to establish a quality mark to designate timber and timber products made from sustainably managed forests in order to deter people from buying tropical timber. The Dutch government subsequently went a step further: it announced that, beginning in 1995, it would only allow imports of tropical timber produced from sustainably managed forests.

At a meeting of the GATT Council, the Austrian action was strongly attacked by the Association of South East Asian Nations—two of whose members, Malaysia and Indonesia, account for 80 percent of global tropical timber exports. They argued that it was both "unilateral and discriminatory," since the labeling requirement applies only to imported (that is, tropical) wood.[95] Since Austria itself is an important timber producer and exporter, they claimed that the real purpose of the labeling scheme was to encourage consumers to switch from products made of tropical woods to ones using temperate (that is, Austrian) timber. Austria's GATT representative responded that the new regulations "arose solely out of a concern to promote the sustainable management of tropical forests."[96] While no formal complaint was filed with the GATT, Austrian trade officials felt that if one was filed, they would lose. Under pressure from the GATT as well as from Malaysia and Indonesia, Austria agreed to drop its mandatory labeling requirement. However, it did retain a provision in the original statute that permits *all* timber producers to apply for a quality mark which certifies that their wood was harvested according to the principles of sustainable development. For its part, the Dutch Ministry of Economic Affairs has concluded that its ban is incompatible with Article XI of the GATT.

The European Parliament has called upon the Union to halt all imports of tropical hardwoods originating in Sarawak, Malaysia, on the grounds that logging in that region is proceeding at "a devastating pace."[97] It has also requested that the Union promote conservation by limiting the importation of hardwoods to countries which had adopted Forestry Management and Conservation Plans. The effect of this last proposal would be to involve the Union in negotiating quotas with each producing country, which it already does for a number of agricultural products, though for economic rather than environmental reasons. However, both the Council and the Commission have resisted these pressures from the Parliament on the grounds that it would be inappropriate for the Union to act outside of the international frameworks provided by the International Tropical Timber Agreement, the GATT, or CITES. According to the Commission, "Import restrictions unilaterally applied by the Community might . . . benefit other consuming countries without doing much to save tropical forests from destruction."[98]

Consistent with this policy, the EU strongly criticized a 1985 Indonesian ban on the export of unprocessed tropical timber from its rainforests. Disputing Indonesia's claim that the "ban [was] an integral part of a long-term program for conservation and management of its forest resources," the EU claimed that its real purpose was to protect Indonesia's wood processing industry, by requiring that the manufacture of "value added" product such as furniture take place in Indonesia rather than in Europe or Japan.[99] They argued that the export ban violated Article I of the GATT, which requires foreign and domestic industries to be treated equally.

The Indonesian ban, like the Canadian salmon and herring handling requirement, may well have had as much to do with domestic politics and economics as environmental protection. The Indonesian government in fact admitted that the ban's purpose was to force Indonesian exporters to switch to higher-valued products such as plywood or rattan furniture.[100] Moreover, according to the *Economist,* one of the ban's main effects was "to drive many small producers out of business," thus handing a "lucrative monopoly" over to a well-connected businessman who "controls access to export licenses for processed wood."[101] However, the ban was strongly supported by international environmental organizations on the grounds that it would help reduce logging in the rainforest. In fact, export bans have become common in the forests sector. In addition to Indonesia, other countries, including the Philippines, Malaysia, Canada, and the United States, have banned exports of raw logs, thus requiring domestic processing. While justified as conservation measures, all these export restrictions also have protected domestic wood processors.

The CAFE Dispute

In 1993 another trade dispute involving an American government regulation surfaced between the European Union and the United States. The EU requested the convening of a dispute settlement panel on the

GATT consistency of American corporate average fuel economy (CAFE) standards, the so-called gas-guzzler tax, and a tax on luxury automobiles. The former two taxes were environmental/conservation measures, while the third was a revenue one. The EU's complaint was promoted by the fact that the burdens of all three fell disproportionately on European car companies; while European cars accounted for only 4 percent of the American market in 1991, they contributed 88 percent of the revenues collected by American luxury taxes and CAFE penalties.[102] Out of total revenues of 558 million dollars from all three taxes, 494 million fell on European cars.

CAFE standards, which were originally established in 1975 and subsequently tightened in 1980, are designed to promote fuel efficiency. They are based on the miles per gallon achieved by a sales-weighted average of all vehicles produced by a manufacturer. If a manufacturer's vehicles fall below this standard, which in 1993 was 27.6 miles per gallon, they are subject to a penalty. Although the penalty applies equally to all car makers doing business in the United States, it has been paid exclusively by European limited-line premium car makers. Since all American automobile firms make a full line of cars, they have been able to avoid the tax on their less fuel-efficient luxury cars by averaging their fuel economy with the rest of their fleet. Japanese car firms have been able to avoid the tax because they mostly make smaller, more fuel-efficient vehicles.

The penalties imposed on European car manufacturers have been substantial. Between 1985 and 1989, BMW paid fines totaling $32 million, Mercedes-Benz paid $85 million, and Jaguar paid $27 million.[103] Only one major high-end European car exporter, Saab-Scania, met the 1989 CAFE standards and that was because it only offered cars with four-cylinder engines.[104] Thanks to the CAFE standards, U.S. consumers are required to pay an additional $1,800 for a Jaguar XJ-S V-12 and $1,500 for the Mercedes 560SEC sport coupe. According to one car executive, "It seems if you're already spending $67,000 on a car you wouldn't worry about another $1,200 for the gas guzzler, but it's a factor."[105] A. B. Shuman, public relations manager for Mercedes-Benz of North America, claims that CAFE rules "are really made for the Big Three. The problem for Europeans is that they're not full-line manufacturers. They don't have little cars to balance out the higher-consumption cars."[106]

Following unsuccessful consultations with the United States, the EU requested the formation of a dispute panel. In its complaint to the GATT, the EU argued that "the CAFE regulations are biased toward the full-line manufacturers and limited-line manufacturers that produce mostly small vehicles."[107] The EU claimed that because CAFE penalties fell only on imported cars, they violated the GATT's national treatment provision. The EU further argued that the 1978 gas guzzler tax, which was based on a threshold fuel economy standard of 22.5 mpg—was discriminatory and was not based on any objective or reasonable criteria. Finally, the EU claimed that the $30,000 cutoff for the luxury tax was both "capricious" and discriminatory, since in 1990, the year the tax was introduced as part of the 1990 budget reconciliation bill, more than 80 percent of the vehicles subject to it were imports.[108]

In fact, the means chosen by Congress to improve fuel efficiency were in part designed to prevent further erosion of the market share of American automobile manufacturers and thus protect domestic jobs. However, the main competitive threat to the American automobile industry at the time the CAFE standards were enacted came not from Europe but from Japan. Ironically, the real beneficiary of the regulations imposed by Congress on the American automobile industry during the 1970s, including both fuel economy and automobile emission requirements, were Japanese manufacturers. They had pioneered the design and development of both fuel efficient and low-polluting vehicles and were more readily able to meet American regulatory standards than American manufacturers. And they too have been largely exempted from CAFE penalties. However, during the 1980s American car manufacturers have supported maintaining the formula for calculating CAFE standards in part because of its effect on European luxury car imports.

The *Financial Times* predicted that "should the United States lose this case, it would face as much an outcry as the so-called 'tuna-dolphin decision.'"[109] But much to the surprise of most observers, in October 1994 the GATT dispute panel ruled in favor of the United States. Employing similar reasoning to the GATT panel decisions in the U.S.-Canadian conservation cases and the Thai cigarette case, it held that product regulations were GATT-consistent as long as they did not *explicitly* discriminate on the basis of country of origin and were necessary to protect public health or the environment. However, the panel decision may well have been affected as much by political considerations as legal ones, since it was released shortly before the American Congress was due to vote on the Uruguay Round agreement.

The Terms of the Debate

The growing number of environmentally-related trade initiatives and disputes has helped to precipitate a heated debate over the appropriate relationship between trade and environmental policy—one with important policy implications. This debate is only partially about the compatibility of particular technical provisions of the General Agreement with the strengthening of environmental regulation or with the logic of the dispute panel's ruling in the tuna-dolphin case. Rather, it reflects a more profound clash of culture and world views between the trade community and environmentalists.

For the former, who tend to be economists, the liberalization of international trade has been and remains critical to the enhancement of global welfare; it is also a necessary, though certainly not sufficient, condition for the improvement of environmental quality. They view the world trading system as fragile: they fear that any significant relaxation of GATT principles in the interests of environmentalism will result in a major upsurge of protectionism, thus undermining the considerable improvement in both living standards and environmental quality that has taken place in the postwar period.

Environmentalists hold a very different perspective. Their formative experience is not the breakdown of the world economy during the 1930s but what they perceive as the increasing environmental degradation of the last few decades. For the environmental community, it is the ecosphere, not the global trading system, which is fragile and in need of maintenance and repair. They regard the economic expansion and increased interdependence of the postwar period as being in large measure responsible for the deterioration of the global environment.

While both communities in principle prefer multilateral accords, many environmentalists believe that in the absence of such accords, unilateralism has an important role to play. But they want the ability of nations to influence the environmental policies of their trading partners to go in only one direction—to permit greener nations to affect the regulations of less green countries, but not the reverse. They thus care less about the principle of national sovereignty than about raising national environmental standards, through whatever means.

For many environmentalists, the GATT panel ruling in the tuna-dolphin case demonstrated the inadequacies of GATT rules to allow nations to address legitimate environmental concerns. Even before the GATT panel had issued its ruling, a number of environmental organizations had begun urging that the GATT be amended to take into account the growing importance of environmental issues. A discussion paper published by the World Wildlife Fund two months before the tuna decision noted that the original 1947 GATT agreement was "negotiated without any express references to the environment," adding that, "on the occasions when the GATT has been amended and strengthened, it has also been without reference to environmental concerns."[110] Not surprisingly, GATT dispute panels have been interested in and have developed expertise "only in the objective of liberalizing trade," and have ignored the implications of their rulings on environmental protection.[111]

The tuna-dolphin decision had clearly made the case for reforming the GATT even more compelling. "If a 19-year old conservation law not generally perceived to be protectionist in intent could be viewed by a GATT panel as a fundamental violation of world trade rules, then it became easy to explain to the public why such rules were in need of reform."[112] At demonstrations in front of the American Capitol, environmentalists carried posters depicting a monstrous "GATT-zilla," with a dolphin in one arm and a canister dripping DDT in the other, chanting GATT's new meaning: "Guaranteeing a Toxic Tomorrow."[113] Friends of the Earth argued that the GATT is "fundamentally at odds with environmental protection," and urged that it either be suspended or dramatically modified.[114] The Earth Island Institute claimed that "without substantial overhaul, GATT will pose a grave threat to environmental protection laws throughout the world."[115]

A number of environmental organizations have proposed a new GATT article to guarantee "environmental conditionality—the idea that countries should not be penalized for taking measures that conflict with GATT rules, if their main purpose is to protect the environment."[116] They also urged that the World Trade Organization (WTO) be instructed to give "high and formal priority to environmental concerns," in particular to sustainable development.[117] In addition, they have demanded that GATT dispute-settlement procedures be reformed to make them more open and permit the introduction of evidence about the impact of trade rules on environmental regulations and standards.

The Response of the GATT

The Uruguay Round agreement which concluded in 1994 did not attempt to address any of the specific issues raised by the tuna-dolphin dispute, let alone the broader questions concerning the future relationship between trade and the environment. But largely as a response to the criticism of the GATT by environmentalists, it did explicitly acknowledge one principle which had formerly been implicit. The preamble to the Standards Agreement, which was now incorporated into the provisions of the WTO, marks the first mention of the word "environment" in the GATT itself. It states that each country "may maintain standards and technical regulations for the protection of human, animal, and plant life and health and of the *environment*."[118] It also notes that a country should not be prevented from setting technical standards (which include environmental regulations) "at the levels it considers appropriate," a phrase meant to discourage nations from harmonizing standards in a downward direction.[119] In addition, the Agreement on Subsidies and Countervailing Measures permits governments to subsidize up to 20 percent of one-time capital investments to meet new environmental requirements, provided that its subsidies are "directly linked and proportionate" to environmental improvements.[120] This provision makes the granting of environmental subsidies somewhat easier.

At the same time, in an effort to reduce the use of national consumer and environmental regulations as nontariff barriers, the Uruguay Round agreement also requires that national standards or "technical barriers to trade" "not be more trade-restrictive than necessary to fulfill a legitimate objective, taking into account of the risks nonfulfillment would create."[121] Significantly, an earlier draft had imposed a stricter test—it had required that standards be the "least trade restrictive available"—but this was modified at the insistence of the United States.[122] Thus, on balance, both the language of the Uruguay Round agreement, along with the reasoning of the dispute panel in the second tuna-dolphin case, and the GATT's decision in the CAFE dispute suggest a softening of the GATT's scrutiny of national protective regulations that interfere with trade. In this sense, the GATT has become slightly greener.

Revising the GATT's rules to better reconcile free trade and environmental protection will be high on the agenda of the post-Uruguay Round of trade negotiations. Indeed, this process has already begun. In 1991, acting on the suggestion of the members of the European Free Trade Association, the GATT agreed to convene its Working Group on Environmental Measures and International Trade, which had been established in 1971 but had never met. EFTA members stated that they wanted "a rule-based analytical discussion on the interrelationship between trade and environment . . . to ensure that the GATT system was well equipped to meet the challenge of environmental issues and to prevent disputes by . . . interpret[ing] or amend[ing] . . . certain provisions of the General Agreement."[123] At the GATT's April 1994 ministerial meeting, at which the results of the Uruguay Round were formally ratified, a resolution was approved which committed the soon-to-be-established World Trade Organization to undertake a systematic review of "trade policies and those trade-related aspects of environmental policies which may result in significant trade effects for its members."[124]

The convening of the GATT working group had initially been opposed by some developing countries which had misgivings about having the GATT examine environmental issues. They feared that the GATT rules would be weakened to permit developed nations wider latitude in restricting imports on environmental grounds from developing nations. However, there was a strong consensus among most GATT signatory nations that it was important for the GATT to address the increasingly important linkages between trade and regulatory policies. Indeed, the turnout of delegations for an informal meeting of this working group appeared to set a GATT record.[125]

Among the most important tasks of the WTO's Trade and Environment Committee, the successor body to the GATT Working Group, will be to examine the GATT consistency of the seventeen international environmental agreements that provide for enforcement through trade restrictions. For as the GATT's annual report conceded, the General Agreement's principles needed to be carefully re-examined "to make certain that they do not hinder multilateral efforts to deal with environmental problems."[126]

What made this task an urgent one was that the GATT panel ruling in the tuna-dolphin case had raised questions concerning the GATT compatibility of three highly visible and extremely important multilateral environmental agreements: the Convention on International Trade in Endangered Species of World Flora and Fauna (CITES), the Basel Convention on Hazardous Wastes, and the Montreal Protocol, which restricts the production and sale of chlorofluorocarbons (CFCs). Indeed, this was one of the reasons why many environmentalists had found the implications of the ruling of the GATT dispute panel so disturbing. All three treaties violate the GATT's most-favored-nation clause by imposing more restrictive provisions on GATT signatories who do not comply with their provisions than on those that do. In the case of the former two agreements, trade controls and restrictions are central to the objectives of the treaties themselves: their purpose is precisely to *restrict* international trade. In the case of the Montreal Protocols, trade restrictions are critical to the treaty's enforcement mechanisms.

The oldest agreement that the working group plans to examine is CITES, which went into effect in 1975 and currently has more than 100 parties.[127] CITES seeks to protect endangered species by restricting international trade in them. Depending on which appendix a particular species falls into, commercial international trade may be absolutely prohibited, maintained at levels consistent with the species' biological carrying capacity, or require an export permit. Additions and subtractions to each appendix are decided biannually by a two-thirds vote of signatory nations.

GATT rules do not prevent a nation from banning the domestic sale of a product and enforcing this ban at its borders, since those actions may be consistent with the GATT principles of nondiscrimination and national treatment. Moreover, CITES rules ban the import of the endangered species itself—not products produced in ways which harm an endangered plant or animal. But what if CITES were to allow limited international trade in ivory? Could a nation discriminate between ivory imports from nations with responsible and irresponsible elephant conservation practices? Or would that constitute a "process" restriction?

In fact, an American action under CITES nearly did provoke a trade dispute with Japan. During the early 1980s the U.S. Commerce Department found that Japan was contributing to the extinction of the hawksbill sea turtle by encouraging the domestic manufacturing of eye-glass frames, mirror handles, combs, and other objects made from the animal's shells. The United States, which had itself banned imports of turtle shells in 1973, threatened to ban imports from Japan of all animal products, including more than $300 million in fish, as well as pearls.

What made this dispute somewhat complicated is that while the hawksbill sea turtle was listed as an endangered species in Appendix I of the CITES convention, Japan had filed a reservation over this classification, meaning that Japan was not bound to protect this particular species. In addition, the GATT compatibility of the American trade restriction was dubious, since while GATT rules require that all like products (such as frames made from turtle shells) be treated alike, the United States was seeking to treat this imported product differently (that is, based on its country of origin). A trade conflict was averted when Japan responded to public and diplomatic pressure by agreeing to limit its imports of the protected turtle species.

Another important international environmental agreement, the Montreal Protocol, also contains provisions that may violate GATT rules. Although the GATT requires nations to treat all their trading partners equally, the treaty provides for the banning of imports of CFCs from those nations that have not endorsed the Protocol. In addition, since the Protocol commits signatories to determine the feasibility of banning or restricting "the import of products produced with, but not containing, controlled substances" from nonsignatory nations, it violates the tuna-dolphin panel's prohibition on import restrictions based on production standards.[128]

But the Protocol's trade restrictions are critical to the treaty's enforcement. Absent trade restrictions, nonsignatory nations might produce goods using ozone-depleting chemicals for sale in nations that had signed the Protocol. While none of these trade restrictions pose a problem if all GATT signatories which produce CFCs also are signatories to the Montreal Protocol, what if a nation had signed the former agreement but not the latter? Privately, GATT officials have informed the drafters of the Montreal Protocol that the environmental agreement is GATT-consistent, since the harms it is designed to prevent are global in nature and therefore do directly affect the health of citizens in all nations. Moreover, to date, all major CFC producers have signed the Protocol. But concern nonetheless persists.

GATT rules also pose potential problems for the 1987 Basel Convention on the Control of Transboundary Movements of Hazardous Wastes and Their Disposal. This convention, which went into effect in May 1992, is designed to control international trade in wastes. It restricts movements of hazardous waste between nations, unless they have a bilateral agreement that meets the terms of the convention. Not only does this provision violate the GATT rule against nondiscrimination, but in the final stages of negotiations the convention was expanded to include "other wastes" as well. Since the latter includes scrap metals, which are commercially valuable, the agreement could well lead to significant disruptions in international trade as well as numerous trade disputes.

No nation has yet challenged the GATT compatibility of a trade restriction taken pursuant to an international environmental agreement, and it is possible that international pressures may prevent any nation from ever doing so. But since the number of environmental agreements is steadily increasing, as is the number of GATT-WTO signatories, the possibility for a conflict between GATT rules and those of various international environmental treaties is real.

Numerous proposals have been advanced to permit the use of trade restrictions to protect environmental quality outside of a nation's physical borders—without opening the floodgates to protectionism disguised as environmentalism.[129] Essentially these proposals require that such restrictions meet a number of criteria. For example, they must address environmental problems that are global in scope, they must be matched by domestic measures, they must not be intended to protect domestic producers, and they must command significant international support.

However, any effort to change the WTO's rules to allow its signatories wider latitude to use trade restrictions to influence environmental standards outside their legal jurisdiction will be strongly opposed by less developed nations, who view the use of any production standards for imports as a new form of protectionism. Principle 12 of the Rio Declaration issued at the 1992 U.N. Conference on Trade and Development states that "unilateral actions to deal with environmental challenges outside the jurisdiction of the importing country [should] . . . be avoided."[130] This view was echoed by a U.N. General Assembly resolution, which cautioned that incorporating environmental decisions into development policy should "not serve as a pretext for creating unjustified barriers to trade."[131]

A second set of equally controversial issues which the Committee plans to address involves the trade effects of packaging and labeling requirements, both of which have been rapidly increasing. Almost all developed countries, as well as the EU and a number of states and provinces in North America, have adopted such regulations. As the EU's experience with Denmark's bottling and Germany's packaging regulations reveals, eco-packaging rules frequently have significant trade effects: whether by necessity or intention, they almost invariably serve to disadvantage importers. For their part, national or local eco-labeling requirements can also present obstacles to trade, especially if their definition of sound environmental practices is tailored to the capacities and practices of domestic firms or reflects domestic environmental concerns. Moreover, foreign producers are generally excluded from participating in the design of national eco-labeling standards, and they often find it more difficult for their products to be granted green labels.

The eco-labeling and recycling regulations and requirements of developed countries have been strongly criticized by developing nations, which view them as increasingly important trade barriers. They want packaging and labeling requirements to be subject to stricter scrutiny by the WTO. At the same time, these regulations have been strongly defended by developed nations, for whom they represent an effective way both of improving the environmental practices of producers in their own country as well as around the globe and, not incidentally, of protecting domestic producers.

Conclusion

What has been the impact of the GATT on environmental standards? In one sense, it is inappropriate to ask if the GATT has contributed to strengthening environmental regulation, since that is not its purpose; it is only a trade agreement. But it is certainly appropriate to assess the *effect* of the GATT's rules on the ability of nations to strengthen either domestic or international regulatory standards.

There are two ways in which the GATT might have served to

weaken environmental standards. One has to do with the international equivalent of the Delaware effect. By reducing tariffs in general and preventing nations from taxing imported goods produced according to laxer regulatory standards, the GATT might have prevented greener nations from enacting regulatory standards as strict as their citizens preferred. The second has to do with the role of dispute settlement panels in finding national environmental regulations to be GATT-inconsistent. In fact, neither had a significant impact.

The Delaware effect has not materialized at the global level, in part because the costs of compliance with most environmental standards has not been sufficiently large to force greener governments to lower them in order to maintain the international competitiveness of domestic producers. For example, according to a study of the impact of trade on regulation in the United States and Canada, "the assertion that trade liberalization leads to a de facto harmonization of environmental standards as the 'lowest common denominator' is not supported by the evidence . . . United States and Canadian tariffs have been reduced over time to imports from a wide range of countries which have weaker environmental standards, yet there has been no retraction of standards or enforcement based on these imports."[132] A study of firms which have been subject to tight environmental regulations in seven countries concludes that "the industrial sectors which spend the most on pollution control generally maintained their international competitiveness between 1970 and 1980," while the OECD reports that "very little evidence exists of firms being transferred abroad in order to escape the more stringent environmental regulations at home."[133]

Nor have GATT restrictions on the use of regulations as nontariff barriers to trade interfered with the steady strengthening of national, or in the case of the EU, regional environmental standards. Since the GATT's establishment more than forty-five years ago, nations have issued literally tens of thousands of production and product environmental regulations, yet only a handful have been found to be inconsistent with the GATT.[134] Nor do GATT rules prevent nations from acting to preserve natural resources located outside of their borders, providing these conservation efforts are taken in conjunction with domestic restrictions on either production or consumption. Neither has the GATT prevented a steady increase in the number and scope of international environmental agreements. Thus to date, the GATT has been largely irrelevant to the steady strengthening of local, national, and international environmental standards.

While the number of trade disputes involving environmental regulations has recently increased, they still encompass only a small proportion of all trade conflicts that have come before the GATT. To date, only seven out of the slightly more than one hundred trade disputes that have come before dispute panels have involved either environmental or consumer regulations. It is true that four of these have been decided since 1990, and doubtless there will be others. But this certainly does not suggest that the international trading system and environmental regulation are on a collision course. Nonetheless, a number of these disputes have been important. What has been their actual impact on consumer protection and environmental quality?

Two of these disputes were commercial conflicts between the United States and Canada; their resolution had no environmental consequences. In the case of a third dispute, brought by Canada, the EU, and Mexico against the excise tax provisions of American Superfund legislation, the American regulation was upheld.

What about the GATT dispute panel's ruling against Thailand's restrictions on sales of American cigarettes? In fact, this decision has not adversely affected the health of the Thai people. Ironically, by encouraging the Thai government to impose the strictest controls on cigarette marketing of any capitalist nation in Asia in order to keep the American market share low, the filing of the suit by the United States may even have enhanced health in Thailand. For the Thai government's efforts to restrict the market share of imports required it, under GATT rules, to impose *equally* strict restrictions on their domestic cigarette monopoly. Consequently, restrictions on cigarette marketing in Thailand are more severe after the GATT ruling than before, and the American market share there is among the lowest in Asia.

Ironically, Thailand, the only nation whose cigarette restrictions were challenged by the United States under the GATT, has been far more successful in limiting both American cigarette sales and total cigarette consumption than Japan, Taiwan, and Korea, which opened up their domestic markets as a result of bilateral negotiations with the United States. Contrary to expectations, and much to the disappointment of the American tobacco industry, the American share of the Thai cigarette market has remained at less than 3 percent.

In the case of American CAFE standards, virtually all policy analysts agree that they are far less efficient and effective than gasoline taxes in improving fuel economy. Gasoline taxes are, of course,

GATT-consistent. Thus, a ruling against the United States in this dispute would not have compromised the effectiveness of American efforts to improve fuel economy; it would only have required the United States to change their form. Indeed, assuming that the United States then chose to increase gasoline taxes, it would have made them *more* effective. The fact that American environmental quality might well be enhanced if CAFE standards had been successfully challenged under GATT rules suggests that less trade-restrictive regulations are not necessarily less effective.

More generally, the WTO's new "least trade-restrictive" test can be understood as the international equivalent of the EU's "proportionality" standard: both subject national regulations to tighter international scrutiny. But as the experience of the EU demonstrates, there is nothing about the application of this principle that forces nations to weaken their domestic standards, though it may well force them to revise their form in order to make them less discriminatory. Equally important, both principles have a significant role to play in restricting the use of national regulations whose real purpose is to protect domestic producers rather than consumer welfare or environmental quality. But in any event, the American CAFE regulations were held to be consistent with American obligations under the GATT.

This leaves the most important case, the tuna-dolphin dispute. Ironically, for all the furor surrounding this decision, it actually had virtually no impact on dolphin mortality. For the most significant reduction in dolphin deaths took place took place *prior* to the American trade embargo. Between the passage of the Marine Mammal Protection Act in 1972 and the banning of tuna imports from Mexico in 1990, annual tuna mortality in the eastern tropical Pacific had declined by approximately 90 percent. Indeed, between 1986 and 1991 the number of dolphins killed by Mexican fishing vessels dropped by nearly two-thirds. Moreover, there was no evidence that dolphins were endangered at the time the embargo provisions of the MMPA were enforced.

In essence, the tuna embargo is based on a moral argument, not an environmental one. America has as much right to demand that Mexicans protect dolphins as India has to demand that U.S. cattle ranchers eliminate their slaughter of cows. In this context, it is significant that while America is certainly not the only nation whose citizens care about international wildlife protection, not a single nation supported the American position in its trade dispute with Mexico. This was not so much because they did not care about dolphins; concern about dolphin mortality certainly existed in the EU as well. Rather, the noticeable lack of international support for the United States in its dispute with Mexico stemmed in large measure from the fact that the United States had acted unilaterally. America was the only nation that banned tuna imports from foreign nationals.

Moreover, this dispute took place between two nations with significantly different levels of economic development. It is one thing for a rich nation to seek to impose its environmental priorities on another rich one; the numerous disputes among Canada, the EU, and the United States over their respective conservation policies fall into this category. But it is quite a different matter for a rich nation to insist that its environmental standards be matched by those of a much poorer one, especially one whose access to the markets of the world's richer countries is critical to its ability to improve domestic living standards. In fact, the United States had long been pressuring Mexico to liberalize its economy and open up its domestic markets to international competition, an irony not lost on Mexico's business community.

Still, the tuna-dolphin case does raise an important issue: do GATT rules unreasonably interfere with the ability of nations to address environmental problems which occur outside of their jurisdiction? In point of fact, notwithstanding that they violate the letter or the spirit of the GATT, politically powerful and affluent green nations have frequently employed the threat of withdrawing market access—or, on occasion, have actually withdrawn it—to pressure other nations into changing their environmental policies. For example, the United States has effectively used the threat of trade sanctions to pressure a number of its trading partners to adopt policies toward the conservation of sea turtles, whales, and dolphins similar to its own. And in the face of trade restrictions by the EU, Canada reformed its policies toward the killing of seal pups. The EU has also successfully employed trade restrictions to persuade the countries of the former Soviet Union and the United States to ban the use of leghold traps for wild animals.

It is important not to confuse the GATT with an American regulatory agency or the European Commission: it is not a global trade police which seeks out protectionists. While the GATT does require nations to adhere to their commitments under the agreement, it only intervenes when a complaint is filed by a signatory nation which believes that its interests have been harmed. There are clearly important political and social pressures in the international community for more responsible environmental policies in a number of areas, including wildlife conservation, which have discouraged nations from filing formal complaints over potential or actual GATT violations. For example, the United States could challenge the EU's leg-trap ban, but for domestic political reasons has not done so. Moreover, the emphasis placed by the GATT dispute panel in the second tuna-dolphin case on the legitimacy of multilateral trade restrictions suggests that dispute panels are unlikely to strike down trade restrictions that command substantial international support. In sum, international law consists of norms as well as rules.

The use of trade restrictions to affect the environmental policies of other countries can be viewed as the regulatory counterpart of "voluntary" import and export agreements for products such as textiles, steel, and cars. These violate the spirit of the GATT but not its letter since they are officially "voluntary." Thus, nowithstanding the GATT's commitment to national sovereignty, the United States, and the EU as well, have repeatedly used their control over access to their domestic markets to force their trading partners to strengthen their environmental standards.

However, the tuna-dolphin panel dispute ruling, while not officially adopted, does appear to have had a chilling effect on the use of trade restrictions for environmental purposes. For example, it has prevented both the EU and Austria from imposing restrictions on tropical timber imports, while the United States hesitated for more than a year before ratifying an international agreement on wild birds because of concerns about its GATT consistency. And the International Convention for the Conservation of Atlantic Tuna backed away from adopting a trade-based enforcement mechanism because of its potential GATT consequences.

In some cases these restraints make sense, but in others they do not. After all, trade restrictions are often not the most effective way to strengthen environmental standards. For example, rather than protecting tropical forests, trade restrictions on timber exports may produce the opposite results. As Esty notes, "By limiting the markets in which tropical timber can be sold, trade restrictions by some countries will reduce demand for the product, thereby lowering the price of tropical timber and potentially forcing exporting countries to cut more trees to maintain much-needed export revenues."[135] Nonetheless, the panel ruling in the tuna-dolphin case did expose an important shortcoming in the relationship between trade rules and environmental regulations. The sharp distinctions drawn by the GATT dispute panel in the first tuna-dolphin case between products and processes, and domestic and extrajurisdictional regulations, whatever their basis in GATT jurisprudence, represent a crude way of defining nontariff barriers. After all, many domestic product regulations often affect the way imported products are produced.

Like the EU, the GATT faces the difficult challenge of reconciling its commitment to trade liberalization with the support of some of its greener members for stricter regulatory standards that may interfere with trade. However, the response of the two institutions has differed markedly. What has enabled the EU to strike an appropriate balance between trade liberalization and the maintenance or strengthening of regulatory standards has been its ability to both strike down trade barriers and establish common regulatory standards for its members. But the GATT only has the authority to do the former. To date, its power has been used only negatively: it has told nations what they *cannot* do. In this sense, the WTO's current authority resembles that of the EEC under the Treaty of Rome: it remains basically a trade agreement.

Accordingly, if nations wish to strengthen one another's regulatory standards, they must do so outside the GATT framework, by signing international environmental agreements. These treaties can be seen as the international counterpart of the EU's Article 100, the basis for the harmonization of the regulatory standards of the member states: they provide a legal vehicle for extrajurisdictional regulations. But it is far more difficult for large numbers of nations with diverse resources and priorities to adopt and enforce international environmental treaties than it is for the EU to harmonize national regulations for fifteen mostly neighboring countries with relatively similar income levels. Moreover, while the EU's rules were rewritten in 1987 to facilitate the harmonization of regulatory standards by establishing a system of weighted voting, no comparable change has taken place within the global community; environment agreements still bind only the nations that sign them. The result is a persistent imbalance between the GATT's authority to protect world trade and an equivalent set of international rules to protect global environmental values.

The California effect does exist at the global level, as evidenced by the successful efforts of both the United States and the European Union to make access to their markets contingent upon changes in the environmental practices of their trading partners. But current GATT rules do limit its scope. Specifically, the GATT has prevented greener nations from taxing imported manufactured products on the basis of the environmental harms caused by the way they are produced. And it has also discouraged, though not prevented, restrictions on imports of animals and animal products for similar reasons. These rules could of course be changed. "Greening the GATT" does not mean making the World Trade Organization into an international environmental regulatory agency. Rather, what it would essentially mean is giving the world's greener powers wider latitude to enact regulations or trade policies that influence the environmental standards of other GATT signatories.

But while some incremental changes in GATT rules may well occur, no significant change is likely. The GATT is a far more unwieldy institution than the European Union: it is comprised of more than nine times as many members who have much less in common with one another. Equally important, the greening of the EU was made possible by the backing of three of the its more important member states, Germany, the Netherlands, and Denmark. But the GATT's more powerful members do not share a similar commitment to its greening. The Clinton administration has at times expressed its support for linking trade liberalization with stronger domestic environmental regulations, as it has expressed interest in linking trade liberalization to improvements in third world labor standards. But the administration does not appear committed to actively supporting such a significant change in the GATT's rules.

At the same time, the EU, notwithstanding its own internal greening, remains strongly opposed to any effort to "green the GATT," in part out of fear that any relaxation of the GATT's strictures against the use of trade restrictions to strengthen the environmental standards of other signatories would provide an excuse for American unilateralism. Moreover, the fact that such a disproportionate number of regulatory-linked trade disputes have pitted the United States against the

EU does not augur well for future cooperation between the world's two greenist international players. And Japan, the GATT's other major signatory, has evidenced no interest in changing the GATT's rules.

A third and final factor operating against the greening of the GATT is that the GATT, unlike the EU, operates by consensus. Thus, the opposition of less developed nations to what they perceive as ecoimperialism is also likely to make any significant changes in GATT rules highly contentious. In this context, the expansion of the GATT to include developing nations such as China will likely weaken rather than strengthen the prospects for its greening. As a result, the California effect is likely to remain more limited at the global level.

-5-

Food Safety
and International Trade

Another dimension of the relationship between international trade and protective regulation can be seen in disputes over agricultural products. While agriculture was largely excluded from a number of the provisions of the GATT, international trade in agricultural products has grown considerably during the postwar period, expanding by more than 800 percent between 1962 and 1993. At the same time, the percentage of food imports affected by nontariff barriers increased from 56 percent in 1966 to 89 percent in 1986.[1] These nontariff barriers, which include food safety and processing standards, have played a critical role in protecting domestic markets for agricultural products. Proposals to liberalize agricultural trade have, in turn, been opposed by some farmers and consumer organizations on the grounds that they threaten to compromise national health and safety standards. Indeed, in no other area of trade and regulatory policy have Baptist–bootlegger alliances been so pervasive, or politically important.

The Standards Code

The GATT sought to limit the use of product standards as nontariff barriers from the very outset. Article I, the most-favored nation clause, requires nondiscriminatory treatment of imported products from different GATT signatories, while Article III stated that such products be treated no less favorably than domestically produced goods with respect to any laws or requirements affecting their sale.

150

These articles covered pesticides and food additives as well as rules protecting animal or plant health—often referred to as Sanitary and Phytosanitary (S&P) Measures. Article XX permits nations to use these measures to restrict imports only if they are "necessary to protect human, animal or plant life or health."

However, Article XX did not specify any criteria to determine whether or not a particular standard was "necessary." As a result, as long as a country treated domestic and imported products alike, it has enjoyed substantial latitude to enact whatever regulations it chose. In many cases, these regulations, while neutral on their face, effectively discriminated against imported products. Yet throughout the 1970s, national standards and certification systems were subject to virtually no effective multilateral supervision.[2]

As a result, even as tariffs on manufactured goods diminished, the relative importance of standards and regulations as trade barriers expanded. This was in part due to the significant expansion of national regulations in the areas of consumer and environmental protection and energy conservation. In some cases, national standards and certification systems were deliberately designed or discretely used to keep out imports, while in others differences among national standards increased production costs by requiring firms to design or test products differently for different markets.[3] Since virtually all internationally traded products were subject to some form of regulation, standard, or certification, many exporters were experiencing increasing difficulties in gaining access to foreign markets.

In an effort "to cooperate in keeping protectionist pressures within limits," four codes on nontariff barriers were adopted during the Tokyo Round of trade negotiations, which concluded in 1979.[4] One of these was the Agreement on Preventing Technical Barriers to Trade, commonly referred to as TBT or the Standards Code. The Code made the national-treatment provision of the GATT more specific by committing signatory governments to ensure that national technical standards, regulations, testing procedures, and certification rules "were not prepared, adopted, or applied with a view to creating obstacles in trade."[5] While not a part of the GATT itself, by 1984 it had been signed by approximately one-third of the General Agreement's signatories.

The Standards Code did not attempt to create or harmonize regulations or standards for individual products. Rather, its purpose was to ensure that existing and new "technical regulations and standards did not create unnecessary obstacles to international trade."[6] These regulations and standards primarily referred to product characteristics, such as levels of quality, safety, performance, and so on. While the Standards Code was developed primarily for the purpose of regulating industrial standards, its provisions also applied to regulations on pesticide residues as well as food inspection and labeling requirements. Signatory nations agreed to use relevant international standards except when they deemed these standards inadequate to protect public health. In addition, they agreed to notify other governments when they issued regulations which were "not substantially the same" as that of a relevant international standard.[7]

Like the GATT itself, the Code established a dispute settlement mechanism. Whenever a signatory nation enacted regulations or standards that may "have the effect of creating unnecessary obstacles to international trade," the party adversely affected has the right to institute dispute settlement procedures.[8] If the affected parties are unable to reach agreement within three months, the Code provides that either party may request the Committee on Technical Barriers to Trade to establish either a technical expert group or a panel of international legal experts knowledgeable about the Standards Code.[9] The group or panel would then decide, and issue a report on, whether the technical standard under review violated any provision of the Standards Code. If the report concludes that the standard contravenes the Code, it would then require that it be either eliminated or replaced by a regulation that was Code consistent. The full Committee would then decide whether to adopt the report. However, the Committee was given no real enforcement powers; and thus enforcement depended primarily upon the good faith of the signatories.[10]

No formal dispute proceedings have been brought under the Code. However, it has played a modest role in reducing technical barriers to trade for a number of manufactured products; it has also worked closely and effectively with a number of regional standardizing bodies to harmonize national testing and certification standards. During its first decade of operation, the Code help settle some trade disputes involving technical standards. One such dispute involved a complaint brought by the European Community, Austria, Switzerland, and the United States against Japan.

In 1986 the Japanese Consumer Product Safety Association, a private industry group, issued a set of standards for ski equipment that differed from those of European and American manufacturers, who held 50 percent of the Japanese market. An EC representative complained that "its application would have adverse effects on the market penetration that had been achieved by exporters."[11] Japanese officials explained that Japan needed distinctive ski safety standards because the snow in Japan was different; due to Japan's unique geothermal activity, it was wetter. European and American officials disputed the scientific basis of this claim, arguing that "snow . . . came primarily from water evaporated over oceans."[12] In March 1987 the dispute was resolved when Japanese agreed to "harmonize the SG [safety goods] mark system of ski equipment with the relevant international standards."[13]

Another trade dispute between Japan and the United States involved the use of product standards and certification requirements to restrict imports of metal baseball bats. The Japanese had refused to grant American manufacturers access to Japan's safety certification for athletic equipment; this meant that each imported piece of equipment had to undergo a safety inspection check, thus creating considerable uncertainty for American manufacturers. The United States charged Japan with violating the TBT Code and requested a committee investigation. The Japanese responded by requesting bilateral consultations. The result was an agreement which guaranteed U.S. access to Japan's certification system. Japan also agreed to amend sixteen of its laws governing certification—a decision which the U.S. trade representative characterized as "the most significant development in the [U.S.-Japan] bilateral relationship since the conclusion of the Tokyo Round."[14]

In other cases, however, the ability of the TBT Code to resolve trade disputes over the use of consumer standards as trade barriers have proved more intractable. The beef hormone controversy between the United States and the EC is the most important example of such a dispute. It was in large measure the frustration of the United States over the inability of the Standards Code to resolve its complaint against the EC that led the United States to propose a strengthening of the GATT's discipline over sanitary and phytosanitary standards in the Uruguay Round.

The Ban on Hormone-Treated Meat

The origins of this trade dispute date from 1980, when newspaper articles reported that babies in Italy were growing oversized genitals and breasts because they had eaten veal treated with hormones. European public opinion was outraged, and large numbers of consumers began to boycott veal.[15] In France, a boycott of hormone-treated veal organized by the French Federal Consumers Union resulted in a 70 percent decline in veal purchases.[16] While the hormone used by the Italian farmers had already been banned in both Europe and the United States, the EC found itself under considerable pressure to place additional restrictions on the use of hormones in animal husbandry.

In July 1981 the Council of Ministers voted to ban the use of thyrostatics and stilbenes, two hormonal substances that were generally considered to have harmful effects. This ban included DES (dimethyl stilbenes), significant residues of which had been discovered in Italian baby food. As it turned out, the connection between DES, which was commonly administered to dairy cows as a growth supplement, and the injuries suffered by Italian babies was never scientifically established. However, DES is considered a carcinogen and its use had previously been banned by most important dairy-producing countries, including the United States.[17]

The EC also considered imposing a ban on five additional growth hormones, three natural and two synthetic. But the Council of Ministers resisted imposing any further restrictions on hormone use because of opposition from Britain, Ireland, and France, whose farmers made extensive use of hormones as growth stimulants for slaughter animals. The Council did vote, however, to prohibit any member state from marketing any new hormones, pending further action by the EC. It also established a scientific inquiry to examine the safety of the five disputed hormones.

The Commission's scientific investigation was conducted by the Scientific Working Group on Anabolic Agents in Animal Protection. The Working Group, in turn, consulted a number of other EC technical advisory bodies, including the Scientific Committee for Food, as well as sixty of the most distinguished veterinary and food scientists in Europe. The Working Group concluded that under appropriate conditions, such as good husbandry practices and limits on maximum doses, the three naturally occurring steroid hormones presented no danger to human health. However, due to lack of adequate scientific data, it was unable to reach any conclusion on the health effects of the two artificial hormones, Trenbolone and Zeranol. A subsequent more extensive inquiry, held in 1984 and 1985, concluded that the two artificial hormones were "harmless for consumers."[18] However, the EC Commission canceled the Working Group's meetings before it could issue its final report.

Notwithstanding the conclusions of its scientific advisory bodies, the EC found itself under growing pressure to ban the use of all growth-promoting hormones. This pressure stemmed from two sources. The first was the Community's commitment, expressed in the 1985 White Paper, to create a single European market by removing nontariff barriers among its member states. Many of these national regulations restricted trade in food, beverages, animals, and plants, among them national rules governing the use of hormones (see Chapter 2).

Because regulations governing the use of hormones had not been harmonized, each member state remained free to establish its own rules governing their use. Half of the EC's member states had banned all five disputed substances, while the other six had authorized the use of at least one of them. The result was an extensive array of barriers to intra-Community trade. For example, the French prohibited the use of natural hormones in lamb production, while the British permitted their use in order to regulate lambing dates. Consequently, the French had periodically restricted imports of British lamb. Not surprisingly, among the most enthusiastic supporters of these restrictions were French sheep farmers, who found it difficult to compete with their more efficient British counterparts. Italy, in turn, was forced to devote considerable resources to policing its border with France, since the Italians were among the first nations to ban the use of all hormones, while the French continued to permit their use in beef.

The continued disparity in national laws regulating hormone use and the border checks that invariably accompanied them thus represented a significant obstacle to the creation of a single European market. Moreover, since the extent to which hormone use *did* affect the health and safety of consumers was precisely the focus of contention, mutual recognition was not a viable solution; nations that had banned hormone use on health grounds remained unwilling to permit the import of products that contained it. In light of the importance of livestock farming to the EC—half the farms in the Community raised animals—as well as the extensive amount of intra-Community trade in beef, the Community had been attempting to establish a common veterinary policy even before the hormone controversy erupted. Heightened public awareness of the potential health hazards of hormone use in a number of member states now made this task even more urgent.

The second reason why the EC moved toward a total ban on hormones was consumer pressure. In principle, the EC could have prevented divergent national hormone regulations from interfering with intra-EC trade by permitting the use of one or more of the five hormones that its scientific advisory body had concluded were harmless—perhaps supplementing this directive with a labeling requirement to maximize consumer freedom of choice. But this in turn would have required half the member states to relax their standards for the sale of hormone-treated beef—an option made impracticable because of public pressure.

Throughout the first half of the 1980s European consumer and environmental groups waged a vigorous campaign to prohibit the use of all growth hormones in animal production. In part because of their efforts, the health hazards of hormone use became a highly visible and emotional issue. The campaign to ban hormone use was led by the Bureau of European Consumer Unions (BEUC), a coalition of national consumer unions which lobbies the EC on issues affecting consumers. BEUC argued that the hormones created major health problems for consumers. While it accepted the conclusion of the EC's first scientific inquiry that some of these problems could be avoided if the hormones were used appropriately, the Bureau contended that it was not practicable to enforce the recommended restrictions on hormone use since it was very difficult to detect their presence in processed meats. Accordingly, it concluded that the only way of ensuring adequate protection of public health was to prohibit their use entirely. The BEUC's tough position was buttressed by consumers who were increasingly interested in "natural" foods. They were willing to pay a premium for these products, including hormone-free meat.[19]

The Bureau also pointed out that permitting the continued use of growth-inducing hormones made little economic sense since the EC had a large surplus of beef. Consequently, the more meat produced by European farmers, the more the EC was required to spend on storing surplus production. Calculating that half of the EC's 400,000 tons of stored beef was due to hormone-based production, BEUC concluded that "the only economic advantage of using hormones is to make profits for those who produce and use them."[20]

The European Parliament, where European consumer and environmental groups enjoy considerable influence, became a focal point of opposition to hormone use within the EC. In 1985, when the Commission proposed allowing the use, under strictly controlled conditions, of the three natural hormones for fattening purposes, the EP strongly registered its objection, and the Commission backed down.[21] The Parliament also firmly opposed a compromise that would have permitted nations to maintain their own regulations for at least some of the disputed hormones; they insisted on harmonized standards. Finally, in early 1985 the Council of Ministers approved a resolution committing it to harmonize hormone use throughout the EC.

As it approached a decision on the five disputed hormones, the EC was divided. The Netherlands, Greece, and Italy favored a complete ban; they had already prohibited the use of all growth hormones and wanted the Community to do likewise in order to ensure a common market for meat as well as protect the economic interests of their inefficient beef producers. While Germany did permit its farmers to use hormones, its strong domestic green movement persuaded it to join the antihormone camp. For their part, Britain and Ireland favored the continued use of all five hormones. Britain's powerful farming lobby claimed it needed to use Trenbolone and Zeranol for managing young beef bulls, while farming interests in Ireland feared that a ban would only lead to the creation of a black market in hormones. France and Denmark also opposed a general hormone ban. However, as antihormone sentiment increased in Europe, some of the nations that permitted hormone use began to fear that their continued use of hormones would place their producers at a competitive disadvantage vis-à-vis the rest of the Community, since consumers might begin to shun their "tainted" beef and veal.

By the time the EC was ready to vote on a hormone ban, the only important constituency still firmly opposed to it was the European Federation of Animal Health. This federation represents thirty-one pharmaceutical companies, including the subsidiaries of a number of large American firms, as well as European national associations of veterinary medicine manufacturers. It argued that "authorized products which have been guaranteed by scientists all over the world to be safe, effective and of the highest quality cannot be banned for purely subjective reasons," and it urged the EC to accept the advice of its own scientific inquiries.[22]

In December 1985 the Council adopted a directive extending its ban on the use of hormones to include the five controversial substances omitted from its 1981 directive. Hormones could be administrated only for therapeutic uses. The Council stated that "assessments of [the hormones'] effect on human health vary and this is reflected in the regulations governing their use . . . this divergence . . . is a serious barrier to intra-Community trade." They concluded that banning "the use of hormonal substances for fattening purposes . . . [would] ensure that all consumers [would be] able to buy the products in question . . . [and would] bring about an increase in consumption."[23]

The Council reasoned that a complete ban on hormone use represented the best way of resolving the distortions in intra-Community trade created by divergent national regulations. In light of the pressures from consumers, it made more political sense to force some member states to tighten their standards than to require others to lower them. The ban thus represented an important victory for European consumer and environmental organizations; their concerns, rather than the judgment of the Commission's own scientific advisory bodies, had carried the day. As Franz Andriessen, the EC's farm commissioner put it, "Scientific advice is important, but it is not decisive. In public opinion, this is a very delicate issue that has to be dealt with in political terms."[24] The EC's commitment to integration thus led to a strengthening of European consumer protection standards.[25]

Foreign Reaction to the Ban

The hormone ban applied not only to beef and veal from cattle raised within the Community, but to all beef and beef products imported into the twelve member states as well. In view of the differences in regulations for hormone use within Europe, it is not surprising that similar differences existed between the EC and its major trading partners.

Most of the EC's major trading partners were relatively unaffected by the ban. Since Brazil had authorized only one of the five hormones, its cattle industry could easily adapt to the Community's new requirements. By contrast, because Australia permitted the use of all five, it opposed the EC ban. However, the economic consequences for its meat industry were modest, since 90 to 95 percent of Australian cattle were raised on grassland, where there are few economic benefits to using hormones. Moreover, a number of Australian farmers specialized in the production of hormone-free meat, and the government had developed an elaborate monitoring and inspection system to certify their meat as hormone-free. In any event, the Australian annual beef quota to the EC was only 3,000 to 4,000 tons.

Like Australia, Canada also formally opposed the EC's hormone ban, but since its beef exports to Europe only amounted to 161 metric tons in 1987, or less than 0.02 percent of its total beef production, the economic effect of the EC directive was also negligible. For its part, Argentina produced large quantities of high quality Hilton beef without the use of hormones. It anticipated that by increasing the demand for "clean" beef, the ban would actually enable it to increase its sales to European butcher shops and steakhouses. Consequently, Argentina supported the ban as a way of increasing its share of the European beef market at the expense of other exporters to the Community.

The American stake in the dispute was considerably different. Not only was the United States the largest exporter of beef to the EC—it shipped 120 million dollars' worth of beef annually during the mid-1980s—but in contrast to the EC's other major trading partners, less than 10 percent of American meat exports to Europe were produced without hormones. During the year following the ban, U.S. exports of beef to the EC dropped by nearly 80 percent. Primarily as a result of the ban, U.S. exports of beef and beef products to the EC fell from a high of 76,000 tons in 1982 to an estimated low of 4,500 tons in 1990.

The use of all five hormones was permitted by the U.S. Food and Drug Administration. According to the FDA, the three natural hormones are metabolized by the cow and leave no residue differentiable from internally produced hormones. Their implantation can only be detected by testing for abnormal hormone levels. To protect public health, the FDA has established tolerance levels for these hormones: "The amount of added hormone from an average daily intake of meat may not exceed 1 percent of the daily production of that hormone."[26] This standard is actually rather conservative, since only 10 percent of the hormones ingested by humans are actually absorbed by the human body; the rest are drowned by the body's own hormones. Similar standards exist for the two synthetic hormones, whose use is easier to detect since they do leave residues in meat.

Hormones are critical to American beef production. Approximately two-thirds of all American beef cattle spend an average of 150 days on a feedlot. When they arrive on the feedlot, they are generally implanted with a bee-sized hormone pellet behind the ear, which supplies additional hormones to those naturally produced by the animal. This pellet, which costs approximately $1.50, enables the steer to convert feed more efficiently, and thus reach its 1,100 pound desired weight 20–25 days faster than it would otherwise. In addition, because the hormones increase muscle growth while reducing fat, animals implanted with hormones contain an average of 50 pounds more meat. According to the U.S. Department of Agriculture (USDA), "the increased production efficiency combined with the higher lean meat percentage gave the farmer an economic benefit of $80 per head," or an estimated $650 million per year.[27]

American meat exports to Europe consisted primarily of varietal meats, such as livers, kidneys, hearts, and tongues. They were used in popular European foods such as pate, kidney pies, sausage, tripe, and blood pudding, where they were valued by European consumers because of their tenderness and by European producers because the uniform size of U.S. parts permitted them to standardize the production of processed food. Unfortunately for the United States, these parts of the animal also tend to be relatively high in hormones. To supply the European market with varietal meats from cows that had not been treated with hormones, American producers would have had to alter the production of 7 million animals per year. But this was not economically feasible, since each steer contained only about $25 worth of varietal meats. American farmers did not believe that these meats could command a high enough price in Europe to justify the increased costs of hormone-free production.

American efforts to comply with EC meat processing standards also suffered from another difficulty. As part of its effort to establish uniform health and sanitary standards for meat processed in the EC during the 1980s, the Community had enacted a number of Third Country Meat Directives. These directives required that meat imported into the Community be produced in plants whose inspection systems and regulations were identical to those established by the EC for its member states. Inspectors were sent from Europe to certify individual plants. However, by the end of 1987, only 90 out of 1,400 American meat plants and cold storage facilities had been certified.

On July 14, 1987, the Meat Industry Trade Policy Council filed a complaint with the United States trade representative under Section 301 of the Trade Act. Their complaint charged that the EC's Third Country Meat Directives imposed an "unjustifiable and unreasonable restriction" on U.S. meat producers by limiting the number of plants certified to ship meat to the EC.[28] Following this complaint, the number of certified American plants increased slightly, reaching 125 by the end of 1989. However, this failed to satisfy either the American meat industry or American trade officials.

The EC hormone ban thus emerged in the midst of an ongoing dispute between American meat producers and the EC. Not only did the hormone ban present another obstacle to American meat exports to the European Community, but it threatened to destroy the value of the millions of dollars already spent by a number of American slaughterhouses to alter their facilities and processes in order to secure EC certification.[29] While the certified slaughterhouses could, in principle, have processed untreated beef, it was uneconomical for them to do so for two reasons: their production runs were relatively small, and it was both expensive and cumbersome to separate hormone-free from hormone-injected beef.

The ban on hormone-treated beef was originally scheduled to go into effect on January 1, 1987. However, in order to allow time for additional negotiations with the United States, as well as to permit the sale of the Community's accumulated stock of hormone-treated beef, the EC agreed to a one-year transitional period. In December 1987, following protests by a number of foreign suppliers, the EC agreed to delay the ban's application to third country (non- EC) producers for another year.

In December 1988, in a further effort to diffuse criticism from the United States, the Council of Ministers voted to exempt meat intended for pet food from the ban. This accounted for about one-sixth of American meat exports to the Community, mostly to France. Finally, in January 1989 the hormone ban was applied to all beef and veal marketed in the European Community for human consumption, regardless of where it was produced.

The Basis of the Dispute

The United States objected to the EC's ban on the sale of beef produced with growth hormones on the grounds that the ban had no scientific basis; it therefore represented an unnecessary obstacle to trade. The Americans argued that any test of meat for purity should be based on whether or not it contains residues of harmful chemicals, not on whether the animals from which it came were ever fed hormones. In fact, according to American officials, "most animals [raised in America] were weaned from hormones well before they are slaughtered."[30] They pointed out that even the EC's own scientific advisory bodies had given the five disputed hormones a clean bill of health.

The Americans contended that rather than protecting the health of European consumers, the ban in fact endangered them by encouraging an illegal market in hormones in Europe. Dr. Lester Crawford of the USDA's Food Safety and Inspection Service noted that "control measures for detecting illegal products and preventing them from getting into the food chain are largely ineffective."[31] U.S. officials cited a number of reports from Europe which indicated that a large-scale black market in hormones had developed in Germany, Belgium, and Wales. "Some reports claimed that two-thirds of meat inspections in Italy revealed evidence of illegal use of banned hormones, and that 90 percent of Belgian beef production had been illegally treated."[32] The Americans argued that these direct injections into portions of the cow consumed by humans represented a far greater threat to human safety than growth hormones implanted in a cow's inedible ear, and then released slowly into the rest of its body.

The Europeans, in turn, countered that the EC was within its rights to enact whatever regulations it deemed necessary to protect consumers, regardless of their impact on trade, since "every country has the right under world trade rules to restrict imports for health reasons."[33] As French Minister of Foreign Affairs Edith Cresson put it: "This isn't a way to avoid the importation of meat; it's a matter of health."[34] Jean François Boittin, France's permanent representative to the GATT, noted that the "ban simply represents the EC bowing to public pressure." He observed that while many scientific authorities had judged hormone-treated beef to be harmless, "the public is still opposed to the meat."[35] An EC official stated, "Europe is democratic, it takes account of the needs of consumers, of political consensus within the Parliament and the vote of the Council."[36] This view was echoed by Hans-Jurgen Zahorka, a West German member of the European Parliament, who stated that "the public consensus [in Europe] is that meat without hormones is better."[37] According to Derwent Renshaw, the EC's agricultural attaché, "No matter what the scientists say, I'm afraid we Europeans prefer to eat our meat free of hormones."[38] The EC's agricultural commissioner noted: "Not all political decisions are based on science."[39] He added that the ban was "no more a trade barrier than was Prohibition."[40]

To illustrate this latter point, Sir Roy Denman, the EC's ambassador to the United States, repeatedly raised the issue of American restrictions on unpasteurized cheese from Europe in interviews with the American press. The United States does not permit the sale of cheeses made from unpasteurized milk. (It was the rumor about an EC proposal to impose a similar restriction that so outraged the residents of Camembert.) The Americans do make an exception for soft French cheeses, such as brie, but only if they are baked first, which, Denman observed "makes brie taste as much like real brie as apple juice tastes like a dry martini."[41] Yet he noted that the Europeans had never demanded a scientific inquiry into the dangers of eating brie from unpasteurized milk. Rather, "they have accepted that Americans have expressed a democratic preference for hygiene over taste, however eccentric or unnecessary."[42] Why should European preferences not be accorded similar respect?

This position was echoed by the Association of Italian Food Processors. In an ad placed in an American publication, Italy's tomato exporters stated: "There is no established scientific basis that the pesticide Alar is harmful to human health; however, consumer perception has effectively banned its use in the United States. Is it then the function of the U.S. Trade Representative to discipline European consumers for perceiving that feeding cattle with growth hormones is undesirable and a hazard to health?"[43]

The Europeans also denied that the ban was protectionist, since it treated both domestic and imported products alike. Moreover, most foreign suppliers of beef to Europe were "able and willing to provide documentation that whatever meat is shipped to the EC was hormone free."[44] Denman pointed out that "the United States could export hormone-free beef. That is what virtually all our other major suppliers. . . have already decided to do."[45] Moreover, for the EC, the ban was important because of its connection to the creation of a single European market. The "1992" program required that significant progress be made toward the adoption of common regulatory standards. What mattered was not whether these standards met with the approval of the scientific community, let alone whether they were similar to those of the United States; rather, what was critical was that they facilitated the free movement of goods *within* Europe. In the words of the Council of Ministers, the ban was necessary because of "distortion of competition in intra-Community trade."[46]

The ban was also closely linked to another important Community policy, namely the Common Agriculture Program. By eliminating hormone use, the EC reduced the productivity of European beef producers and thus the supply of beef. This in turn helped protect the economic interests of small, inefficient cattle producers by raising the price of beef, and at the same time reduced the subsidies the Community was required to provide them. The latter had in fact become quite substantial; the EC's subsidies to beef farmers had increased by more than 56 percent between 1980 and 1987. The EC's spending on beef rose almost 25 percent between 1987 and 1988, just as the issue of hormone use was emerging.[47] At the same time, EC beef exports were declining and imports were increasing. Thus, while the ban may have been primarily enacted as a result of pressures from consumer groups and public opinion, it also served another important EC objective, namely, reducing Community beef stockpiles and subsidies.

The Hormone Ban and the Standards Code

From the outset, the American strategy was to refer the hormones dispute to international arbitration. In the fall of 1986 the Americans challenged the EC ban in the Codex Alimentarius Commission. The Codex Commission had been established in 1962 by two United Nations bodies, the Food and Agriculture Organization and the World Health Organization. Its purpose was to develop international standards for food and agricultural products to both facilitate international trade and protect public health. Its technical Committee on Residues of Veterinary Drugs in Food agreed with the United States that the EC ban represented "a classic example of a nontariff barrier with no scientific basis whatsoever."[48] Its Technical Committee on Food

Additives and Contaminants likewise gave the five growth hormones a clean bill of health.

However, the Commission itself, which is the vehicle for government acceptance—or nonacceptance—of the recommendations of its technical committees, was reluctant to become embroiled in the conflict between the EC and the United States. Like the EC Council, it chose to ignore the recommendations of its own scientific bodies; the Commission turned down the American request that it declare the disputed hormones safe.

In January 1987, the date the hormone ban was originally scheduled to go into effect, the United States requested consultations with the EC under the Standards Code. After six months of fruitless negotiations, the United States requested the formation of a group of technical experts to examine the scientific basis for the EC's ban, as provided by Article 14.9 of the Technical Barriers to Trade Code. However, this request was blocked by the EC, which argued that the Standards Code applied only to product standards, not to processing and production methods (PPMs). The EC was willing to participate in a review of the Code's applicability to PPMs—an offer which the United States in turn declined. The United States responded by invoking section 301 of the Trade Act of 1974, which authorizes it to restrict imports from nations that have engaged in unfair trade practices.

The legal dispute between the United States and the EC revolved around a number of issues. The first concerned the question of intention to discriminate. The EC argued that in order to prove the Code was violated, the United States must first demonstrate, rather than simply assert, that the EC had adopted the hormone directive "with a view" toward restricting imports. Since the hormone ban was not discriminatory on its face—it applied equally to domestic and foreign producers—the EC contended that the Americans could not meet this criterion. Nor could the Americans offer any evidence that the principal impetus for the EC hormone ban was to restrict imports. The United States countered that the issue of nondiscrimination was irrelevant. For the Code covered more than intentionally discriminatory trade actions; it applied to any technical regulations that "have the effect" of creating obstacles to international trade.

A second dispute focused on the distinction between product standards and process and production methods. The Europeans argued that the Code applies only to the former. Their position was based on an explanatory note to Annex I, which explicitly excludes from the agreement "codes of practice," commonly understood to refer to PPMs—a provision which the EC had insisted upon in the Tokyo Round. The EC contended that the use of growth hormones in cattle-raising was a PPM, not a product characteristic, and therefore did not fall under the Code's jurisdiction. The language of the ban is consistent with this interpretation. Thus, the directive prohibits "the use of hormonal substances for fattening purposes," while the import prohibition refers to "meat from animals which have been administered growth hormones."[49] Nowhere does the directive ever refer to restrictions on either the sale or import of meat *containing* growth hormones.

The United States countered that the EC was engaged in a legal subterfuge. After all, the real purpose of the directive was to affect the characteristic of a product: it was enacted precisely in order to make all beef sold in Europe hormone-free. Since the EC could have achieved this objective just as easily through a product specification, which would then have fallen under the Standard Code's purview, the fact that the directive was instead drafted as a PPM was, according to the Americans, evidence of the EC's attempt to circumvent the Code. The Americans argued that since virtually every technical regulation could be written as a PPM, accepting the legality of the EC's directive would make the Standards Code irrelevant. American negotiators further contended that had the EC established a hormone-tolerance level for beef products, American exporters would had have no difficulty meeting it—however strict—since U.S. regulations prohibit hormones from being administrated sixty days prior to slaughter. Consequently, all artificial hormones wind up being flushed out of the animal's system before it is killed, while natural hormones cannot be detected in processed meat in the first place.

These technical issues aside, the underlying basis of the dispute between the United States and the EC was whether or not the directive was an "*unnecessary* trade barrier." Both the Standards Code and the GATT itself allow nations to enact trade barriers that "are necessary to ensure . . . the protection of human . . . life or health," provided that they are nondiscriminatory or act as a "disguised restriction on international trade."[50] Accordingly, even if the EC directive was considered a product regulation, and thus fell within the terms of the Standards Code, it would still be consistent with the Code if it was "necessary" to "protect human life or health."

The United States conceded that the Europeans were well within their rights to establish appropriate hormone tolerance levels and to test imported meat to make sure that its hormone content fell below those limits. But what the EC was attempting to do went beyond legitimate concerns about product safety; rather it was trying to dictate to Americans how they should produce a particular product—in the absence of any scientific evidence that American production methods resulted in an unsafe product. According to an FDA official, when used properly the traces of naturally produced hormones in meat are so minuscule that "a pregnant women would manufacture several million times more estrogen a day than if she ate a pound of beef each day."[51]

The EC countered that there was no scientific evidence that hormone-treated meat *was* safe. Since European consumers were fearful that such beef might cause cancer, "there is some basis for the belief that an absolute ban is better than a low threshold for hormone presence."[52] In short, since the United States could not prove that the use of hormones presented absolutely no risk, the European ban was justified. Why should the citizens of the EC tolerate the presence of substances in imported foodstuffs that they sincerely consider to be harmful "absent *conclusive* proof of [no] deleterious health effects."[53] Moreover, even if the fears of European consumers were exaggerated, that did not make them illegitimate; after all, were not governments entitled to protect the psychological as well as the physical well-being of their citizens?

The Trade Dispute Escalates

As negotiations proceeded, a temporary compromise was reached; the United States rescinded its 301 sanctions, while the EC delayed its implementation of the ban. These negotiations, however, remained deadlocked, and the EC continued to refuse to refer the dispute to the Committee on Technical Barriers to Trade. On January 1, 1989, the EC implemented its ban on American meat exports valued at $120 million, though, as previously noted, in a conciliatory gesture the Council of Ministers agreed to exempt from the ban the $20 million worth of beef imports intended for pet food.

The United States responded by imposing retaliatory tariffs of 100 percent on $100 million worth of EC agricultural exports to the United States. Agriculture Secretary Yeutter stated that while he regretted that the United States had been forced to retaliate against the EC's ban on meat treated with growth hormones, "we have tried repeatedly to bring this issue to a scientific dispute panel under the GATT in order to have it resolved; however, our European counterparts have consistently blocked our efforts."[54]

The EC, in turn, selected a range of American agricultural exports worth about $96.7 millon for possible counter-retaliation, but agreed to delay temporarily the implementation of this sanction. It also filed a complaint with the GATT against the United States, charging that the American tariffs were illegal because the EC ban was consistent with the GATT's national treatment rule.

In January 1989 Texas Agricultural Commissioner Jim Hightower wrote to the EC's ambassador in Washington offering to provide state-certified hormone-free beef. He claimed that Texas ranchers alone could supply the EC with the roughly 35,000 head of cattle that the EC purchases annually. Hightower argued that the continued American opposition to the ban primarily served the interests of the "three firms who control 70 percent of the grain-fed beef in this country."[55] The offer of the Texas ranchers was sharply criticized by the American Meat Institute, which stated that their members stood "solidly behind the Bush administration's efforts to end the unjustified EC hormone ban."[56]

Nonetheless, the American position did soften somewhat. James Baker, the recently appointed American secretary of state, was concerned that the Bush administration's relations with the EC not get off to a bad start. Thus, U.S. officials indicated that they would begin to explore ways of giving the EC hormone-free beef. Specifically, USDA officials agreed to work with Hightower to develop a certification process for hormone-free beef.

In February the United States and the EC agreed to establish a high-level task force to help diffuse the conflict. On May 3, 1989, it announced an interim arrangement. The United States would agree to assist the EC in certifying that American beef exports were hormone-free. But American officials would only serve as information disseminators. They would not participate in the inspection process since to do so would be to imply that current American inspection procedures were inadequate; it might also undermine the confidence of American consumers in the safety of hormone-implanted beef. However, this compromise only applied to the 15 percent of American beef exports that were high quality. The remainder was in the form of offal, which American officials claimed would be virtually impossible to certify as coming from hormone-free cattle.

In return, the EC announced that it would postpone its implementation of counter-retaliatory duties. The Americans responded by agreeing to reduce their overall level of retaliation by the amount of any additional hormone-free beef shipped to the EC from the United States. Subsequently, the United States proposed, and the EC accepted, an increase in American exports of beef from dairy cows. (American regulations then prohibited the treatment of dairy cows with growth hormones.) Since this agreement, both beef and veal exports to the EC have increased by approximately 4 million dollars, and the United States has proportionately reduced its tariffs on the targeted EC agricultural products.

The American Stake

Following the pet food exemption and an increase in sales of high-quality hormone-free beef to the EC, the total of American exports affected by the hormone ban amounted to somewhat under 85 million dollars. While this represented a significant portion of U.S. meat exports to the EC, U.S. meat exports to the EC represented less than 5 percent of total American meat exports, which were worth approximately 1.3 billion dollars in 1988, 90 percent of which went to Japan. (Total annual American beef production amounts to 20 billion dollars.) Moreover, the decline in meat exports to Europe was more than compensated by a surge in meat exports to Japan, Canada, and Mexico.[57] In addition, the hormone dispute affected less than 0.1 percent of total U.S.- EC trade. In short, by any objective measure, the European beef hormone ban was economically unimportant. Why then, did the United States oppose it so vigorously?

There were several reasons, each of which suggests the potentially high stakes involved in this controversy. First, the Americans feared that the European ban on meat hormones would become the first in an on-going and ever-increasing series of stricter regulatory requirements by the European Community, whose effect would be to keep more and more American products out of Europe. As Food and Drug Commissioner Frank Young put it, the enactment of the hormone ban suggested that as the EC moved to harmonize regulatory requirements in order to create a single European market, "it is not necessarily the most sensible rule that will prevail, but . . . the most stringent."[58] The ban thus seemed to confirm America's worst fears about the emergence of "Fortress Europe"—that the liberalization of Europe's internal market would be accompanied by an increase in external trade barriers.

Second, the ban seemed to augur poorly for American efforts to liberalize global trade in agriculture. A major priority for the United States in the Uruguay Round of GATT negotiations, which was beginning at about the time the hormone controversy unfolded, was to persuade both the EC and Japan to reduce their agricultural subsidies and open up their domestic agricultural markets. The EC hormone ban seemed to point in the opposite direction, signaling a move toward increased agricultural protectionism.

The United States was also concerned that the ban would both legitimate and encourage the increased use of health standards as nontariff barriers on the part of America's other trading partners. For if the EC could successfully exclude an American agricultural product on what the Americans considered to be arbitrary grounds, might not other America's trading partners, especially Japan, be encouraged to seize upon this precedent to do likewise?[59] From the American perspective, the EC had established an impossibly high standard, one which threatened to make the Standards Code a dead letter, since proving a negative—in this case that a chemical substance is 100 percent safe—is often impossible.

The result of allowing the beef hormone ban to stand would thus be a new wave of restrictions on American agricultural exports. In short, for the United States, the hormone ban represented the first step down a slippery slope. As the American Secretary of Agriculture Yeutter remarked, "If we permit [the hormone ban] . . . to occur, in the [EC] or elsewhere, then we've opened up a gigantic loophole in the GATT which will result in major impediments to agricultural trade throughout the world for years to come."[60]

The administration's position on the EC hormone ban was also influenced by domestic concerns. American consumer organizations, while generally critical of the use of hormones in beef production, had not campaigned for a ban on their use. Those American consumers who considered growth hormones undesirable purchased hormone-free beef, which was becoming increasingly available. However, American government officials feared that the EC ban would encourage American consumer organizations to begin a campaign for a ban on the use of the growth hormones in the United States as well.

Finally, the hormone ban struck at a critical source of American comparative advantage, namely, its technically advanced agricultural production. If beef made from cows which had ingested growth hormones could be banned, what about processed food made with chemical additives, produce sprayed with postharvest chemicals, or bioengineered food products—all of which regulatory authorities outside the United States might choose to ban following the logic of the EC? Even more importantly, what would happen to the global market for all the advances in biotechnology on which American companies were currently working and in which the United States enjoyed a comparative advantage?

In this context, it was not simply American farmers and food processors who stood to lose current and future markets, but also the American companies who produced agricultural technology. If other nations forbade their farmers or food processors from employing these new technologies, they too were threatened with the loss of export markets. The result would be to discourage research and innovation in agricultural biotechnology since manufacturers would be unable to commercialize their scientific discoveries.[61]

Nor were these concerns academic. For no sooner had the hormone ban been enacted than all four fears—of a Fortress Europe, of an increase in agricultural protectionism, of demands for stricter domestic regulation, and of additional restrictions on improvements in agricultural productivity—became crystallized around another issue. It also involved growth hormones, but for milk cows rather than beef.

The Controversy over Milk Production

Bovine somatotropin (BST) is a naturally occurring protein which can also be produced synthetically. When injected into cows, it increases their milk production by between 12 and 25 percent, or approximately 500 pounds per year. In August 1989 the European Commission proposed to the Council of Ministers a moratorium on the use of BST. This proposal was not primarily based on health and safety considerations. For although some dairy farmers and retailers in Europe had expressed concerns about customer acceptance of milk produced from hormone-treated cows, the EC's Committee for Veterinary Medicinal Products had given the hormone a clean bill of health. Rather, the proposal was based on the fear of Community officials that BST's introduction would undermine the competitive position of small-volume dairy farmers and thus hasten the long-term consolidation of the dairy-farm sector. Most dairy farmers in the EC, especially in Germany, are small producers who have benefited from extensive subsidies under the Common Agricultural Program. In addition, the oversupply of dairy products has been one of the EC's most chronic problems. Until the late 1970s nearly half of the Community's agricultural subsidies was spent on dairy products, although during the second half of the 1980s subsidies to this sector were progressively reduced. However, the use of BST threatened to increase these surpluses once again.

EC Agricultural Commissioner Ray MacSherry urged the Commission to withhold approval of BST because it violated the EC's newly established fourth criterion for the approval of production-enhancing substances. In addition to the three current criteria—safety, quality, and effectiveness—the EC decided to evaluate new agricultural technologies on the basis of "social and economic need." MacSherry claimed there was no socioeconomic need for BST.[62] He expressed concern that the drug would lead to a "serious distortion of competition," since its benefits might not reach many small farmers. His position was supported by a number of organizations representing European dairy farmers. Another EC official noted that the Commission feared a "consumer backlash" if it approved BST. He stated: "It's not easy to explain to consumers that everything is all right when you are injecting drugs into cows."[63] Thus, the EC's ban on the introduction of BST, like the hormone ban, reflected a convergence of interests between small, inefficient European farmers—and the Common Agricultural Program which subsidized them—and European consumer groups.

The United States immediately voiced its strong opposition to an EC-wide ban on the use of BST. It claimed that, like the hormone ban, it violated the Standards Code. Indeed, according to one United States trade official, "this BST ban could potentially be far worse than the hormone ban. It might be used by a government to give itself license to prohibit the import of almost any product." United States Trade Representative (USTR) Carla Hills stated that she was "troubled by a growing attitude in Europe and elsewhere that technological developments which encourage greater efficiency in agricultural production are socially undesirable."[64]

United States Agriculture Secretary Yeutter noted that an EC ban on BST "would certainly contravene our mutual objective of achieving international harmonization in the sensitive area of food safety."[65] He claimed it "would also add fuel to the fires for those who wish to have public policy decisions made on the basis of emotion and political pressure."[66] Another American official warned that the EC's decision to review a new biotechnology product on the basis of its "social and economic implications . . . could set a very dangerous precedent."[67]

What concerned the United States was not so much the ban's impact on imports of products from BST-treated American dairy cows—which the USTR estimated would affect only approximately 25 million dollars of American dairy exports—but the prospect of the loss of a much larger market for sales of the hormone itself within Europe. Four American-based firms (Monsanto, American Cyanamid, Eli Lilly, and Upjohn) had invested considerable sums in developing growth hormones not only for dairy cows but also for pigs, poultry, and sheep. A European ban on BST appeared to be the first step in closing off the entire global market, which industry officials have estimated at 500 million dollars—with the EC accounting for between one-third and one-half of this total.[68]

Furthermore, an EC ban on the sale of milk from cows that had been injected with BST might well make it more difficult for the hormone to be approved for general use in the United States, where a similar coalition of small dairy farmers and some consumer groups were campaigning to delay its approval on grounds echoing those of its opponents within the EC.[69] In August 1989, shortly after the hormone ban went into effect for imports, the EC, in response to American pressures, agreed to postpone the implementation of a moratorium on the use of BST. Instead, in September it adopted a proposal for a 15-month evaluation period to allow for scientific studies of BST and consultations with third-party countries. The following year, the

Council requested member states to prohibit the administration of BST to dairy cows on their territory until the end of 1990. This ban has subsequently been extended. However, in January 1994 the FDA formally approved the use of BST, thus once again creating a divergence in food safety regulations between the United States and the European Union.

Other Conflicts between the Union and the United States

These controversies over beef and dairy hormones are part of a series of ongoing trade disputes between the European Union and the United States that have revolved around health and safety standards for agricultural products. In 1990 it was the Europeans' turn to complain about American use of "arbitrary" safety standards to restrict agricultural imports. In the fall of that year, the Environmental Protection Agency announced a ban on imports of French and Italian wines which contained residues of a fungicide called procymidone. The EPA acted in response to an American law which prohibits the use of any chemicals in food for which toxicity levels have not been established. Because the chemical is not used in the United States, no tolerances for it existed. Although it is approved for use in twenty-six countries, its manufacturer, the Sumitomo Corporation, never attempted to register the chemical with EPA, hoping that it would not show up in toxicity tests. The chemical is used on about 20 percent of French and 10 percent of Italian grapes; the EPA ban affected 20 percent of American wine imports from the two countries, worth approximately 150 million dollars.

While high doses of procymidone do produce cancer in both rats and mice, there is no evidence that the residues found in the European wine represented a health risk. According to the Sumitomo Corporation, an individual who consumes two glasses of wine containing the residue each day for fifty-two years would have an increased cancer risk of no more than one in two million. The limit for the chemical established in the Codex Alimentarius is five parts per million, more than ten times as high as the highest level found in imported wines. Accordingly, Sumitomo, European wine exporters, and a number of American wine importers petitioned EPA to establish an interim tolerance level in order to avoid a major disruption in trade.

But William Reilly, the EPA's administrator, found himself under pressure by American environmental and consumer groups to maintain the ban; the latter argued that according to American regulations, processed foods, which include wine, cannot contain any carcinogens, however diluted. Not surprisingly, his decision to maintain the ban outraged French winegrowers, who denounced the ban not only as a trade restriction—it was announced just before shipments were to begin for the Christmas season—but also as "a paranoid over-reaction to an imagined hazard."[70]

The following year EPA moved to diffuse this trade conflict by establishing an interim four-year tolerance standard of 7 ppm for grapes grown before 1990. While its action was denounced by American consumer groups, who accused the EPA of "elevating trade concerns over its public health mandate," the agency stated that the trade implications of its decision had affected not its substance but its timing.[71] Regulatory officials explained that "because of the overwhelming trade issues," EPA had decided to "deviate from its usual administrative practice" and expedite its rule-making proceedings.[72] Reilly stated that "our review of the data base available indicates that the level of residues of this pesticide that have been found in wine should not pose a serious risk to consumers."[73]

Disputes with Japan over Agriculture

Japanese regulatory politics and policies have also been a recurrent source of friction with its trading partners. Like the European Union, Japan has long protected domestic agricultural producers through the use of quotas, prohibitions, and tariffs. In addition, exports of agricultural products to Japan have been significantly impeded by Japan's health and sanitary regulations.[74] Japanese consumer organizations have frequently opposed trade liberalization on the grounds that Japan's "hard-won safety standards and inspection procedures could be compromised."[75] The views of many Japanese consumers that outsiders cannot be trusted to screen products for safety as carefully as do Japanese authorities have been both echoed and reinforced by producers opposed to allowing additional agricultural imports into Japan.[76]

Food Additives

Japan's regulations governing food additives have been a recurrent source of trade friction, especially with the United States. The two nations define food additives differently. Under the terms of Japan's

1946 Food Sanitation Law, only synthetic chemicals are considered additives; these consist primarily of flavors or colors added to food in the process of manufacturing or for the purpose of processing or preservation. The United States Food, Drug and Cosmetic Act defines additives to include not only synthetic chemicals but also natural products, flavoring agents, colors, hormones, antibiotics for animal feed, agricultural chemicals, materials of food containers, and detergents.

While both the Americans and the Europeans regulate the use of synthetic and natural additives in an identical manner, the Japanese have different regulations for synthetic and natural additives. (The latter consist primarily of additives which are natural products or which are purified only by physical or biological processes.) Natural additives have historically been relatively unregulated in Japan: no governmental approval is required before they are introduced, there are no restrictions on the quantities in which they can be consumed, and, until recently, manufacturers have not been required to list them on food packages.

According to an official of the Food Chemistry Division of Japan's Ministry of Health and Welfare (MHW), "There are no regulations [for natural food additives] because historically these additives were made from ordinary food . . . like color from cabbage."[77] Moreover, Japanese food processors make extensive use of natural additives. In 1984, according to the Japan Food Additives Association, natural additives accounted for 58 percent of all additive sales in Japan.[78] Between 700 and 2,000 unregulated natural food additives are regularly used in food sold in Japan.

In contrast, Japanese standards for the approval of synthetic or chemical additives are among the world's strictest. Japan permits the use of fewer synthetic or chemical additives than any other developed nation. Depending on how a chemical additive is defined, between 50 and 200 more synthetic chemicals can legally be added to processed food in the United States than in Japan. While there are virtually no synthetic additives whose use is permitted in Japan but not the United States, a large number of commonly used additives in the United States are not permitted in Japan. The Japanese government refuses to allow the import of foods containing even traces of such additives.

Opposition to the use of chemical additives in processed food has long been a focus of the Japanese consumer movement. In the early 1970s a consumer boycott was organized against canned goods containing cyclamates, following a decision by the MHW to extend the deadline for a ban on the use of this artificial sweetener. A public opinion poll held shortly after the boycott found that "dangerous food additives" was one of the problems that the public most wanted the consumer movement to pursue.[79] In 1972 the Japanese Diet passed a resolution calling for restricting the use, on health and safety grounds, of synthetic additives in food. As a consequence, the number of synthetic additives approved for use in Japan did not increase for more than a decade.[80]

The Japanese government's restrictions on synthetic food additives have made it much more difficult for both American and European food processors to export processed foods to Japan. According to the Foreign Agricultural Services of the United States Department of Agriculture, "Japan's restrictive food additive regulations . . . seriously impede exports of high value products to Japan. Many food additives which are commonly used in the United States, such as Red 40 food coloring, cannot be used in Japan . . . In some cases United States companies have been able to reformulate products for the Japanese market but in many cases exports are impossible because such reformulation is not economically or technically feasible."[81]

During the 1980s, changing Japan's food additive regulations became an important priority of American trade negotiators. In 1983, as a result of intense pressure from the United States, the Japanese government agreed to permit the use of ten additional synthetic food additives—in addition to the artificial sweetener aspartame (which was already being produced by a Japanese company in Japan, but only for export). As a result of this decision, the number of permitted synthetic additives increased from 336 to 347. At the time, American officials expressed their hope that the number of synthetic food additives approved for use in Japan would gradually increase "at the rate of one or two a year."[82]

However, MHW's policy shift was strongly criticized by Japanese consumer groups and environmental organizations, who accused the Japanese government of sacrificing the health of the Japanese public in order to relax trade tensions. Nihon Shoshisha Renmei, the Consumers Union of Japan (CUJ), charged that "the deliberations carried out by the MHW were very slipshod."[83] In June 1986 it issued a report claiming that many of the chemical additives approved for use by the Japanese government were either harmful or had been insufficiently tested. According to a CUJ food-additive specialist, none of the chemical food additives approved for use in Japan had undergone adequate long-term toxicity tests. Moreover, four had been banned in other countries as carcinogens, and twelve were known mutagens.[84] Kazuya Fujiwara of Seikyoren, the National Association of Consumer Cooperatives, added that the Japanese currently were eating 4 kilograms of chemical additives per capita annually. He stated: "There are now 100,000 kinds of man-made chemicals in the world. Nobody knows what effect they will have on us or our children . . . We want to decrease the number of chemicals we consume and come into contact with."[85] To date, there has been no further increase in the number of synthetic additives permitted in food sold in Japan.

Food Labeling

Japan's food labeling requirements have also been a source of both trade friction and domestic controversy. While the United States has long required that all additives, whether natural or synthetic, be listed on the labels of the food products in which they are used, historically, processed food sold in Japan has been required to list only 20 percent of the more than 300 synthetic additives permitted for use. In 1983 the MHW announced its first major change in food additive labeling requirements since the Food Health Law was first passed in 1948.[86] It issued regulations requiring that a total of seventy-eight additives be identified by name, seventy-three of which were also required to have their uses clearly stated on the product's labels.

In 1987 a MHW panel recommended a more sweeping change in Japan's food labeling requirements. According to the *Japan Times,* "The MHW decided to set up the panel because product labeling in Western countries are more comprehensive than in Japan and consumer organizations have been complaining that consumers cannot find out which additives are used in food products under the current system."[87] It proposed to increase the number of food additives required to be identified on product labels to 300, or 86 percent of all the chemical and synthetic additives currently used in Japan. It also proposed to make the labeling requirements more comprehensive.

While the panel's recommendations were supported by both Japanese food processors and consumer groups, they were greeted with dismay by Japan's major trading partners. Foreign government officials contended that because processed food exported to Japan contained a relatively large number of chemical or synthetic additives, they would be placed at a competitive disadvantage: the packages of many imported products would now contain lengthy descriptions of their contents, while the packages of most domestically produced products—which still primarily used natural additives—would remain "blank." Since many Japanese consumers believe that foods processed without additives are "no-risk" products, they would now be even less likely to purchase imported processed food. In effect, they argued that *reducing* the divergence between Japanese and foreign American food labeling requirements would disadvantage food exporters. In response, the Japanese government agreed to delay the introduction of the new labeling requirement.

Food Safety Standards

Japan's Food Sanitation Law has also been a source of trade tensions between Japan and its major trading partners. As an example, because the Japanese have classified mineral water as a soft drink rather than as plain water, it has been necessary for it to be sterilized before entering Japan. As a result, after Evian mineral water was bottled, it had to be shipped 600 kilometers to a special heat sterilization plant before it could be exported.[88] The Japanese government also required that mineral water be placed in glass rather than plastic containers—which are twice as expensive and more costly to ship—because the latter are insufficiently heat resistant. However, in June 1986 the Japanese government, faced with a rapid increase in consumer demand for imported mineral water, agreed to exempt some imports from the sterilization requirements.[89]

In 1992 a trade dispute broke out between Japan and Italy over the former's ban on Italian wine. After United States authorities found that some Italian wines shipped to the United States contained traces of methyl isothiocyanate, a widely banned insecticide, Japan announced that it would prohibit sales of all wines made from the same two grapes or grown from the same region as the wine produced by the offending wineries. Italian trade officials complained that "it was wrong to penalize thousands of wineries," many of them small-scale producers.[90] However, Japanese government officials contended that "tests had to be carried out on all the wines because no guarantee could be given that they were safe."[91]

Foreign firms have also complained that some Japanese safety standards for imported agricultural products are unreasonably strict. For example, because the Japanese have established a "zero-tolerance" level for prohibited insects, some Canadian products have been denied entry on the grounds that Canadian export certificates only identify their agricultural products as "substantially free" of the prohibited insects.[92] Japanese prohibitions on the sale of American apples in Japan have been a source of contention between Japan and the United States for more than two decades. Japanese officials have justified the ban on imports of this product on the grounds that they have not received adequate assurances that American pest-control technology is adequate. According to an official from the Ministry of Agriculture, "Japan is an island country and naturally we have to be very careful not to let harmful insects or diseases previously unknown to this country enter our territory. It is a matter of course that we must have stricter quarantine requirements than countries where such pests already exist."[93] Japanese apple growers have strongly opposed lifting the import ban on the grounds that harmful moths and pests from imported United States fruit might endanger their crops.

American officials have invited Japanese agricultural inspectors to visit the United States to confirm the validity of United States pest-control technology. However, the latter have declined this invitation, leading James Parker, minister-counselor for agricultural affairs at the United States Embassy in Tokyo, to conclude that "this is not a technical issue . . . [but] a nontariff trade barrier." Parker argued that while the Ministry has every right to be concerned about protecting Japanese apple growers, "using phyto-sanitary rules to prevent the import of products is basically a violation of international GATT principles."[94] In 1993, after apple growers in the state of Washington had spent more than decade setting up 3,500 acres of orchards to meet Japanese pest control standards, Japan still refused to admit American apples. At a food fair in Japan, American apple growers had an empty display with the sign, "Empty boxes, empty promises."[95] According to one apple grower, "We've gone through every hoop they have asked us to go through and we're just fed up."[96] They urged the American government to apply trade sanctions against Japan. However, in the fall of 1993 the Japanese government assured officials from the Clinton administration that it would allow American apples into Japan. Finally in January 1995, the first American apples arrived in Japan.

Pesticides

Because Japan has relatively little arable land compared with the United States, Japanese agriculture is far more intensive. Consequently, Japanese farmers make far more extensive use of preharvest pesticides than do farmers in the United States. A 1990 study reported that American farmers use 4 tons of fertilizer and 0.08 tons of pesticides per square kilometer, while Japanese farmers employ 37.7 tons of fertilizers and 1.55 tons of pesticides—nearly ten times the American rate—per square kilometer.[97] Japanese farmers thus use slightly more than half of the quantity of pesticides of their counterparts in the United States—even though the land acreage under cultivation in Japan is only 1.3 percent that of the United States.[98]

However, because most Japanese food is consumed soon after it is harvested and relatively close to where it is grown, Japanese farmers do not generally use postharvest pesticides. By contrast, American food is usually shipped long distances after it is harvested—both within and outside the United States. As a result, American farmers make extensive use of postharvest agrochemicals—which include pesticides as well as fungicides—in order to prevent crops from perishing while being stored and transported and to preserve its physical appearance at the point of sale. The use of these agrochemicals is particularly extensive for agricultural products exported from the United States to Japan because of the long distances these commodities must travel. Moreover, in contrast to preharvest pesticides, postharvest chemicals are more likely to leave detectable residues on the food purchased by consumers.

The extensive use of postharvest agrochemicals in the United States has fostered concern in Japan about the safety of imported food. Tsuji Machiko, a member of the People's Research Institute on Energy and Environment, attacked proposals to open up the Japanese rice market to the United States on the grounds that "American rice is grown with many dangerous agricultural chemicals. In addition, many chemical substances are used to kill insects during transportation and at quarantine stations in Japanese ports."[99] Tsuji specifically cited carbofuran, which is used in the United States to kill insects, but which is not registered in Japan, and methyl bromide, a fumigant used on rice during transportation from the United States, which she characterized as "an extremely poisonous gas."[100]

The lead article in the November-December 1988 newsletter of the Consumers Union of Japan was headlined, "California Rice is Full of Agricultural Chemicals: Far More Dangerous Than Imported Flour."[101] Its author, Takamatsu Osamu, who is associated with Tokyo Metropolitan University, wrote that "there is a strong possibility that the California rice . . . expected to be imported into Japan is contaminated with post-harvest chemicals." After noting that none of the postharvest chemicals used on wheat in the United States is regulated in Japan and that only one of those used on rice is regulated, Takamatsu concluded that "Japan is completely unprotected from post-harvest chemicals."[102]

Nonetheless, four years later, in response to international pressures, the MHW announced the first major change in Japanese pesticide standards in thirteen years. It established new, more permissive safety standards for residual levels in agricultural produce for thirty-four farm chemicals. Government officials explained that the new standards "were based on international criteria . . . [and] are within the acceptable daily intake standard in Codex."[103] Their action was promptly denounced by Japanese consumer groups, who claimed that a number of the standards were too lenient and endangered public health. Koa Tasaka, a professor specializing in farm chemicals at International Christian University in Tokyo, described the new regulations as "a move to avoid trade friction," and claimed that they were "set with political rather than scientific considerations in mind."[104]

Consumer Protection and Protectionism

The fears of Japanese consumers about the safety of imported foods have been strongly encouraged by Japanese farm organizations. In 1988 the Central Union of Agricultural Cooperatives (Zenchu) produced and distributed a video entitled, "You Still Eat That Stuff?"[105] The film showed pictures of American oranges and grapefruit being heavily doused with insecticides such as ethyl dibromide (EDB) and toxic preservatives as well as rice being treated with dioxin prior to its shipment to Japan. Even more dramatically, it linked visual images of deformed human fetuses and children with strange diseases with citrus from the United States decaying on Japanese docks. The film's narrator noted that "Children's diseases are increasing in tandem with the rapid increase of imported foods and food additives." He asked rhetorically, "Can this really be a simple coincidence? If Japanese consumers are being poisoned, is it good to have open trade with the United States?"[106]

The video was strongly denounced by United States Agricultural Secretary Richard Lyng, who had seen a privately dubbed English version, as being "malicious" and "full of lies."[107] Ironically, the effect of Lyng's remarks was to significantly increase the Japanese public's interest in the film. Zenchu spokesmen reported that following the secretary's remarks, "we started getting endless inquiries from agricultural cooperatives, labor unions, consumer groups, women's groups and schools."[108] By the end of July, the cooperative had sold 4,000 copies, while another 40,000 pirated copies were believed to be in circulation. Encouraged by the film's popularity, Zenchu began to work with interested consumer and women's groups to have the film shown throughout Japan.

Their campaign apparently struck a responsive chord among the Japanese public. One Japanese journalist noted in 1988, "The fear of foreign food has taken hold of Japanese consumers, and like the rice issue, is growing beyond the reach of reason."[109] The following year, in the midst of the debate over beef liberalization, another film was made by a Japanese producer association; it depicted a typical family becoming physically ill after eating a meal which included imported beef. After criticism from both the United States and Australia, circulation of the film was halted. Japanese government officials advised agricultural producers to employ more subtle means to influence public opinion.[110] In 1990 the Central Council of Dairy Farmers ran a series of full-page ads in several Japanese newspapers expressing concern about the safety of "foreign-made food" and arguing that only "domestic milk is safe."[111] This campaign had been provoked by a decision of the Ministry of Agriculture, Forestry and Fisheries to import 3,000 tons of butter as an emergency measure. Following complaints by both the EC and the French government, Japan's Fair Trade Commission announced that it would investigate whether the ad violated the Law against Misleading Representation.

In 1992 the Foundation for Japan's Prosperity, which, like the

Consumers' Union, has close links to farming groups, produced yet another video on the subject of the health hazards of agricultural imports. Entitled *Imported Rice Is Dangerous,* the film compared the fate of weevils in imported and domestic rice. While virtually all the weevils added to both American and Australian rice perished within a week, "the weevils in the Japanese rice lived happily ever after."[112]

A survey among Japanese housewives conducted in August 1992 by the Ministry of Agriculture, Forestry and Fisheries found that more than half of the women believed that food imports should be frozen at current levels to ensure safety.[113] Nearly half expressed concern that imported food contained harmful additives. When asked what should be done to ensure the safety of imported food, 60 percent of the respondents wanted Japan to keep imports at current levels.

The concerns expressed by Japanese consumers and consumer organizations about the safety of imported foods have not had a major impact on Japanese trade policies; Japanese policies toward agricultural imports reflect primarily the political influence of Japanese farmers and their long-standing close ties with Japan's dominant political party, the Liberal Democratic Party. But Japanese agricultural producers, like their counterparts in other capitalist nations, have continually sought to justify the use of both tariff and nontariff barriers on the grounds that they are necessary to protect the health of the Japanese public. And their campaign against agricultural trade liberalization on health and safety grounds has been both supported and legitimated by Japanese consumer groups, with whom they enjoy close, mutually supportive ties. Moreover, while Japan has progressively liberalized its policies toward agricultural imports, nontariff barriers still affect 25 percent of its food imports and 16 percent of its agricultural imports.[114]

Reforming the Standards Code

As the ongoing trade disputes over the use of agricultural standards as nontariff barriers between the European Union and the United States and between Japan and its trading partners demonstrate, existing international institutions and rules have proven relatively ineffective in reducing the role of sanitary and phytosanitary (S&P) measures as trade barriers. Indeed, the real significance of the hormone dispute was what it revealed about the limitations of the Standards Code.

Current Shortcomings

Most obviously, the Code excluded process and production methods. In addition, it effectively assigned the burden of proof to the exporting nation, which must prove either that the actions of the restricting government were deliberately protectionist or that the trade barrier was not necessary.[115] However, meeting the latter test is extremely difficult, as it is very hard to prove a negative. Rarely is an exporting nation in a position to guarantee that the consumption of a particular foodstuff poses absolutely no risk to the consumers of the importing nation. For these reasons, the dispute resolution mechanics established by the Standards Code have been rarely utilized.

The other international institution which has attempted to promote world trade in agricultural products is the Codex Alimentarius, an international standards-setting body established under the auspices of the United Nations. As of the mid-1980s, 129 nations were participating in the Codex. Working through twenty-eight committees and two export groups, it has developed voluntary standards for a wide variety of S&P standards, including pesticide levels in foods, the processing and packaging of food additives, and labeling and nutritional information for consumers. However, although these standards have, on occasion, served as a reference point for national regulatory policies, most notably by less developed nations seeking to gain access to developed country markets, most nations have not adopted them.[116]

There are a number of reasons why reducing the role of food safety and production regulations as trade barriers has proven extremely difficult. To begin with, national standards vary considerably due to differences in methods of food production as a result of climate and geography as well as national differences in diet and food preparation. In addition, it is often difficult to achieve consensus on assessments of the safety of food standards. Since they are frequently the subject of considerable debate within nations, it is not surprising that they have often been the focus of equally heated debate among nations as well.

Because food safety standards do directly affect public health, consumers tend to be relatively aware of them, and consumer groups are apt to monitor them carefully. Throughout the industrialized world, public awareness of and anxiety about the health effects of food additives, pesticides, high-technology agricultural production, and the like has increased substantially in recent years. Many consumers and consumer groups do not trust their own governments to adequately protect the safety of their food supply; they are even less inclined to defer to the scientific judgments of a foreign government. Indeed, if consumers around the world tend to hold one belief in common, it is that their nation's food safety and production standards—like its culinary traditions—are superior to those of other nations. And as the EU's response to American criticism of its hormone ban revealed, they do not relish being told what levels of risk are appropriate for their citizens.

Finally, it is impossible to separate trade conflicts over the role of S&P standards from the broader debate over the liberalization of agricultural trade. Farmers who are unable to compete on international markets enjoy considerable political strength in a number of nations. And they have frequently attempted to justify protectionist policies on health and safety grounds, which in turn has enabled them to form coalitions with consumer groups. Alliances between farmers eager to protect their domestic markets and national consumer groups have become common in the EU, Japan, and the United States.[117]

Prompted by its frustration over the inability of the Standards Code's rules and proceedings to resolve—or even address—the EU's hormone ban, as well its larger economic interest in liberalizing agricultural trade, the United States proposed strengthening the Standards Code in order to limit the ability of nations to use S&P regulations for protectionist purposes. As former United States Agriculture Secretary Yeutter put it: "It is politically impossible for Americans to persuade the EC to reverse their hormone standards now, at least as long as there is no international agreement on what kinds of treatment are safe."[118] He added: "We can't fool around for the next 25 years waiting for these international bodies to get standards done. If you have an area like pesticides that's just crying out for standards . . . the GATT ought to have its own standards and then apply them."[119]

Nor has the United States been alone in its concerns about the role of S&P standards in restricting market access. Indeed, each of the major participants in the Uruguay Round negotiations on agriculture, with the exception of Japan, which is not an agricultural exporter, claimed that the phytosanitary and sanitary standards of their trading partners represented barriers to imports.[120] For example, both Australia and New Zealand have criticized the EU's Third Country Meat Directives as well as its hormone ban, while some Union members have complained about the blanket bans instituted by the United

States against imports from countries with geographically limited incidence of hoof-and-mouth and other diseases.

The EU has in turn criticized the import bans imposed by Australian state governments to prevent the introduction of diseases and pests; they regard these bans—many of which restrict the import of all agricultural products, including semiprocessed and processed foods, from a particular country—as unjustified trade barriers. The EU has expressed similar unhappiness with the increasing number of American state pesticide regulations, claiming that state-specific laws could "unjustifiably discriminate or disguise restrictions on trade, thereby unjustifiably increasing fragmentation of the United States market."[121] (Indeed, this view has also been expressed by some American officials. For example, testifying before Congress in opposition to California's "Big Green" initiative—which was subsequently defeated—Agriculture Secretary Yeutter asked: "How can we get international harmonization when we can't get it here at home?")[122]

The Uruguay Round Agreements

Largely at the initiative of the United States, a limitation on the use of S&P regulations as trade barriers was incorporated into one of the later drafts of the Uruguay Round agreement. Commonly referred to as the "Dunkel draft," after GATT Secretary-General Arthur Dunkel, its basic purpose was to plug a major loophole in the Standards Code, namely, its lack of an analytical framework for determining when a technical regulation that restricts trade is "necessary." According to the GATT Secretariat, "Sanitary and phytosanitary measures, by their very nature, may result in restrictions on trade. All governments accept the fact that some trade restrictions are necessary and appropriate in order to ensure food safety . . . But governments are sometimes pressed to go beyond what is needed for health protection and to use sanitary and phytosanitary restrictions as a way of shielding domestic producers from international competition."[123]

The Secretariat predicted that "such pressure is likely to increase as the use of other trade barriers will be reduced by the Uruguay Round negotiations." It added that restrictions on food products and agriculture "which are not required for valid health reasons can be a very effective protectionist device, and because of its technical complexity, a particularly deceptive and difficult barrier to challenge."[124]

The Uruguay Round agreement, which was concluded in April 1994, significantly strengthened the newly established World Trade Organization's oversight of national regulations and standards in a number of respects. First, it required all WTO signatories to abide by a new Agreement on Technical Barriers to Trade, thus effectively making the agreement into part of the WTO itself. This change meant that compliance with the Standards Code would no longer be voluntary on the part of WTO signatories (see Chapter 4). It also subjected technical barriers to trade to normal GATT dispute resolution procedures, which were also tightened. Second, it established a separate Agreement on Sanitary and Phytosanitary Measures, which also applied to all WTO signatories.

The Agreement on Sanitary and Phytosanitary Measures represents an ambitious effort to establish international discipline over national and subnational food-related standards. Most important, it replaces the GATT standard of national treatment by a new principle, which one commentator has labeled "international treatment."[125] Nations are required to base their S&P measures on "international standards, guidelines and recommendations, where they exist."[126] In the case of food, the Committee on S&P Measures, established to implement the agreement, is instructed to work closely with and rely upon the scientific and technical advice of the Codex Commission. Measures that conform to Codex standards are presumed to be consistent with the rules of the World Trade Organization.

A government is not required to follow these standards in determining the level of risk its citizens must bear. "Nations retain the power to select their preferred level of protection."[127] But if a nation chooses not to be guided by international standards, its regulations must meet the following tests to be WTO-consistent: they must be "necessary," "not maintained without sufficient scientific evidence," and based on appropriate risk assessments.[128] In addition to effectively placing the burden of proof for justifying departures from international standards on the importing nation, the S&P agreement also adds a "trade restrictiveness" test, based on the Thai cigarette case: a nation may not use its own standard if "there is another measure reasonably available, taking into account technical and economic feasibility, that achieves the appropriate level of protection and is significantly less restrictive to trade."[129]

The S&P agreement also requires nations to avoid "arbitrary or unjustifiable distinctions" for different products or processes, if these have the effect of placing foreign products at a de facto disadvantage.[130] National governments are required to take all reasonable measures to ensure compliance with the agreement by other than central government bodies. Finally, the agreement explicitly covers processing and production methods, thus subjecting both the EU's beef hormone ban and its Third Country Meat Directives to WTO scrutiny.

The Politics of Harmonization

The Agreement on S&P Measures in the Uruguay Round agreement represents part of a much broader effort on the part of both the WTO and the international business community to promote the use of international standards in order to prevent unnecessary obstacles to international trade. The Uruguay agreement is intended to strengthen the power and prestige of the large number of international organizations which set technical, health, and safety standards for industrial and agricultural products.[131] The agreement on technical barriers, which covers nonfarm goods, both requests countries to use international standards where they exist and encourages them to participate in the activities of the 28-plus international standards-setting bodies. This provision is extremely important, since diverse national technical standards represent a significant obstacle to global production and marketing. In fact, over the last decade there has been an increase in technical barriers to trade among OEC D countries.[132]

This increased support for global standards stems in part from the success of regional trading blocs, of which the EU is the most important, in facilitating trade by harmonizing national regulations and standards. Having in many cases achieved the benefits of a single EU standard—after enormous effort—European producers now wish to capture the competitive advantage of a single global standard, thus avoiding the additional costs of meeting separate standards for their domestic and international markets. Since 1991 the EU's standard-setting bodies have worked closely with their international counterparts to establish common EU and global standards. Both the TBT and the S&P agreement can thus be seen as efforts to extend the EU "1992" program to the global level.

In a number of important respects, the S&P agreement draws upon EU jurisprudence. Most obviously, it seeks to harmonize domestic national regulations in order to facilitate trade by relying on the scientific advice of technical bodies: in this context the Codex Commission represents the global counterpart of the EU's Scientific Commission on Foodstuffs. The S&P agreement, like Article 36 of the Treaty of Rome, permits nations to maintain their own, stricter standards, but these in turn are now subject to scrutiny by an international body. Finally, the agreement employs a slightly less stringent version of the EU's proportionality test to assess the legitimacy of standards which restrict trade, namely, the "least trade restrictive test."

While, historically, American firms have not taken much interest in global standards due to the huge size of their domestic market, the growing importance of international trade to the American economy has prompted increased support for international standards on the part of American business as well. Significantly, much of the domestic political support for the S&P agreement came from American exporters of grain, wheat, fruit, and vegetables. More broadly, both agreements reflect the political strength of internationally oriented firms, who increasingly favor international standards.

There is, however, an important difference between technical standards for manufactured products and for agricultural products. With some notable exceptions, the former are of interest only to producers; the latter, however, frequently raise health and safety issues. For this reason, while the Technical Barriers to Trade Agreement has attracted little public interest—though some of its provisions were modified as a result of pressures from environmentalists (see Chapter 4)—the Agreement on S&P Measures has been much more controversial. Indeed, even as it was being negotiated, it was repeatedly denounced by many consumer and environmental organizations, especially in the United States, on the grounds that it would "promote downward harmonization."[133] An official of the Community Nutrition Institute stated in 1991: "The term 'reasonable scientific justification' offers a misleading sense of objectivity, suggesting that it is the one and only one scientifically reasonable response to food safety hazards. But food safety laws are not just scientific—they also reflect the level of risk that society in willing to accept in its food supply. [The S&P Agreement is based] on the false proposition that decisions can be determined exclusively by experts on scientific grounds . . . We are concerned that . . . this language . . . could unduly restrict government action to protect the environment and consumer."[134]

While American public interest groups stated that they feared that the agreement would be used to undermine stricter American food safety standards, such as the Delaney Clause's prohibition on the use of any carcinogenic chemical additive in processed food, their counterparts in Europe expressed concern that the agreement would be used to undermine stricter European food safety standards, such as the EU's beef hormone ban.[135] Both, however, agreed that the Codex Commission could not be depended upon to protect consumers, since its membership was dominated by the representatives of multinational food exporters and chemical manufacturers. According to a report issued by a British food safety organization, 81 percent of nongovernment participants on national delegations to the Codex came from industry between 1989 and 1991, while only 1 percent represented consumer organizations.[136]

To reassure American consumer organizations, during the final weeks of the Uruguay Round negotiations the Clinton administration insisted on a number of modifications to the original Dunkel draft. Thus, while the earlier draft had provided that S&P measures must "not be maintained against available scientific evidence," the final text states that standards cannot be justified "without sufficient scientific evidence."[137] And to attempt to prevent the agreement from resulting in the downward harmonization of S&P Standards, the United States succeeded in adding an explanatory footnote which stated that "there is a scientific justification if, on the basis of an examination and evaluation of available scientific information . . . a Member determines that the relevant international standards . . . are not sufficient to achieve its appropriate level of protection."[138] According to USTR Michael Kantor, these changes mean that the agreement "safeguards United States animal and plant health measures and food safety requirements [by recognizing] the sovereign right of each government to establish the level of protection . . . of health deemed appropriate by that government."[139] However, these changes failed to satisfy a number of American consumer groups, which continued to strongly oppose American ratification of the Uruguay Round agreement (see Chapter 6).

Impact on Safety

What is likely to be the impact of granting the Codex Commission a larger role in setting national, or, in the case of the EU, regional food safety standards? More specifically, how will it affect current American food safety standards?

There are numerous differences between current American and Codex standards; however, contrary to the claims of some American consumer groups, the former are not significantly stricter. According to a report prepared by the General Accounting Office, almost two-thirds of the Codex standards cannot be compared to those of the United States, because either the United States has no standard, or the standards are defined differently.[140] In addition, American regulations cover 230 pesticides for which they are no Codex standards. In all of these cases, the Codex will have no impact on American standards.

Of those standards which are comparable, American standards do tend to be stricter, although not in all cases. If tolerance residues for pesticides are used as the basis for comparison, the United States has stricter standards in 19 percent of the cases for which there are comparable standards; the Codex in 34 percent. On the other hand, based on acceptable daily intake, American standards are stricter in 66 percent of the cases, and the Codex is stricter in 16 percent. Among the pesticides that EPA has rated as probable carcinogens, American standards are stricter in 55 percent of the cases, the Codex, in 16 percent. However, in most of these cases, these differences are relatively minor.

For those standards based on tolerance residues in which the United States and Codex standards differ from one another by more than a factor of ten—only about 8 percent of the cases fall into this category— the Codex tolerance exceeds the United States tolerance about as often as the United States tolerance exceeds that of the Codex.[141] On the other hand, for standards based on acceptable daily intake, the American standards are at least ten times lower than those of the Codex in 16 percent of the cases; the obverse is true only 2 percent of the time.[142]

The Agreement on S&P Measures clearly has the potential for affecting some American regulations. For example, the standards for risk assessment established by American regulatory statutes vary widely, ranging from zero risk in the case of food additives covered by the Delaney Clause to more flexible limits for pesticide residues established by EPA. Moreover, American nutritional label requirements are more extensive than the Codex voluntary food labeling guidelines. Clearly, much of the impact of the S&P agreement will depend on precisely which of the American regulatory requirements that exceed those established by the Codex Commission are challenged in WTO dispute settlement proceedings and the way the Committee on S&P Measures interprets the various provision of the agreement.

Nevertheless, given the American government's regulatory record, there is something rather ironic about its taking the initiative to demand that its trading partners base their food safety standards on internationally recognized scientific principles. For there are few nations whose regulatory procedures and standards have been so frequently divorced from any scientific rationale. In fact, there are literally scores of American consumer and environmental standards that have as little—if not much less—scientific basis as the EU's beef hormone ban which the United States challenged so strongly.[143] If anything, American regulatory agencies have in recent years been far more responsive to the emotional fears of consumers and the organizations that claim to speak for them than have their counterparts in the EU.[144]

The clearest American counterpart to the beef hormone ban was the successful media campaign waged by an environmental group, the Natural Resources Defense Council, to ban the use of the pesticide Alar (daminozide). (The Codex standard allows residues up to 5 parts per million on produce.)[145] As a result of panic by consumers, U.S. apple growers suffered loses of approximately $100 million dollars, roughly the same as that experienced by U.S. beef exporters as a result of the EU's hormone ban. Yet subsequent studies by experts at the American Medical Association, the Office of Technology Assessment, and the World Health Organization have concluded that "in the trace amounts present on apples, Alar poses no real threat to human health."[146]

Thus, stricter standards are not necessarily safer standards; many American health and safety standards provide the public with few or no benefits. Subjecting some American food safety and processing regulations to international scientific scrutiny might well result in changes in domestic regulatory standards and procedures that advocates of American regulatory reform have long urged; and in those cases in which American standards are weaker than international ones, it might even strengthen them—thus leading to a California effect for some California agricultural exports.

But even if the S&P agreement does result in weakening some American or EU food safety standards, it also has the potential to strengthen food safety standards on a global basis. For although its provisions do not expose nations with standards lower than international ones to formal WTO scrutiny, it is likely to increase pressures on all agricultural exporters to adopt Codex standards—for the obvious reason that doing so will now significantly facilitate their ability under the WTO to demand that their products be accepted in the markets of developed countries. From this perspective, just as the harmonization of environmental and consumer regulations within the EU has significantly strengthened the regulatory standards in the majority of member states, so is the S&P agreement likely to lead to a steady improvement in the food safety standards and production practices in the majority of WTO signatories, though the precise extent of this dimension of California effect remains to be determined.

The adoption of the Agreement on S&P Measures, by forcing nations to define and justify their standards for food safety in an international forum, will likely reduce many of the more blatant uses of health and safety standards as nontariff barriers—just as has occurred in the EU. And this will in turn help liberalize trade in agricultural products. In particular, it may well facilitate agricultural exports to Japan, many of whose S&P standards really are disguised forms of protectionism. Significantly, Japan's recent changes in its pesticide residue standards were made in anticipation of the S&P agreement. In the long run it may also contribute to an international consensus regarding standards for at least some products and production processes and help persuade national regulatory authorities that standards can be equivalent without being identical. Thus, the agreement can be seen as part of a broader movement toward the globalization of regulatory standards for traded products.

At the same time, the actual impact of the agreement on food safety and processing standards may well prove more modest than its critics fear or its proponents anticipate. The Codex Commission has operated in relative obscurity in large measure because its standards have been voluntary.[147] But as they acquire standing in international trade law, they will be subject to increased scrutiny, particularly as the Codex comes to play a more important role in determining standards in such controversial areas as pesticide residues, additives, food hygiene, and labeling. Just as environmental groups became more aware and critical of GATT dispute settlement procedures following the tuna-dolphin decision, so has the Agreement on S&P standards increased public criticism of the decision-making procedures of the Codex Commission. Consumer groups in the developed nations are likely to demand, and may well be granted, a more important role in shaping Codex policies.

As the decision of the EU's Council of Ministers to ignore the decisions of its own scientific advisory body in the case of beef hormones indicates, scientific assessments are not always acceptable to regulatory officials since the latter must also contend with domestic pressures from both producers and nongovernmental organizations. Thus, the impact of this agreement, at least with respect to those standards that attract public interest or which have a significant effect on global market shares, may be not so much to change national standards as to move the debate over them from the national to the international level.

Indeed, the "politicization" of the Codex has already begun. Significantly, in spite of strong pressure from the United States, the Codex Commission has not adopted the recommendations of its own scientific advisory committees that it officially approve the use of the five growth hormones whose banning by the EU helped create a more important role for the Codex in resolving international disputes over divergent S&P standards in the first place. And it has not done so because of the EU's insistence that "standards can not and should not be solely based on science and that consumer preferences should be taken into account."[148]

Ultimately, the power of the world's major agricultural producers, the largest of which is the United States, will determine the actual impact of the S&P agreement on the harmonization of world safety standards for agricultural products. To the extent that there is a consensus among them, then progress will be made in reducing the role of sanitary and phytosanitary standards as nontariff barriers to trade in agricultural products. But if they disagree among themselves, especially with respect to regulations with high public visibility, subjecting national S&P regulations to international discipline is likely to prove far more difficult.

-6-

Baptists and Bootleggers in the United States

During most of the postwar period, the policy arenas of social regulation and international trade were distinctive. While business interests have historically played an important role in shaping policy in both arenas, until recently interest groups promoting health, safety, and environmental regulation paid relatively little attention to trade policy. For example, of more than a score of books published by Ralph Nader and his associates during the late 1960s and early 1970s criticizing virtually every aspect of American health, safety, and environmental regulations, none examined trade policy. Consumer and environmental organizations played no role in the fierce debates surrounding American trade policy during the 1960s and 70s.

However, over the last fifteen years public interest groups have become increasingly active participants in the making of American trade policy. They have sought to restrict the export of a number of products, formed alliances with producers opposed to trade liberalization, and criticized the impact of proposed trade agreements on consumer health and safety. While their policy impact has been mixed, they have succeeded in placing the relationship between American trade and regulatory policies firmly onto the domestic political agenda.

There are important similarities in the public interest movement's motivations with respect to trade and regulatory policies. In both cases, they are interested less in promoting the economic interests of consumers than in protecting consumers, and the environment, from harm; both the domestic and international regulatory policies they favor tend to make products more rather than less expensive. More

196

generally, their suspicion of international markets parallels their mistrust of domestic ones. Just as they have often supported intervention in domestic markets to improve environmental quality and consumer protection, so they have frequently endorsed restrictions on international commerce to achieve similar goals.

Restricting Exports

In both the EU and Japan, nongovernmental organizations have frequently supported restricting imports on health, safety, and environmental grounds. However, a unique feature of American public interest organizations has been their long-standing campaign to use similar arguments for restricting the *export* of various products. This effort dates from the late 1970s, when the muckraking magazine *Mother Jones* published an article entitled "The Corporate Crime of the Century," which described numerous products that had been banned by American regulatory officials but which had subsequently been "dumped" on unsuspecting third world consumers.[1]

The most widely publicized such product was children's pajamas that had been manufactured with the flame retardant Tris. After being prohibited for sale in the United States by the Consumer Product Safety Commission on the grounds that Tris was a potential carcinogen, 2.4 million garments made with the chemical were exported, primarily to developing countries. The action greatly disturbed both the public and many American legislators.[2] Similar criticisms were made of the export of pesticides, such as DDT, which had recently been banned in the United States.[3]

In response to these and other exposés of America's "double standards," Congress expanded the scope of several statutes that regulated hazardous products in the United States to include exported goods. In 1979 Congress approved amendments to the Flammable Fabrics Act, the Federal Hazardous Substances Act, and the Consumer Product Safety Act, which required foreign governments to be notified before consumer goods banned in the United States were exported. A similar amendment to the Federal Insecticide, Fungicide and Rodenticide Act (FIFRA) required exporters to obtain a statement from the foreign purchaser which acknowledged that the pesticide could not be used in the United States before a domestically banned pesticide was exported. The EPA was then required to notify appropriate foreign officials.

In 1980, shortly before leaving office, President Carter accepted the recommendations of an interagency working group established to formulate a comprehensive hazardous export policy for the United States. Executive Order 12,264 strengthened the export notice requirements of existing statutes and established formal exporting licensing controls for "extremely hazardous substances."[4] However, one month later, on February 17, 1981, President Reagan revoked Carter's Executive Order and substituted his own. Entitled "Federal Exports and Excessive Regulation," it directed the Departments of State and Commerce to review American export policy on hazardous exports in order to "find ways to accomplish the same goals at a lower cost."[5] One critic commented, "With a single sentence, the Reagan Administration wiped out two-and-one-half years of study and hard bargaining among more then twenty federal agencies, two sets of Congressional hearings, and the participation of over 100 business, labor and environmental, and consumer organizations here and abroad."[6]

During the 1980s consumer and environmental groups pressed for legislation to restore the Carter executive order, or even to go beyond it. They specifically urged that the FIFRA be amended to require exporters to provide more detailed information to importers and to write labels in the language of the country to which the pesticides were exported. This proposal was supported by a broad and unusual coalition of environmental and industry groups as part of an elaborate compromise designed to both strengthen and streamline the federal government's regulation of pesticides. While the legislation came within a "hair's breadth" of passage in 1986, the coalition eventually split apart over other issues and the proposed law was never acted upon.[7] It was not until 1993, shortly after President Clinton assumed office, that EPA issued a new export policy strengthening notification and labeling requirements for American pesticide exports, and applying notification requirements to additional pesticides.[8] But this initiative was far weaker than the proposed amendments to the 1978 FIFRA amendments which Congress had failed to enact in 1986.

The Export of Cigarettes

Public interest groups have also waged a vigorous campaign to restrict cigarette exports. While American public health groups had been actively campaigning for policies to discourage domestic cigarette sales and marketing since the 1960s, during the late 1980s they began to turn their attention to the health effects of cigarette exports. During the mid 1980s, as part of its effort to increase American exports to Asia, the Office of the United States Trade Representative (USTR) began to scrutinize the policies of America's trading partners that restricted purchases of American-made goods. At the request of the United States Cigarette Export Association, the USTR began to investigate the tobacco regulations of Japan, Taiwan, and Korea. All three countries had large numbers of cigarette smokers. Yet their governments, by enacting quotas and protective tariffs that almost tripled the price of American cigarettes, and by restricting the advertising of foreign brands, had managed to preserve almost their entire domestic market for cigarettes produced and marketed by state-controlled monopolies. Indeed, in Korea the mere possession of an imported pack of cigarettes was illegal.

Between 1986 and 1988 the Reagan administration twice threatened to invoke "301 sanctions" against Taiwan, Korea, and Japan in order to pressure them to eliminate their restrictions on imported cigarettes. As one U.S. trade official put it, "All we wanted was a fair crack at their markets. Just the chance to compete on equal footing with their domestic brands; nothing more, nothing less."[9] These pressures were effective. Japan liberalized its laws in 1986, South Korea in 1987, and Taiwan in 1988. All three governments either reduced or eliminated their tariffs and quotas on imported cigarettes and agreed to permit American and British cigarette companies to advertise their products more widely.

However, as we have seen, a fourth Asian country, Thailand, proved more recalcitrant. Its 1966 Tobacco Act prohibited cigarette imports without a license, and the government had issued no new licenses for ten years. It also imposed higher taxes on imported cigarettes and banned all cigarette advertising. In 1990 the United States filed a complaint with the GATT on the grounds that Thailand had violated the GATT's national treatment clause. While a spokesman for the USTR conceded that since "tobacco products are harmful, countries have a sovereign right to protect the health of their citizens . . . [what] Thailand has done is create a monopoly under which they alone sell cigarettes. It is simply discriminatory."[10]

Thailand sought to defend its trade restrictions under Article XX of the GATT. It claimed that they were "necessary" to control domestic cigarette smoking and protect its citizens from U.S. cigarettes, "which had additives that might make them more harmful than Thai cigarettes."[11] However, its case was weakened considerably by the fact that Thailand had only banned cigarette advertising after American firms had begun to increase their marketing efforts in Asia. Moreover, the government monopoly's harsh tobacco blend is generally considered both more unpleasant and more harmful than American brands. Nonetheless, the Thai government argued that its ban on imported cigarettes "served to control a social ill."[12] An official stated: "The cigarette exporters make it sound as if all they're going to do is come in and get smokers to switch brands. But what they do is, they come in and target women and children, who generally do not smoke in Asian societies, and increase the number of smokers."[13]

The GATT dispute panel ruled that Thailand's restrictions on cigarette imports were not "necessary," since it had alternative ways of protecting the health and safety of its citizens which were less GATT inconsistent. However, it did allow Thailand to retain its recently enacted ban on all cigarette advertising, as the ban was nondiscriminatory. The latter decision constituted something of a setback to the United States, which had argued that Thailand's ban constituted a de facto trade barrier, as it made it more difficult for newly introduced (that is, foreign) brands to gain market share. One American cigarette industry official asked rhetorically: "What would have happened to Toyota and Nissan if GM and Ford had allowed their cars in but then banned auto advertising? I don't think that would be fair."[14]

As part of its effort to resist American pressure to give up its monopoly over the domestic market, the government of Thailand had approached American antismoking activists for help. According to Alan Davis of the American Cancer Society, "The Thais came to us and said: 'Your government is trying to force U.S. cigarettes down our throats.'"[15] The result was one of the more bizarre Baptist–bootlegger coalitions, a "strange de facto alliance . . . between the local tobacco monopoly . . . and antismoking forces."[16] However, it had no effect on American trade negotiations; the USTR insisted on filing its complaint with the GATT.

But the ongoing efforts of Asian governments to keep out American cigarettes have been strongly supported by the American public health community. U.S. Surgeon General C. Everett Koop characterized the American position as "unconscionable . . . deplorable . . . the height of hypocrisy," and described the export of tobacco products as a "moral outrage."[17] Scott Ballin, of the American Heart Association, argued that "the U.S. government should not be in the business of encouraging exportation of cigarettes . . . Every country including the United States, should be doing everything possible to discourage [their] use worldwide."[18] Representative Chet Atkins (D-Mass.) stated that by allowing American manufacturers to export cigarettes without the health warnings required under American law, "Washington is sending Asians a message that their lungs are somehow more expendable than American lungs."[19]

In response to strong congressional criticism of the USTR's effort to promote cigarette exports, the General Accounting Office conducted an investigation. A 1990 GAO report found "no evidence" that the USTR had given tobacco product cases preferential treatment over other types of trade complaints.[20] It noted that the industry's complaints were well-founded and that the USTR's decision to pursue them was "consistent with current trade policy criteria." However, the report also observed that the efforts of both the USTR and the Department of Agriculture to promote cigarette exports were inconsistent with the American government's support of global health programs, such as the World Health Organization's smoking prevention program. It concluded that the inconsistency of American policy stemmed from the fact "that trade and health policies are developed independently of each other."[21]

The American tobacco industry responded that there was no evidence that cigarette consumption trends overseas "are affected by whether or not the U.S. product is there."[22] Industry officials noted that most Asian countries have made little effort to discourage cigarette smoking, which, with the exception of Hong Kong, remains dominated by domestic brands. For example, the label required on cigarette packages sold in Japan reads, "Please Do Not Smoke Too Much For Your Health," while in Taiwan the best-selling government-produced brand is called Long Life.[23] According to Owen Smith, president of the U.S. Cigarette Export Association, "If U.S. manufacturers are inhibited from offering cigarettes in overseas markets, we will only be giving business back to the domestic monopolies."[24]

The "Circle of Poison"

Like their counterparts in Japan, American consumer and environmental groups have also become increasingly concerned about the health effects of pesticides sprayed on imported food. Citizen groups in both countries have tended to regard imported food as less safe because of the gap between foreign and domestic regulatory standards for pesticide use—a gap compounded by the inadequacy of border inspections in both countries. In Japan, consumer groups have allied with farm organizations to oppose the relaxation of barriers to agricultural imports. In America, a similar coalition, with similar objectives, has emerged. However, it has also had a second political focus: it has sought to protect American consumers, along with foreign workers, by restricting American pesticide *exports*.

Like cigarettes, American pesticides are highly competitive on global markets; American exports account for one-quarter of the $17 billion world pesticide market. U.S. chemical companies export between 400 and 600 million tons of pesticides annually—approximately one-third of their domestic production.[25]

While the 1978 amendments to FIFRA did impose some controls on pesticide exports, they were interpreted loosely. According to Michael Synar (D-Okla.), the EPA "created a loophole big enough to drive a Mack truck through."[26] At hearings held by the House Energy and Commerce Committee's Subcommittee on Environment, Energy and Natural Resources, Synar stated: "The subcommittee's investigation found that when it comes to the export of unregistered pesticides, foreign governments have been kept in the dark, the public has been kept in the dark and the agencies responsible for inspection of U.S. food imports have been kept in the dark."[27]

Environmentalists have long criticized American policies regarding pesticide exports.[28] Sandra Marquardt, pesticide coordinator for Greenpeace, considers it "outlandish that current pesticide law permits the uncontrolled export of these dangerous products."[29] Jay Feldman, who heads the National Coalition Against the Misuse of Pesticides—a coalition of more than 300 organizations—argues that "U.S. corporations must be held accountable for standards of health and safety in this country and must uphold those same standards around the world."[30]

But while the impact of American pesticides on public health and environmental quality in foreign countries has caused widespread indignation, the more politically potent case against pesticide exports has focused on their impact on American consumers. This issue was first raised in 1979 in an article in *Mother Jones* entitled "The Boomerang Crime," which argued that American consumers were still being exposed to many of the pesticides that had been recently banned in the United States.[31] Many of these banned chemicals, including DDT, were produced in the United States for export. Farmers in other countries sprayed the chemicals on fruits and vegetables, which were in turn exported to the United States, thus completing what was characterized as a "circle of poison"—a phrase made popular by a 1981 book by that same name.[32]

Approximately one-quarter (by weight and volume) of American chemical exports have not been approved for domestic use; they have been banned either because of health reasons or because no application was submitted for their approval in the first place as they are not appropriate for domestic conditions. As exports of pesticides from the United States have increased in recent years, so have American imports of fruits and vegetables. Fresh fruit imports more than doubled between 1979 and 1986. Currently, one-quarter of the fruits and vegetables consumed by Americans are imported; during the winter months this figure increases to 50 percent.[33]

While the FDA is responsible for monitoring the safety of imported as well as domestic foods, the former system of regulation is highly uneven. According to a 1986 Government Accounting Office study, less than one percent of the estimated one million food shipments that enter the United States each year are checked for dangerous pesticide residues.[34] Yet according to federal agents, 6.1 percent of all food imports tested violate American safety standards, double the rate for domestic produce.[35] When the Natural Resources Defense Council ran its own tests on coffee beans, all of which are imported, it found "multiple illegal chemical residues on every sample taken."[36]

Many imported crops contain pesticides whose use has been banned in the United States.[37] In other cases the pesticides found on imported produce are legal in the United States but either exceed U.S. approved levels or are sprayed on crops for which the United States has not approved their use. According to the GAO, a total of 110 pesticides without U.S. tolerance levels are used overseas.[38] In addition, "at least twenty pesticides, potential carcinogens, are undetectable with FDA tests used to find residues in food."[39]

In America as in Japan, the safety of imported food has emerged as an important political issue. In 1984 Congressmen Frank Horton (R-N.Y.) argued that "there is no justification for a double-standard system under which American producers must use only U.S.-registered pesticides and meet the tolerance levels recommended by the EPA and enforced by the FDA, while foreign producers are not subject to equivalent regulation and enforcement."[40] Three years later, the journal *Food Processing* reported that "Congress and Federal regulatory agencies are becoming increasingly concerned about the safety of imported foods."[41] That same year, the *Wall Street Journal* published a front-page article entitled, "As Food Imports Rise, Consumers Face Peril from Use of Pesticides."[42]

In 1990 Senator Patrick Leahy (D-Vt.) and Representative Michael Synar (D-Okla.) introduced the Pesticide Export Reform Act. It required that imported foods be accompanied by documentation describing which pesticides have been used on them in order to facilitate American border inspections. It also amended FIFRA to impose a total ban on the exports of pesticides not approved for use in the United States. Leahy argued that, "because FDA waves through virtually all imported foods without inspection, these chemicals often end up on America's dinner tables."[43] He added: "If EPA says it is too hazardous for a pesticide to be used on American-grown food, then it is too hazardous to be used on foreign-grown food."[44] Their legislation was backed by Greenpeace, the Consumers Union, and the National Wildlife Federation.

Largely at the initiative of Senator Leahy, who chairs the Senate Agriculture Committee, his amendment was included in the farm bill reported out by the Senate Agriculture Committee and passed by the Senate in the fall of 1990. A somewhat weaker version—which permitted the export of unregistered pesticides as long as they had been registered for use in at least one of the twenty-four OECD countries—was adopted as part of the House farm bill.

The Leahy-Synar amendments, as well as both the Senate and House versions of the farm bill, were strongly opposed by the American chemical industry. Jay Vroom, the president of the National Agricultural Chemicals Association, described the amendments as a form of "environmental imperialism" and warned that their passage would provoke a trade war that would undermine the American chemical industry.[45] He contended that restricting American exports would increases sales of foreign produced pesticides, many of which are more dangerous than those manufactured in the United States. The chemical industry argued that one reason why many pesticides were not registered for use in the United States was not because they could not meet American regulatory standards; rather, there was simply no demand for their use in the United States. Now, in order to continue to export them, American manufacturers would have to go though the trouble and expense of applying for American regulatory approval.

Finally, the bill's critics contended that American jobs would be sacrificed since the passage of the Leahy-Synar amendment would either force American chemical firms to shift production to other countries or encourage foreign farmers to purchase chemicals produced in their own country or imported from Europe. Industry lobbyists began to refer to the legislation as "the circle of jobs bill."[46] In a letter to Leahy, EPA Director William Reilly and Agriculture Secretary Clayton Yeutter contended that "the restrictions on exports will disrupt trade which will be worth several hundreds of millions of dollars per year and which undoubtedly support a large number of American jobs. These impacts cannot be justified, given that [the bill] . . . is unlikely to result in significant gains for human health or the environment."[47]

The Bush administration also strongly opposed the amendment, since it threatened to undermine its efforts to develop international standards for pesticide use in the Uruguay Round of GATT negotiations. John Wessel, director of the FDA's Contaminants Policy Staff, argued that the passage of the "circle of poison" legislation has "the potential of bringing international trade to a halt. If there is a need for providing a level playing field for farmers, then it should be the responsibility of the Codex Committee on Pesticide Residues rather than an individual country."[48]

Due to aggressive lobbying by both the chemical industry and the Bush administration, the pesticide export provisions in both the House and Senate versions of the farm bill were eliminated in conference committee. Yet what is striking is how close each came to being enacted. What made this possible? How, after so many years of complaining in vain about the "circle of poison," had antipesticide political forces suddenly acquired such influence? In particular, how did Leahy's amendment pass the Senate Agricultural Committee, traditionally dominated by agricultural producers?

The explanation is a simple one. Many American farmers have come to realize that restrictions on pesticide exports are in their economic interest. Restricting American pesticide exports deprives overseas agricultural producers of an important competitive advantage; they no longer are able to use pesticides that do not meet strict American health and safety standards or which, for various reasons, have not been approved in the United States. This, in turn, is likely to make it more difficult for them to produce fruits and vegetables for the American market. Stricter labeling requirements for imported produce perform a similar function; it increases the cost of access to the American market.

In both cases, the playing field between third world farmers and their American competitors would become more nearly level: both would now face equivalent pesticide restrictions. As Congressman Leon Panetta (D-Calif.) wrote in defense of the Leahy-Synar bill: "California fruit and vegetable producers have met the toughest food safety standards in the country. However, foreign produce has not had to meet these same strict standards. I believe that this double standard is not fair to . . . domestic producers who are competing with foreign producers for a share of the market."[49] His position was supported by Republican Senator Pete Wilson of California. Echoing the view of the Western Growers Association, Wilson argued that "export of dangerous pesticides creates a competitive inequity between foreign and American farmers and growers."[50]

Thus, the increase in public concern about the safety of imported food has created a community of interest between public interest lobbies and many American farmers, the latter standing to benefit financially from whatever success the former achieves in "protecting" American consumers from unsafe agricultural imports.[51] While to date this alliance has not prevailed in its efforts to restrict pesticide exports, it remains politically potent. Pressure to restrict American pesticide exports is likely to persist.

Logging Exports

While efforts to restrict exports of both American cigarettes and pesticides have been unsuccessful, a coalition of producers and public interest groups did succeed in restricting the export of logs from state-owned lands. American sawmills in the northwest have suffered economically as a steadily growing share of the logs harvested in the northwest have been shipped directly to Japan. The Japanese prefer to import the raw logs and then cut them in their own mills; this both supports their domestic mill industry and enables the logs to be cut according to their particular specifications. In order to preserve employment in the dying sawmills of their region, Senator Robert Packwood (R-Ore.) and other legislators from the Pacific Northwest began to urge that log exports from state lands be banned. (Exporting logs from federal lands is already prohibited.) This proposed export restriction was initially opposed by the Bush administration on the grounds that it was protectionist.

But an important change occurred after June 22, 1990, when the Bush administration decided to list the spotted owl as an endangered species. This decision threatened to severely restrict logging in the Pacific Northwest and Rocky Mountain states. The U.S. Forest Service estimated that the log-cutting restrictions necessary to protect the habitat of the endangered birds would cost 20,000 jobs in the timber and logging industries.[52] However, following the spotted owl decision, the campaign of the sawmill operators for export restrictions gained a significant political ally in the American environmental movement.

Environmentalists now argued that the shortage of logs available for processing in domestic lumber mills was due not to the logging restriction imposed to protect the owls, but rather to uncontrolled log exports. They supported an export ban on unprocessed timber from state-owned lands because it would help reduce demand for American lumber products, thus helping to preserve the owl's habitat. In addition, by promising to create upwards of six to seven thousand additional jobs in sawmills, it would soften the economic impact of protecting the spotted owl. In short, an export ban would help protect both the spotted owl *and* American workers.

The Bush administration, under pressure from both environmentalists and the logging industry, saw the export ban as a way of pleasing both constituencies. In August 1990 President Bush signed into law the Customs and Trade Act of 1990, which, among its other provisions, imposed a permanent ban on unprocessed timber exports from all public lands. In signing the bill, the President stressed its environmental significance: "There can be no doubt that high levels of export of unprocessed timber have contributed to the decline in habitat that caused this species [spotted owl] to be listed as endangered."[53] While the legislation also authorized the President to suspend the ban if it was found to violate American obligations under any trade agreement, the legislation was carefully drafted in such a way as to qualify under the GATT's Article XX. Thus, it explicitly linked the export restriction to comparable restrictions on domestic consumption. While the Japanese did not file a formal appeal with the GATT, they viewed the ban as essentially a protectionist measure designed to save American jobs at the expense of Japanese ones.

Trade Equity

A persistent concern of both the American business community and American environmentalists has been the gap between American environmental standards and those of other nations, especially developing ones. American producers exposed to international competition claim that the relatively high costs of compliance with domestic environmental standards places them at a competitive disadvantage; in effect, laxer regulatory standards abroad constitute a subsidy. Environmentalists in turn argue that it is morally irresponsible for Americans to consume goods produced in a manner that destroys the environment of other countries. At the same time, they are worried that American producers may use the higher costs of compliance with domestic standards to pressure for their relaxation. Accordingly, the existence of "pollution havens" appears to threaten environmental quality not only outside the United States but within it as well, since, if American environmental laws appear to harm American competitiveness—by making American products more expensive than imported ones— public support for strong environmental protection might diminish.[54]

The result has been a community of interests between "eco" and economic protectionists, which has received considerable support in Congress. Of the forty-eight bills on environmental matters introduced in the 101st Congress (1990–91), thirty-one included trade restrictions, suggesting that many lawmakers believe that trade contraction rather than expansion is the best way of improving environmental quality.[55]

A resolution submitted to the House of Representatives stated: "It should be the policy of the United States to seek in trade negotiations the adoption and enforcement of effective and equivalent environmental standards and controls among the nations of the world . . . the President should seek, through the Uruguay Round and the next GATT round, agreement on mechanisms under which the United States and its trading partners can eliminate or reduce competitive disadvantages resulting from differential national environmental standards and controls."[56]

During the debate over the Clean Air Act Amendments of 1990, Senator Slade Gorton (R.-Wash.) submitted an amendment that imposed a tariff on "any product imported into the United States that has not been subject to processing, or manufactured from a process, which does not comply with the air quality standards of the Clean Air Act."[57] He argued that "we live in one world . . . [the United States] should do everything we can to encourage policies which are similar to our own in the rest of the world, whether it has a direct impact on air quality in the United States or not."[58] The amendment was narrowly defeated by a vote of 52 to 47.

Following the defeat of the Gorton amendment, Senator Frank Lautenberg (D.-N.J.) introduced an amendment to Section 301 of the United States Trade Act of 1974 to expand the definition of unreasonable acts, policies, or practices to include any practice that "constitutes a failure to establish effective natural resource protection and effective pollution abatement and control standards to protect the air, water and land."[59] He also proposed legislation specifically making access to the American market contingent on improvements in the environmental polices of developing countries. Under his proposed Global Environmental Protection and Trade Equity Act, in order to be eligible for trade preferences under either the U.S. Generalized System of Preferences or the Caribbean Basin Initiative, developing countries trading with the United States would have to institute and enforce effective pollution-control programs.

The following year another piece of legislation was introduced which aimed at creating both a "level playing field" for domestic producers and improving environmental standards outside the United States. The International Pollution Deterrence Act of 1991 defined pollution as an impermissible subsidy, and authorized the imposition of countervailing duties against countries whose pollution policies did not meet domestic American production standards.[60] It also provided that half of the duties collected be placed into a Pollution Control Export Fund, to be used to assist developing countries in purchasing

American-made pollution-control equipment. The remainder of the import duties would be used to provide financial assistance to American companies to develop pollution control technologies. The bill's sponsor, Senator David Boren (D-Okla.), informed the Senate: "The bill recognizes that a country's failure to require and enforce meaningful pollution controls constitute a subsidy no different, but more dangerous than practices such as cash grants to money losing State enterprises which have long been actionable under U.S. law. By making such absence countervailable, we allow U.S. companies to level the playing field by removing the cost advantage derived from freedom to pollute."[61]

The principle underlying all three bills was essentially similar. As the AFL-CIO put it: "Products made in an environmentally unsafe manner constitute an unfair trade practice."[62] Each bill was supported by a coalition of environmentalists, trade unions, and protectionist producers. They were also all strongly opposed by the USTR on the grounds that they would violate American obligations under the GATT. For while the Standards Code permits nations to impose countervailing duties when firms engaged in international commerce have been the beneficiary of government subsidies, neither the Code nor the GATT explicitly addresses the issue of subsidy by *omission*.[63] A tariff on goods from nations whose pollution control standards differed from those of the United States would clearly violate the GATT's national treatment provision—to say nothing of its highly disruptive effect on international trade. From the perspective of the GATT and supporters of trade liberalization, it represents the ultimate "ecoprotectionist" nightmare.

As a result of pressures from environmentalists as well as American fishermen, the United States has restricted imports of some fish products that are either produced in environmentally harmful ways or which threaten to deplete fishing stocks in international waters (see Chapter 4). However, the United States has not to date restricted the import of any manufactured product because of the environmental consequences of its production outside the United States; none of the legislative proposals discussed above have been enacted. But the pressure to do so is likely to persist, largely because such measures are strongly supported by unions, many environmentalists, and segments of American industry.

Agricultural Liberalization

One of the most important policy goals of the United States in the Uruguay Round was to liberalize trade in agricultural products. It attempted to achieve this objective through two policy proposals: the "double zero plan," which prohibited restrictions on the production, consumption, and prices of agricultural products, and an agreement restricting the use of sanitary and phytosanitary standards as nontariff barriers. This American initiative divided the American farming sector.

The American proposal was supported by those export-oriented sectors which stood to benefit from an across-the-board reduction in subsidies and trade restrictions on the part of both the United States and other food producing industrialized nations. However, it was strongly opposed by those farmers whose products were not competitive on international markets and who therefore favor continued government intervention in agricultural markets, including subsidies and import restrictions. Organizations representing the latter characterized the Bush administration as "a tool of the multinational food processors, which profit from low grain prices and push the use of chemicals to maintain productivity."[64]

Like their counterparts in Japan, uncompetitive American farmers have sought to generate public opposition to agricultural trade liberalization by stressing the linkage between public health and safety and the maintenance of import restrictions. For example, the Farmers Union Milk Marketing Cooperative, which represents 9,800 midwestern dairy farmers who stood to suffer serious financial losses if barriers to milk imports were lifted or dairy subsidies were reduced, urged Congress to "reject any new international trade agreement which puts American consumers and farmers at increased risk from unsafe food imports."[65]

Opposition to the administration's GATT proposals was initially organized by a coalition called the Fair Trade Campaign. Formed during the mid-1980s, shortly after the Uruguay Round of GATT negotiations began, it consisted of various local and national organizations representing the interests of family farmers, including the National Family Farm Coalition—comprised of forty-two grassroots farm and rural advocacy organizations in more than thirty states—and the National Toxics Campaign, a coalition of both local and national environmental and consumer groups. In its opposition to the liberalization of agricultural trade, this alliance focused on the domestic health and safety implications of the harmonization of regulatory standards for food and agricultural products. It claimed that the "harmonization of national rules under the GATT would result in the weakening of hard-won environmental and consumer protections that have become part of U.S. law."[66]

Their criticisms of the impact of the proposed S&P agreement on American regulatory standards were subsequently supported by a wide range of national consumer and environmental organizations. In May 1990 seven of these organizations, including the Natural Resources Defense Council (NRDC), the National Wildlife Federation, Friends of the Earth, and the Community Nutrition Institute, co-signed a letter to USTR Carla Hills expressing their concern that the technical tribunals created by the S&P agreement would have the power to preempt state regulations—many of which were stricter than both national and international standards. According to a NRDC attorney, "The pesticide industry has lost the battle in Congress, in the courts, at the state level and in the court of public opinion. Now industry, with the administration's help, seeks to undermine state and federal pesticide regulations through the back door of international trade."[67] Ralph Nader added: "More than one giant multinational corporation is watering at the mouth over the opportunities presented by the forthcoming GATT Treaty."[68]

In January 1992 twenty-eight national consumer and environmental organizations sent a letter to each member of Congress urging rejection of the Uruguay Round draft text on the grounds that it would seriously undermine U.S. environmental and consumer laws. They claimed that the United States would be forced to harmonize its regulatory standards with the less stringent ones developed by the Codex, thus preempting more stringent state or local environmental laws. They also contended that the draft text codified "the worst elements of the recent GATT tuna-dolphin panel resolution" by placing in jeopardy extraterritorial U.S. environmental laws such as the Endangered Species Act as well as various American laws and treaties protecting the global commons.[69]

The following month Congressmen Henry Waxman (D.-Calif.) and Richard Gephardt (D.-Mo.) introduced a resolution expressing the "sense of Congress" that it "would not approve legislation to implement international free trade agreements if any such agreement jeopardizes United States health, safety, labor or environmental laws."[70] They characterized the harmonization clause of the proposed treaty as a "hidden timebomb with dangerous ramifications" for American regulatory standards.[71] The resolution was endorsed by more than fifty environmental, consumer, labor, and agricultural organizations, and it was passed unanimously by the House in the summer of 1992.

To enhance the visibility of this issue, in the spring of 1992 Public Citizen, along with a number of other consumer and environmental groups, took out full-page advertisements in a number of American newspapers. Headlined in bold letters, "SABOTAGE!" the text cited the GATT's rulings in both the tuna-dolphin and Thailand cigarette cases to illustrate the GATT's role in harmonizing regulatory standards downward in order to further the interests of "multi-national corporations for whom democracy itself is an impediment to *their* free trade." It claimed that if the GATT's powers were further expanded, "faceless trade bureaucrats," acting in secret and with no democratic accountability, would be able to strike down "*thousands* of laws in countries around the world that give priority to clean food and clean water, protect sea mammals and wildlife, preserve trees or other resources, restrict poisonous pesticide sprays, save rain forests and safeguard small farmers from being overpowered by agribusiness."[72]

Carla Hills responded that state and local governments would maintain their right to adopt stricter rules, providing they were based on scientific justification, were applied without discrimination, and were transparent. Hills affirmed that "a state's food labeling statute (such as California's Proposition 65) is not 'arbitrary and unjustifiable' merely because other states do not have such a standard or because other states maintain a standard that is not as stringent."[73] EPA's Linda Fisher claimed that "the United States position in the GATT discussions is that a state may establish its own S&P measures but it should not be permitted to erect discriminatory unscientific trade barriers any more than the United States government or any of our trading partners should."[74] These assurances, though, failed to satisfy a number of environmental organizations. A number of state governments also expressed concern about the impact of the proposed S&P Code.[75]

It is a measure of the importance that the public interest community has come to attach to the linkages between trade and regulatory issues that Ralph Nader, its most prominent spokesman, has made opposition to trade liberalization one of his most important political priorities. Nader argues that "international trade is increasingly being used as an instrument for . . . deregulating food and health safety standards."[76] Agreements to liberalize trade "jeopardize so many of the programs we've been working on."[77] He told the National Press Club in 1993: "Citizen groups who have fought for stronger safety and other standards traditionally have had to deal with the auto industry, the Chamber of Commerce and the federal government. Now they have to deal with the argument that this may violate GATT and NAFTA. It's another tier of extrajurisdictional power, and its much more remote and difficult to deal with."[78]

However, not all public interest groups opposed the GATT agreement. After reading the text of the agreement, the Washington Director of the Consumers Union concluded that it "will protect the right of the U.S. to maintain higher standards than the rest of the world, if we choose to do so," adding, "And we should!"[79] Stewart Hudson of the National Wildlife Federation expressed concern that the coalition opposed to the GATT might be "ultimately successful in achieving objectives that we do not want to achieve." He noted that his organization "was not comfortable with the status quo, where the United States is very protectionist with regard to certain items that are produced in developing countries," adding that "economic protection . . . as it relates to Third World Development, is a very troubling issue for us."[80]

The S&P agreement was subsequently defended by Mickey Kantor, the Clinton administration's trade representative. He expressed confidence in "our ability to maintain our food safety laws and regulations," and stated that he was "disappointed in the continuing misperceptions expressed by some of those who appear to be our vocal critics."[81] However, in response to the criticisms of American consumer and environmental organizations, Kantor did propose a number of modifications in the original Dunkel draft, most of which were incorporated in the final text of the Uruguay Round agreement (see Chapter 5). The purpose of these changes was to reduce the vulnerability of American food safety laws to GATT scrutiny. While they were not as extensive as many American consumer groups had advocated, their incorporation into the GATT reflects the increasing influence of public interest groups in shaping American trade policies.

Conclusion

In a number of respects, the impact of public interest groups on American trade policies has been limited. No important new restrictions have been imposed on American exports of hazardous products in more than a decade, the USTR and the Department of Agriculture continue to promote the sale of American cigarettes overseas, the "circle of poison" legislation remains stillborn, Congress has not imposed penalties on imported products manufactured in ways that violate American environmental standards, and in December 1994 Congress approved the Uruguay Round GATT agreement, which significantly liberalized trade in agricultural products and also exposed American regulatory standards to closer international scrutiny.

The influence of public interest groups on previous trade policies has been limited by two factors. The first has to do with the political influence of export-oriented American producers. Thus, the "circle of poison" legislation was strongly opposed by the American chemical industry, who stood to lose important export markets. And while export-oriented agricultural producers did not actively lobby against it, neither did they support its passage, preferring to harmonize food pesticide standards under the Codex rather than for each nation to seek reenforcement of its own standards. These same agricultural producers were also strong and effective advocates of agricultural trade liberalization through the GATT and the adoption of the S&P agreement. Likewise, globally oriented American firms have not supported legislation which would restrict imports from nations with laxer pollution-control standards; not only do they fear retaliation, but many of the manufactured goods from these countries are produced by their own subsidiaries. By contrast, the restriction on log exports was approved in large measure because *no American company stood to lose by it;* its costs fell exclusively on foreign firms and workers.

The second reason has to do with American obligations under, and commitment to, the GATT. The Bush administration opposed the "circle of poison" legislation because it threatened to undermine its negotiating stance vis-à-vis the Europeans in the Uruguay Round.

Likewise, the Office of the USTR was not about to let the complaints of antismoking activists interfere with its statutory responsibility to challenge the efforts of foreign governments to evade their obligations under the GATT. Significantly, the Bush administration put considerable effort into drafting the language of the log export ban to make it qualify under Article XX of the GATT by emphasizing that the export ban was imposed in conjunction with domestic restrictions on logging. And for its part, the Clinton administration backed the S&P agreement as part of its broader commitment to complete the Uruguay Round.

Still, an important change has taken place in the politics of American trade and regulatory policy—formerly distinctive policy arenas which are increasingly overlapping. Public interest groups have now become active participants in the debate over American trade policies. They now are as critical of the USTR and the American negotiating stance in the GATT as they traditionally have been of the domestic policies of American regulatory agencies. They have become much more aware of the ways in which American trade policies affect public health, safety, and environmental quality in both the United States and other countries. In a sense, the "adversary relationship" has gained a new dimension: in addition to challenging the interests of domestic producers, public interest groups are now challenging both foreign producers and American exporters. Their criticisms of unaccountable GATT dispute panels or of business domination of the Codex Commission echo the complaints they have frequently made of regulatory bodies in the United States.

This development has had two important consequences. First, it has influenced the terms in which American trade policies are discussed and debated: they are now much more likely to include a debate over their impact on health, safety, and environmental regulations than in the past. Second, it has provided producers opposed to trade liberalization with important new political allies in the form of public interest groups. Not only do American NGOs enjoy more political influence than trade unions, but their concerns are more likely to resonate with the American public. In short, the consumer and environmental movements have enlarged the constituency for nontariff barriers to trade.[82] As one activist proclaimed, "When they call me protectionist, I respond, 'Well, if protecting the earth, if protecting the air, if protecting the water, and indeed human life on the planet is protectionist, then I have to admit that I am protectionist.'"[83]

The coalition between public interest groups and protectionist producers has benefited both constituencies. For example, the "circle of poison" bill would not have garnered as much support as it did without the backing of an important segment of the farm community. Likewise, it was the backing of American environmentalists which enabled northwest sawmill operators to persuade the Bush administration to agree to restrictions on log exports: the log export ban protects both the American environment *and* American loggers—at the expense of Japanese wood processing companies. On the other hand, an important reason for the lack of success of the anticigarette lobbies was that no domestic industry stood to benefit by discouraging exports of this product: there were Baptists, but no bootleggers.

Baptist–bootlegger alliances are not, of course, unique to the United States. As this book has repeatedly demonstrated, they have come to play an important role in regulatory and trade politics within the European Union as well as in Japan. But given the relative political strength and influence of the American public interest organizations, they have become particularly significant in the United States. As the Clinton administration's modifications of the Dunkel draft reveals, to date the most important way public interest groups have affected American trade policies has been not so much by imposing additional restrictions on either imports or exports as by making the terms of trade agreements more compatible with the maintenance and strengthening of regulatory standards. Their impact has been particularly important in the case of NAFTA, discussed in the next chapter.

-7-

Reducing Trade Barriers in North America

The impact of trade liberalization on environmental and consumer standards played an important role in the debate over both the Free Trade Agreement, between the United States and Canada, and the North American Free Trade Agreement, which extended the free trade zone to include Mexico. In the case of the FTA, this debate primarily took place within Canada; in the case of NAFTA, it took place largely within the United States. In part due to the political strength of non-governmental organizations in the United States, and in part due to the strength of the United States' government relative to Mexico's, NAFTA is a much greener trade agreement than the FTA. Thus, while the regulatory provisions of the FTA closely resemble that of the GATT, NAFTA bears a closer resemblance to the Single European Act. While the FTA has had relatively little discernible impact on the regulatory policies of either the United States or Canada, NAFTA is likely to contribute to a shift in national regulatory standards and their enforcement toward those of the largest and most powerful North American nation.

The Free Trade Agreement

In early 1986 the United States and Canada began negotiations aimed at reducing or eliminating trade barriers between the two countries. An agreement was finalized in the fall of 1987 and signed by President Reagan and Prime Minister Mulroney on January 2, 1988. On the whole, the American business community strongly supported the

218

FTA, although there was some opposition from various natural resource and agricultural producers. However, neither American consumer nor environmental groups participated in the congressional debate over its ratification.[1] It was approved by Congress in the fall of 1988, acting under fast-track negotiating authority.

The response to the agreement in Canada differed markedly from that in the United States. Following its passage by the lower house, the agreement was stalled in the Senate. Prime Minister Mulroney then dissolved Parliament and called for a new election. This election was dominated by the issue of free trade and the long-term impact on Canadian society of closer economic integration with the United States. Many Canadians expressed concern that the removal of trade barriers to American goods would both overwhelm Canadian producers and undermine Canada's political and cultural autonomy. The leader of Canada's Liberal opposition party claimed that Mulroney had "sold Canada down the river."[2]

The Politics of Ratification

The effect of the trade agreement on Canadian environmental policy figured prominently in the public debate over the treaty. For the most part, Canadian environmentalists strongly opposed the FTA.[3] In particular they objected to the treaty's impact on the conservation policies of both the provincial and central governments of Canada. A clause in the FTA prohibited the Canadian government from limiting exports of nonrenewable resources, including energy, unless domestic sales were similarly restricted. This provision was criticized not only for undermining Canada's control over its natural resources, but for biasing Canada's energy and resource policy toward extraction and away from conservation.[4]

Environmental and consumer groups were also troubled by the agreement's potential impact on Canadian regulatory policies. According to its critics, the agreement's provisions left unanswered some critical questions. For example, would differences in environmental requirements and conservation programs between Canada and the United States be considered "subsidies" and therefore constitute unfair trade practices? Would the agreement require Canada to modify some of its future regulatory standards—either upward or downward—to bring them more in line with those of the United States?

The FTA's commitment to the harmonizing of American and Canadian pesticide standards particularly worried Canadian environmentalists, since they considered American standards to be too lax. Pesticide approval in the United States is based on a balancing of risks and benefits, while the Canadian Pest Control Products Act only focuses on the safety of the proposed pesticide. According to a Canadian environmental lawyer, "The difference between the two approaches . . . explains why there are twenty percent more active pesticide ingredients registered for use in the United States and over seven times as many pesticide products."[5]

Environmentalists also criticized the Canadian government for negotiating a comprehensive trade agreement likely to have a significant impact on the Canadian economy without attempting to assess its environmental ramifications. They were disturbed as well by the Canadian government's statement that "the free trade agreement is a commercial accord . . . not an environmental agreement . . . The environment was not, therefore, a subject for negotiations; nor are environmental matters included in the text of the agreement."[6]

The opposition of Canadian environmentalists to closer economic integration with the United States in part reflected the ongoing and long-standing dispute between Canada and the United States over American "exports" of acid rain to Canada. For more than a decade, the Canadian government had been unsuccessfully pressuring the United States to require coal-burning power plants near the Canadian border to curb their emissions of sulphur oxides. Numerous bills to curb these emissions had been introduced in Congress, but none had been approved due to both opposition from the Reagan administration and a lack of agreement within Congress about how the costs of abatement were to be allocated among the states. In 1988 the Province of Ontario joined with several American states whose forests and lakes were also being damaged, as well as with American environmental organizations, to request that the Environmental Protection Agency enforce Section 115 of the Clean Air Act, which addresses international pollution controls. After EPA refused to do so, a lawsuit was filed, which was still pending while the debate over Canadian ratification of the FTA was taking place.

While public opinion polls reported that the majority of Canadian voters opposed the trade agreement, the Conservative Party won a majority of seats in the new Parliament. As a result, the treaty was officially ratified by Canada in December 1988 and went into effect the following month.

The Terms of the Agreement

The Free Trade Agreement subsumes rather than supersedes each nation's current trade laws or obligations. But while based primarily on GATT and GATT principles, its scope and coverage are significantly greater in a number of respects. The FTA phases out all tariffs between the two countries over a ten-year period. In addition, the agreement applies the GATT principle of national treatment to all government policies that restrict trade. Thus, while each nation maintains its policy independence, whatever policies it enacts must be applied equally to all goods, regardless of where they are produced or the nationality of the firm that produces them. However, these principles apply only to new or changed regulations, not to existing ones— even if the latter violate the principle of national treatment.

The treaty specifies that health, safety, environmental, or consumer regulations are not to be considered trade barriers: it affirms that the "right to maintain regulations to protect human, animal and plant life, the environment . . . is a sovereign issue for each country to decide."[7] However, it also states that regulatory actions whose effect is to restrict trade will only be permitted if it can be demonstrated that they "achieve a legitimate domestic objective," and it specifically precludes the use of standards-related measures as disguised trade barriers.[8] In addition, Article 608 commits the two countries to recognize each other's accreditation systems for testing facilities, inspection agencies, and certification bodies.

Equally important, both nations agreed to coordinate their product standards to reduce their role as trade barriers by establishing "equivalent" (defined as "having the same effect") technical regulations and standards and, in the case of agricultural products, to move toward harmonization.[9] The agreement's chapter on agriculture specifically pledges both nations "to make equivalent or to harmonize, where possible, testing and evaluation procedures, labeling requirements and residue tolerances for certain chemical products," including fertilizers and pesticides.[10]

The FTA also contains a much stronger mandate than the GATT Tokyo Round agreement to ensure compliance with the agreement by subnational governments. This reflects the fact that both the United States and Canada are federal systems in which state and provincial governments play important regulatory roles. The language of the FTA is similar to that of the Uruguay Round agreement: both are required to "ensure that all necessary measures are taken in order to give effect to its provisions, including their observance . . . by state, provincial and local governments."[11] The legislation approved by both nations implementing the trade agreement further states that "its provisions prevail over any conflicting state law."[12]

The FTA established a Canada-United States Trade Commission, whose principle participants are the senior trade officials from each country. It oversees the working of the agreement and resolves disputes arising from its interpretation or implementation. If disputes cannot be settled within thirty days after being referred to the Commission, they are sent to an arbitration panel. FTA dispute panels operate on a strict timetable and their decisions must be accepted by both parties. This latter provision parallels the tightening of dispute settlement procedures in the newly established World Trade Organization.

Conservation Trade Disputes

The first trade dispute between Canada and the United States under the FTA involved a conservation issue whose origins predated the treaty. In 1980 Canada began to prohibit the export of unprocessed herring and salmon. Canadian officials argued that this regulation was necessary to enable them to maintain quality controls over their fish exports and thus ensure their access to a highly competitive international market. During the mid 1980s, the United States complained to the GATT, which in 1987 ruled against Canada on the grounds that Canada had not imposed comparable restrictions on domestic food processors and consumers (see Chapter 4).

Following the adoption of the GATT panel's report on Canadian fish exports, Canada revoked its regulations prohibiting the export of unprocessed herring and salmon. However, it also imposed new regulations. It now required that five species of salmon as well as all commercial harvest of roe herring caught in waters off Canada's west coast be first brought ashore at a licensed fish landing station in British Columbia for biological sampling—after which they could be exported. Canadian officials argued that this requirement was necessary in order to enable them to promote the conservation of these important species, which were being depleted due to inadequate fisheries management.

The United States complained that although the new regulations were worded so that they did not directly affect exports, their clear *effect* was discriminatory since the burden of compliance fell exclusively on exporters.[13] By contrast, fish purchased by Canadian processors would be landed in Canada in any event. Accordingly, the Canadian requirement was really an export restriction due to "the extra time and expense U.S. buyers must incur in landing and unloading, as well as dockage fees and product deterioration."[14] American officials went on to argue that the laws's real purpose was to protect British Columbia's fish processing industry from American competition, since fresh fish has to be processed as soon as it is brought ashore. In sum, "the Canadian landing requirement was an environmental policy acting as a disguised restriction on international trade."[15]

After consultations between the two nations failed to resolve the dispute, the United States had the choice of seeking settlement under either the GATT or the FTA. It chose the latter. But whichever venue it had chosen, the legal basis of the American complaint was identical, since the relevant provisions of the GATT had been incorporated into the FTA.

The dispute panel concluded that the Canadian regulation, while ostensibly an internal measure, was in fact a trade restriction, since it imposed a "materially greater commercial burden on exports than domestic sales." According to the panel, "the cost of complying with the landing requirement would be more than an insignificant expense for those buyers who would have otherwise shipped directly from the fishing grounds to a landing site in the United States."[16]

The second issue addressed by the panel was whether or not the Canadian rule was justified by the "exception" clause of Article XX of the GATT, which also had been incorporated into the FTA. Drawing upon the criteria established by the 1987 GATT ruling on Canada's export ban, the panel argued that for Article XX to be applicable, the *primary* aim of the trade restriction had to be conservation. Employing a cost-benefit test, it concluded that this was not the case, since it was highly unlikely that Canada would have imposed the same requirements "if its own nationals had to bear the actual costs of the measure."[17] Moreover, the landing requirement failed the "proportionality test," since Canada could have achieved the same conservation objectives by exempting a portion of the catch from the landing requirement. The panel specifically suggested that allowing between 10 and 20 percent of the fish catch to be exported directly would not adversely affect Canada's conservation program.

The reaction of the two governments to the panel ruling suggested the depth of their differences over this long-standing commercial dispute. Canada's Ministry of International Trade, Fisheries and Oceans issued a press release that accepted the panel's report, but added that it had "found that a landing requirement is a legitimate conservation measure."[18] American officials, in turn, offered a rather different interpretation. Noting that the panel members had suggested an alternative to the landing requirement, they complained that Canada had read "the findings in the narrowest way possible to maximize protection for west coast interests."[19] Officials from both nations were troubled by the resulting impasse. A U.S. government official predicted that the dispute "could have adverse effects for the FTA," while his Canadian counterpart acknowledged that the dispute over the meaning of the panel's ruling did not augur well for the future of an agreement whose purpose was to liberalize trade.[20]

However, both nations did agree to accept the panel's primary recommendation, specifically that Canada could require that between 80 and 90 percent of fish caught in Canada be processed there, even if they continued to disagree over the meaning of the panel's ruling. Canada continued to insist that the panel had upheld its sovereign right to impose conservation programs; an advisor to the Canadian government told a Senate committee that "Canada had got what it wanted from the panel report because it can still require 80 to 90 percent of the catch to be landed for conservation purposes."[21] American officials in turn also declared "victory," since the panel had upheld their complaint that "the landing requirement was an unfair trade restriction disguised as a conservation measure."[22]

Following additional negotiations both sides announced a compromise agreement: 75 percent of the catch must be first landed in Canada, while the remaining 25 percent could be directly exported. The Americans regarded this outcome as satisfactory, but it upset both the government and fisheries processing industry of British Columbia. B.C. International Business Minister Elwood Veitch predicted that "this decision will have negative impacts on this important resource and the industry that supports it."[23] The executive director of the Fisheries Council of British Columbia complained that "what the panel decision actually does is strike down a legitimate resource conservation scheme and recommend substitution of an expensive, loophole-laden, unmanageable dual reporting scheme."[24] A Canadian environmental lawyer concluded that "the salmon and herring case illustrates that in a contest between environmental and trade objectives, the former is not likely to come out the winner," adding that "the implications of this precedent for other conservation programs are very serious."[25]

The following year another trade dispute broke out between the two countries over fishing rules, this one brought by Canada against the United States. In order to conserve its domestic lobster stocks, the United States had limited the harvesting and marketing of lobsters below a certain size. However, the mixing of smaller Canadian lobsters with American lobsters had made it difficult for American officials to enforce this restriction, since American fishermen frequently used fraudulent documentation to "prove" the Canadian origins of their undersized (and under-age) lobsters. In addition, a number of U.S. lobster fishermen complained that the federal size requirement put them at a competitive disadvantage vis-à-vis their Canadian competitors. Accordingly, in 1989 the United States amended the Magnuson Act to make it unlawful "to ship, transport, offer for sale, sell, or purchase, in interstate or foreign commerce, any whole live lobster . . . at a size below that specified by the Act."[26] This restriction applied to all lobsters, regardless of where they were originally harvested.

This legislation significantly restricted sales of mature Canadian lobster in the United States, since due to the warmer temperature of Canadian waters, Canadian lobsters mature more quickly and reproduce when still relatively small. Canada argued that because the ban on the importation of smaller sized lobsters affected only Canadian imports, the size limitation was, in effect, a "trade restriction which the United States is attempting to disguise as a conservation measure."[27] Canada claimed that the Americans were seeking to deprive them of the competitive advantage they enjoyed because their lobsters matured earlier. According to Canadian officials, nearly one-third of Canadian lobster exports were affected by the prohibition, resulting in an annual loss of 40 million dollars. The United States countered that the minimum size requirement was an internal measure that applied equally to domestic and foreign lobsters, not a border control targeted at imports. And because it treated Canadian and American lobsters alike, it was consistent with the GATT principle of national treatment.

In a divided (3–2) vote, the panel upheld the American position on the grounds that the minimum size provisions enacted by the United States were "primarily aimed" at the conservation of American lobsters.[28] The minority opinion, however, took strong issue with this conclusion, arguing that the United States should have been required to demonstrate that its legitimate conservation objectives could not have been met by alternative measures, such as the special marking of Canadian small lobsters or by requiring that lobsters be sorted by size prior to their importation into the United States.

The minority report also reviewed the legislative history of the amendment to the Magnuson Act. While it found a number of statements that underscored the conservation rationale for the lobster size restriction, it also found evidence that another important purpose of the legislation was to remedy the fact that "U.S. lobster fishermen were at a competitive disadvantage because they were subject to more stringent conservation regulations than the Canadians."[29] The minority report concluded that the United States "had not made their case strongly enough to lead . . . to the conclusion that the measures were primarily aimed at conservation."[30]

By contrast, the majority opinion acknowledged that although the Magnuson Act was in part motivated by perceptions of "unfairness" on the part of American lobster fishermen, this did not render the American size restriction illegitimate; on the contrary, it explicitly acknowledged the legitimacy of these perceptions. Surprisingly, neither the majority nor the minority report chose to address the Canadian claim that its lobsters reached sexual maturity at a smaller size than American lobsters because of differences in water temperature.

Environmental Trade Disputes

Ironically, notwithstanding the fears of Canadian environmentalists that the FTA would force Canada to weaken its regulatory standards, the first environmental dispute between the two countries following the enactment of the FTA was prompted by the relative strictness of

American standards. In 1989, following nearly a decade of public discussion and legal proceedings, the U.S. Environmental Protection Agency banned the use of asbestos on the grounds that it posed an unreasonable risk to health and the environment.

A number of American firms challenged the EPA rule on the grounds that the agency's rule-making procedure was flawed. However, the ban's economic impact on Canadian producers was more serious, since Canada supplied 94 percent of the asbestos used in the United States. Equally important, the Canadian asbestos industry feared that the U.S. rule would create a "dangerous precedent" by encouraging the European Community to establish a similar standard.[31] Subsequently, a Canadian mining company and three Canadian labor unions joined the American plaintiffs in their suit against the EPA ban. They argued that "EPA failed to consider the effect of the ban on foreign firms and their employees who supply the U.S. market."[32] More substantively, they contended that the ban was not based on adequate scientific evidence, as it failed to distinguish among the health hazards of different kinds of asbestos fibers. Both Canadian parties claimed that they had a direct interest in the EPA's rule and that, under the terms of the Toxic Substances Control Act, they were entitled to petition for judicial review.

On May 22, 1990, the Canadian government filed an amicus brief in support of the Canadian litigants. It argued that "American treaty obligations under the GATT granted the plaintiffs legal standing to protest EPA's actions, since the treaty requires nations to indicate that their environmental decisions meet international standards, thus preventing countries from using arbitrary environmental rulings as de facto trade barriers."[33] Canada claimed that because the EPA ban was not supported by sufficient scientific evidence, it constituted an import provision which violated the GATT, as well as an unnecessary obstacle to trade according to the terms of the GATT Standards Code. Canada also argued that the U.S. rule violated Article 603 of the FTA, which prohibits both parties from adopting standards-related measures that create unnecessary obstacles to trade, unless they achieve "a legitimate health objective." According to the Canadian government, "to the extent that the EPA rule bans the importation of products that do not cause unreasonable risks to life or health, the rule is not necessary to achieve a legitimate domestic objective, and therefore runs counter to U.S. FTA commitments."[34]

The Fifth United States Circuit Court of Appeals struck down the EPA rule prohibiting the importation, manufacture, processing, and distribution of most products containing asbestos. However, it based its decision solely on arguments about domestic law advanced by domestic parties. The court denied standing to the Canadian plaintiffs on the grounds that "EPA was not required to consider the effect on people or entities outside the United States"; it further noted that "international concerns are conspicuously absent" from the Toxic Substances Control Act.[35] The court suggested that GATT, not the American judicial system, was the appropriate forum for addressing the effects of American domestic regulations on international trade. Canada did not, however, file a formal complaint with either the GATT or the FTA.

Although American courts refused to hear the Canadian petition, the filing of the suit was politically significant: it marked the first time that American environmentalists became aware of the potential impact of the FTA on domestic regulatory policies. Not surprisingly, American public interest organizations were extremely upset by Canada's effort to use the FTA to undermine an American regulatory policy. According to Ellen Haas, the executive director of the Public Voice for Food and Health Policy, "The Canadian challenge sends a chilling message for U.S. regulators faced with making decisions to ban hazardous chemicals."[36] An article in the *Progressive* predicted that had the Canadian position prevailed, an additional 1,900 American lives would have been lost by the end of the decade.[37] The suit also alarmed Canadian environmentalists, for whom it confirmed their long-standing suspicion about the treaty's potential for abuse by producers seeking to weaken the regulatory standards of their trading partners.

The two nations have also been involved in a series of trade disputes stemming from each other's recycling laws. In each of these cases, environmentalists and domestic producers have found themselves on the same side, both seeking to defend environmental policies that also impeded trade. While there is no federal recycling requirement, thirteen American States have enacted recycling laws to encourage the use of recovered materials in newsprint in order to reduce their urban landfill problem. These laws require that certain types of pulp and paper consumed in the state contain a minimum recycled content, which ranges up to 50 percent. The Canadian pulp and paper industry urged Canada to challenge the legality of these laws. According to the Conference Board of Canada, "From the viewpoint of the Canadian pulp and paper industry, . . . [United States recycling legislation is a] disguised nontariff barrier to trade because Canada does not have the supply of recycled fibre to maintain market share in the United States." Canada's largest pulp and paper firm specifically urged the Canadian government to challenge American newspaper recycling laws "as a ploy of United States newsprint producers seeking to gain competitive advantage."[38]

The American state laws have imposed a real hardship on Canada, which is the world's largest producer and exporter of newsprint. Historically, Canada exported 85 percent of its domestic production—75 percent to the United States and 10 percent to Europe. However, since it is expensive to collect and ship waste paper from urban centers in the United States hundreds of miles to Canadian paper mills to transform it into newsprint and then ship it back to the United States, the American recycling requirements have shifted the location of new newsprint production facilities from proximity to forests to proximity to waste paper. Thus, between 1989 and 1992 the percentage of American newsprint imported from Canada declined from 56.3 to 50.3.[39] Canada, however, has not filed a challenge to the United States under either the FTA or the GATT in part because it is unclear if such a challenge would succeed. Needless to say, American environmentalists, as well as American firms involved in the recycling business, have strongly defended American recycling requirements.

In 1992 another trade dispute emerged between the United States and Canada over recycling, this time with American producers challenging a Canadian regulation. It raised issues strikingly similar to the Danish bottles case, which had been decided by the European Court of Justice four years earlier. The dispute dates from the mid-1980s, when the United States began to complain about Canadian restrictions on the sale of American beer in the province of Ontario, where the American market share was only 4 percent. Following a GATT dispute panel decision which addressed the discriminatory distribution practices of provincial liquor boards, a tentative agreement was reached in the spring of 1992. However, the following week Ontario announced a doubling of the tax on all nonrefillable alcoholic containers to 10 cents a can. This tax increased the retail price of American beer sold in aluminum cans from $19.83 to $24.35 per case.

The Province of Ontario described the levy as a "green tax" whose purpose was to encourage the use of bottles, which are refillable. Provincial officials contended that glass bottles are more environmentally efficient, since they can be used an average of 15–18 times; they are also much less likely to end up in garbage cans and landfills. They claimed that without the additional tax, their province's extensive recycling efforts would be undermined: consumers would switch to less expensive imported beer sold in aluminum cans, thus forcing Canadian brewers, most of whom used bottles, to switch to cans as well. According to a Canadian official: "Ten cents seems to be the correct level to make it an effective incentive to change consumer behavior."[40]

American beer companies, along with American trade associations representing aluminum and can manufacturers, claimed that the Canadian tax was a protectionist weapon disguised as an environmental regulation, since virtually all Canadian beer was sold in bottles, while most beer imported from the United States was sold in cans.[41] The Canadians contended that American brewers could avoid the tax by switching to "environmentally friendly" bottles; the Americans replied that the extra weight made bottles too expensive to ship. They also argued that using aluminum cans actually consumes no more energy than the washing, transportation, and refilling of bottles. As further evidence of the protectionist intent behind the Canadian action, they noted that Ontario had only taxed nonrefillable alcohol containers, not cans of soft drinks, juice, and food—an argument similar to that made by the European Commission in the Danish bottles case (see Chapter 3).[42]

The position of the Province of Ontario was strongly backed by Canadian environmental organizations. Zen Makuch, a lawyer with the Canadian Environmental Law Foundation, argued that "the United States has to play by our rules." He added: "The U.S. system should not be imposed on us, when ours is more environmentally sound."[43] However, a columnist for the *Toronto Star* agreed with the United States, describing the tax as "a smoke screen for protectionism."[44] Since the imposition of the 10-cent tax, the consumption of beer in Ontario in nonrefillable beverage containers has declined by 60 percent.

In July 1992 the United States imposed a 50 percent ad valorem tax on beer from Ontario, though this was due to the continuing impasse over the broader issue of market access rather than to the beer can tax. A year later a comprehensive settlement was reached that removed a variety of barriers to exports of American beer, and the United States rescinded its tax. Due to the intervention of the Clinton White House, which did not want to use the FTA to force the Canadians to rescind an environmental regulation, especially in light of the upcoming debate over the environmental impact of NAFTA, Ontario's beer can tax was allowed to stand—much to the chagrin of American brewers, who have seen their market share fall still further since the imposition of the Canadian environmental levy.[45]

In 1992 another trade dispute broke out over the alleged use of a protective regulation as a nontariff barrier. The previous year, after two decades of pressure by the Food and Drug Administration, Puerto Rico agreed to adopt the system used in the fifty states for certifying and inspecting dairy facilities. This policy change ended Puerto Rico's imports from Quebec, Canada, of ultra-high temperature milk processed for long shelf life. Canada promptly challenged the new Puerto Rican standard as a violation of the FTA. In its brief, the United States stated that the case is "of great significance to the Free Trade Pact as it will be the first to interpret the rights and obligations of the United States and Canada with respect to the enforcement of technical standards designed to protect public health and safety."[46]

The dispute panel issued its decision in June 1993. It noted that although "standard-setting is a significant prerogative of States . . . standards have an effect on imported goods which cannot be ignored."[47] However, it went on to state that the FTA "affords broad discretion in the setting of health standards applicable to imported products," provided that these standards applied equally to domestic and imported products and are not intended to afford protection to domestic producers.[48] Accordingly, it concluded that the American regulation did not violate the FTA.

Criticisms

Environmental and consumer groups on both sides of the border have continued to criticize the FTA. For example, in 1991 American consumer groups blamed the FTA for allowing poisoned meat to enter the United States as a result of the "streamlined" meat inspection system established a month after the FTA went into effect.[49] According to Lori Wallach, a staff attorney with Public Citizen's Congress Watch, "One of the little-noticed results of the Canada FTA . . . was the dismantling of meat inspection along the U.S.—Canadian border."[50] Under the new system, only one truck in fifteen is inspected; the result, she contended, was a "terrifying increase in meat imports contaminated with feces, pus-filled abscesses and foreign objects such as metal and glass."[51] American officials claim that the Canadian meat inspection system is equivalent to that of the United States; the American Food Safety Inspection Service informed Congress that it has "more confidence in the Canadian inspection system's ability to ensure wholesome meat than they do that of other countries."[52] However, in 1991 the U.S. Department of Agriculture agreed to withdraw a proposal to end all American meat inspections along the Canadian border.

For their part, Canadian environmentalists have continued to argue that the FTA has undermined the quality of Canada's physical environment, though their criticism has centered primarily on "the structural and economic realities" of free trade itself, rather than on the impact of the FTA on specific domestic regulations.[53] To date, only one Canadian conservation policy has been successfully challenged under the dispute-settlement procedures established by the FTA: British Columbia's fish landing requirement. And this decision resulted in a compromise.

Nor has the trade agreement affected Canadian pesticide regulations. Indeed, even before the FTA went into effect, American and Canadian regulatory decisions were tending to converge. Of the ten high-profile pesticide controversies that have taken place in either country since 1970, the two countries have responded identically in eight of them.[54] Of the remaining two, the American regulation was stricter in one case, while the Canadian standard was stricter in the other.

Canadian regulatory officials have tended to follow the lead of their counterparts in the United Sates, primarily due to the greater scientific resources available to American officials, the dominance of the American media, and the greater size of the American market. These three factors predate the FTA and overshadow it in significance. In 1990 the Canadian government announced that while it will continue to perform independent regulatory evaluations, it planned to rely more extensively on American data generation and analysis for its re-evaluation of existing chemicals.[55] Moreover, many of the differences between Canadian and American regulatory standards have not affected trade. For example, while Canadian tolerances for chemicals in food tend to be more stringent than those of the United States—in part because of the way they are calculated—these regulatory disparities have had no impact on trade in agricultural products because virtually all residues fall well below both countries' limits.[56]

As in the case of the GATT, the number of actual trade disputes between the two countries remains below their potential number. Significantly, both of the disputes that did come before dispute settlement panels involved fisheries conservation, a longstanding source of conflict between the two countries as well as between the United States and many of its trading partners (see Chapter 4).[57] By contrast, neither of the three controversial issues raised by contemporary environmental policies—the U.S. asbestos ban, the paper recycling requirements of American states, and the Ontario beer can levy—went to a dispute settlement panel. Each government backed down from challenging the other's regulations because neither was willing to risk the political repercussions of challenging a politically popular environmental policy, once again illustrating the role of American and Canadian green pressure groups in affecting the outcome of regulatory-related trade disputes. In the one formal case involving a consumer regulation that did go before a disputes panel—Puerto Rico's milk processing standard—the United States' position was upheld. Thus, with the partial exception of Canada's landing requirement, the FTA's dispute settlement procedures under the FTA have had no direct effect on the regulatory policies of either nation.

Moreover, after the FTA was signed, Prime Minister Mulroney persuaded President Bush to begin negotiations aimed at limiting American "exports" of sulfur dioxide emissions which were producing acid rain in Canada.[58] In March 1991 the United States and Canada reached an agreement to limit air pollution that originates in one country and adversely affects the other.[59] Of equally significance, in March 1992 Canada decided to adopt the automobile emission standards of the United States 1990 Clean Air Act Amendments so that automakers would no longer have to build a separate line of models for export to the American market, illustrating the role of one dimension of the California effect,—the lure of greener markets—in strengthening regulatory standards for traded goods.[60]

NAFTA

The regulatory dimensions of the FTA—at least in the United States—were soon overshadowed by the debate over the environmental impact of the proposed North American Free Trade Agreement (NAFTA), which would extend the FTA to include Mexico. Unlike the debate over the FTA, American consumer and environmental organizations were highly visible participants in the debate over approval of NAFTA. In marked contrast to the experience of their Canadian counterparts a few years earlier, their political impact was substantial.

The Environmental Challenge

Following the conclusion of the FTA, the United States began negotiations with Mexico with the goal of creating a free trade zone throughout North America. Much of the impetus for this initiative came from Mexican President Carlos Salinas de Gortari, for whom the expansion of trade and investment with the United States was critical to his plans to liberalize and modernize Mexico's stagnant economy.

American opposition to NAFTA was spearheaded by citrus and vegetable growers, the American textile industry, and the AFL-CIO, all of whom feared competition from Mexican producers. However, in addition to this expected economic opposition, from the outset much of the criticism of NAFTA focused on the treaty's impact on environmental and consumer protection in the two countries. American consumer and environmental organizations expressed a number of concerns about the proposed agreement.

The first had to do with the environmental impact of Mexico's *maquiladora* factories. As a result of an earlier agreement to permit goods produced or assembled by factories in Mexico located near the American border to enter the United States duty-free, nearly 2,000 factories, mostly American-owned assembly plants, had located in this region. But due to the lax enforcement of Mexico's environmental laws, these plants were generating substantial amounts of pollution, much of it toxic. The National Wildlife Federation regarded the issue of border pollution as its highest priority in U.S.-Mexican environmental relations.[61] The National Toxics Campaign reported that many *maquiladoras* were disposing their hazardous wastes illegally, contaminating rivers and streams.[62] Environmentalists pointed out that contamination levels in the Rio Grande were many times greater than those considered safe for recreational use.[63]

Nor were the effects of this pollution confined to Mexico. Raw sewage dumped into the New River in northern Mexico had been carried across the border to California, while Tijuana's lack of adequate waste disposal had polluted beaches in San Diego. In San Elizario, Texas, where a shared aquifer had been contaminated, 35 percent of the children contracted hepatitis by the time they were eight years old, and 90 percent of adults contracted it by the age of 35.[64] An American environmental writer predicted that "if Bush gets his version of free trade between the United States and Mexico, this systematic poisoning of an entire region . . . could prove impossible to stop."[65]

A second related issue focused on the environmental impact of increased American investment in Mexico in general. Many environmental organizations feared that NAFTA would encourage American firms to take advantage of Mexico's laxer enforcement of its pollution laws to relocate their production throughout all of Mexico, thus further exacerbating Mexico's pollution problems—and at the same time costing American jobs. Craig Merrilees, the San Francisco co-director of a grassroots organization opposed to NAFTA, stated: "We think the experience across the border is the best predictor of what will happen under a broader agreement. It's a wild-West, dump-and-run kind of situation that has turned the 2,000 mile border into one big Love Canal."[66]

A third concern revolved around the trade agreement's impact on American regulatory standards. Many public interest groups feared that a free trade agreement with Mexico would result in downward harmonization of consumer health and safety standards, since America's stricter product standards could potentially be challenged by Mexico as nontariff barriers. Mexico is the largest supplier of produce to the United States, and many pesticides prohibited or suspended by EPA are used by Mexican farmers.[67] In testimony before

Congress on NAFTA, American environmental groups frequently cited the Canadian challenge to the American ban on asbestos as a precursor to the kinds of legal challenges to American regulations that Mexico might mount were NAFTA to be approved.[68]

A fourth related issue—which also drew on the experience of the FTA—concerned the impact of NAFTA on border inspections. According to Lori Wallach of Public Citizen, "If meat from Canada has proven a serious concern to American consumers, the danger of not reinspecting meat from Mexico, not to mention Mexican fruit and vegetables, is many times greater."[69] She warned that "if the Mexico agreement follows the pattern of the U.S.-Canada agreement, effective border inspection would be all but stopped."[70]

The Mobilization of Opposition

For American environmental groups, often frustrated by their inability to have a greater impact on environmental policy outside the United States, the political opportunity offered by NAFTA was unprecedented: the debate over the treaty in the United States provided them a vehicle for influencing the environmental policies of a developing country. As Stewart Hudson of the International Program Division of the National Wildlife Federation put it, "We have to take a stand here and set a correct model."[71] For their part, Mexican environmentalists also saw NAFTA as a unique opportunity: working with their counterparts in the United States to shape the treaty's terms could enable them to dramatically increase their hitherto limited leverage over Mexican environmental policy.

The participation of environmental groups in the anti-fast-track coalition helped legitimate congressional opposition to the extension of presidential fast-track negotiating authority, since "opposing fast-track on environmental grounds was easier than arguing the concerns of labor with the attendant risk of being accused of being in the pocket of 'special interests.'"[72] The environmental issue quickly became a focal point for legislators opposed to trade liberalization.[73] Thus House Majority leader Richard Gephardt (D—Mo.), long a prominent opponent of liberal trade policies, stated in a public letter to President Bush that his willingness to support NAFTA depended not only on the treaty being rewritten to protect American jobs, but also on the inclusion of strict environmental safeguards. He argued that "neither

Mexico nor Canada nor America is benefitted by a system that benignly looks upon massive air pollution, poisonous pesticides and child labor as 'comparative advantages.'"[74] Evoking the "circle of poison" argument, Gephardt stated that American farmers "cannot and should not have to compete against farmers who use pesticides that fail to meet U.S. standards."

As the debate over NAFTA heated up in the spring of 1991, both the Mexican and American governments began to recognize that the environmental critique of NAFTA threatened the trade agreement's approval in the U.S. Congress. To demonstrate his commitment to environmental protection to the United States, President Salinas dramatically closed Mexico City's largest oil refinery, a major source of air pollution. On the American front, two months later, the USTR agreed to appoint five representatives from environmental organizations to its top-level NAFTA advisory committees, and the White House pledged to conduct parallel negotiations to develop a border environmental plan with Mexico.

Following these preliminary concessions on the part of the Bush administration, the Natural Resources Defense Council and the National Wildlife Federation agreed to support an extension of fast-track authorization. While most environmental organizations and consumer groups continued to oppose fast track, the President had succeeded in splitting the environmental movement. The support of the NRDC and the NWF played a critical role in securing congressional approval of the administration's request for an extension of fast-track negotiating authority for both GATT and NAFTA. However, the administration's victory was a close one: fast track passed the House by only thirty-nine votes.

Two months after fast track passed the U.S. Congress, the United States and Mexico released a draft plan committing both countries to cooperate to improve environmental quality along their common border.[75] EPA administrator William Reilly stated that the plan was intended to "reassure those who have concern about the environmental consequences of free trade."[76] It called for additional investment in waste water treatment plants, increased restriction on cross-border shipments of hazardous wastes, and the hiring of more officials to enforce environmental laws in Mexico. The following month, USTR Carla Hills assured environmentalists that NAFTA would not be rushed through until proper safeguards were in place. She promised that the United States was "not going to bend environmental and safety commitments," adding that "we've no intention of letting pesticides come in from Mexico as we wouldn't from Italy or France."[77]

In January 1991 both governments announced an integrated plan to clean up the American-Mexican border. The plan committed approximately one billion dollars over three years—about two-thirds of which would come from Mexico—to build water treatment plants, better roads, and solid waste disposal sites along the border. The plan represented the first large-scale attempt to integrate the environmental strategies of the two governments, and it clearly acknowledged the linkages between natural resources and trade. It included funds to construct a 200 million dollar plant to end the water pollution from Tijuana that had closed San Diego beaches, as well as a 19 million dollar sewage treatment facility in Nuevo Laredo, Mexico. In addition, the World Bank approved loans of 50 million dollars to improve environmental enforcement and 200 million dollars to reduce air pollution in Mexico City. To address the latter problem, Mexico enacted legislation requiring that all new vehicles be equipped with catalytic converters.

To emphasize its own commitment to environmental regulation, and at the same time diffuse environmental opposition to the trade agreement, the Mexican government began a crack-down on polluters, doubling the number of its inspectors along the border and temporarily closing hundreds of *maquiladoras* for failing to comply with Mexican environmental regulations. It also passed legislation requiring all new industries to submit environmental impact reports.[78] Sergio Reyes Lujan, under-secretary of ecology in Mexico, promised that Mexico would not become a haven for polluters. He stated: "There should be no doubt that any factory rejected by the United States will not be acceptable in Mexico."[79] Mexican officials argued that NAFTA would help improve the quality of Mexico's environment, both by making Mexico richer and by removing the incentive for firms to locate along the border rather than in the less crowded interior.

By early 1992 environmental objections to NAFTA were shaping the national debate. David Ortman of the Friends of the Earth expressed his astonishment at the number of members of Congress who supported the demands of the environmental movement that the trade agreement and environmental regulation be explicitly linked.[80] Congressman Bill Richardson (D-N.Mex.), a supporter of free trade, called the environment a "wild card" issue, noting that forty members of the House had voted in favor of fast track with the understanding that the treaty would explicitly address environmental issues. He predicted that "what will decide the free trade agreement will not be the commercial side . . . but the environmental issue."[81] In June 1992 more than two hundred representatives—including fifty-seven who had previously supported fast-track authorization—signed a statement that they would not support an agreement that did not include strong environment and food safety provisions.[82]

Bush administration officials continued to insist that a free trade pact would improve Mexico's environment; EPA head William Reilly argued that NAFTA would provide Mexico with "the money to reduce pollution, apply new technologies, support government programs and pay for inspectors, regulators and prosecutors."[83] While acknowledging that the gap between Mexican and American environmental standards was a legitimate cause for concern, Reilly cautioned environmentalists against holding the trade agreement hostage to force changes in Mexican environmental law—and in doing so play into protectionist arguments and risk the possible defeat of the agreement.[84]

NAFTA was officially signed by the heads of state of all three nations shortly after the 1992 U.S. presidential election. However, upon assuming office, President Clinton declined to submit the trade agreement to Congress. Instead, the administration began to negotiate a number of changes in the agreement, including the addition of a supplementary environmental agreement. The changes were announced in the summer of 1993, when the administration submitted the treaty along with the side agreement to Congress.

The Terms of the Agreement

The specific regulatory provisions of NAFTA go significantly beyond the FTA in three important respects. First, NAFTA makes a more ambitious effort to reduce the role of regulations as trade barriers. Second, NAFTA explicitly attempts to prevent trade liberalization from undermining domestic regulatory standards. Finally, the dispute settlement mechanisms established by NAFTA's side agreement on the environment permit the use of both fines and trade sanctions to enforce its provisions. In brief, NAFTA seeks to prevent its signatory nations from using regulations to gain a comparative advantage either by making them too strict or too lax.

The agreement prohibits any country from lowering its environmental standards to attract investment and does not prevent its parties from imposing stringent environmental standards on new investments, provided they apply equally to foreign and domestic investors. It also requires all three countries to cooperate on improving the level of environmental protection, and it encourages, but does not require, the upward harmonization of regulatory standards.

As the direct response to the concerns of environmentalists over the implications of the GATT decision in the tuna-dolphin case, the agreement specifically states that the provisions of several international environmental agreements—including the Montreal Protocol, the Basel Convention on hazardous wastes, and CITES—take precedence over NAFTA. In some cases, it also allows each nation to continue to enforce "generally agreed international environmental or conservation rules or standards," provided they are "the least trade-restrictive necessary for securing the protection required."[85] While this latter clause essentially echoed the "proportionality" doctrine of the European Court of Justice, it leaves open to question whether trade restrictions can be used to enforce the way a product is made or caught in another country if there is no international environmental treaty—precisely the issue that lay at the core of the tuna-dolphin dispute between the United States and Mexico.

NAFTA also attempts to limit the ability of its signatories to use national standards for protectionist purposes.[86] A Committee on Standards-Related Measures will attempt to develop common criteria for assessing the environmental hazards of products as well as methodologies for risk assessment, while a Committee on S&P Measures will seek to harmonize these standards "to the greatest extent practicable" and to minimize their negative trade effects.[87] This latter provision represented an attempt to address a long-standing series of disputes between Mexico and the United States over their respective uses of S&P standards to restrict trade in agricultural products.[88]

For example, in 1989 Mexico had required that U.S. swine be vaccinated for hog cholera thirty days before export—even though U.S. hogs had been free of this disease for more than a decade. For its part, the United States required that Persian limes grown in Mexico undergo a chlorine-based treatment before export in order to eliminate citrus canker, which Mexican growers claim has been eradicated. The United States has also restricted imports of avocados from Mexico, claiming they contain worms, even though worms have not been found in this fruit in Mexico for nearly fifty years. Thus, like the European Union and the World Trade Organization, NAFTA is intended to contribute to reducing the use of regulatory standards that are little more than disguised trade barriers.

At the same time, because the United States was able to exercise more influence over the provisions of NAFTA than over the final terms of the Uruguay Round GATT agreement, the former's treatment of sanitary and phytosanitary standards is more explicit about each country's right to establish or maintain its own standards of protection. While the GATT states that in choosing its level of protection a nation should attempt to minimize negative trade effects, NAFTA permits each nation to determine its own regulatory standards, subject only to the constraint that they have a scientific basis. Thus, unlike the GATT, NAFTA does not subject S&P standards to the least-trade-restrictive test. Nor does NAFTA permit a dispute settlement panel to substitute its scientific judgment for that of a national government.

Equally important, NAFTA permits each nation to maintain its existing federal and subfederal environmental standards. Products that do not meet these standards can be banned, provided that the country's standards are nondiscriminatory and are scientifically based. New standards can be challenged on the grounds that they are discriminatory in their design or application. If one party questions another's standards, the burden of proof is on the complaining country to show that a regulatory measure was inconsistent with the agreement—in contrast to the GATT, which places the burden of proof on the country which enacted the regulation.

The agreement's most innovative feature is its Supplemental Agreement on the Environment, though this agreement is not part of NAFTA itself. It was negotiated by the Clinton administration with considerable input from U.S. environmental organizations. The Supplemental Agreement establishes a Commission on Environmental Cooperation, headed by a Secretariat and Council composed of the senior environmental officials from each country, and advised by representatives of environmental organizations. Addressing some of the criticisms of GATT dispute procedures made by environmental groups following the tuna-dolphin decision, it extends to citizens the right to make submissions to the commission on any environmental issue, requires the Secretariat to report its response to these submissions, and permits, under certain circumstances, its reports to be made public. In fact, the agreement provides more opportunities for non-business participation than current U.S. trade law, which only permits aggrieved producers to file complaints with or sue the International Trade Commission, the body responsible for enforcing American trade laws.

In addition, the Commission was given the authority to consider the environmental implications of both processes and production methods or, in its words, the "environmental implications of products throughout their lifecycles."[89] While the side agreement does not require any of the three signatories to enact new environmental laws, it does authorize the use of fines as well as trade sanctions if existing laws are not enforced, though only fines can be applied against Canada. Although the Commission is empowered to address any environmental or natural resource issue, the range of issues subject to dispute settlement panels is limited to the enforcement of those environmental laws which are related to trade or competition among the parties. However, as the discussion of EU environmental policies in Chapter 3 reveals, the potential range of regulatory policies that fall within this definition is extremely large; it certainly includes production standards for traded goods. NAFTA thus subjects more national regulatory policies to international scrutiny than any other trade agreement negotiated by the United States.

NAFTA and the FTA

An important reason why environmental issues played a prominent role in the debate over the terms and approval of both the FTA in Canada and NAFTA in the United States has to do with geographic proximity. Because of their common borders, both nations had long been directly affected by the environmental policies of their southern neighbors: the air and water pollution generated by the factories located on Mexico's northern border had created serious pollution problems for the southwest region of the United States, while the pollution generated by American midwestern coal burning utilities had contributed to Canada's acid rain problem. Both sources of cross-border pollution had been the subject of long-standing international negotiations, but no satisfactory solution had been reached by the time the negotiations over trade agreements had begun. Moreover, the existence of long borders had made the monitoring of cross-border trade difficult.

Yet the differences between the debate over the FTA in Canada and the NAFTA in the United States were equally striking. What is distinctive about NAFTA is the extent to which environmentalists in the United States were able to affect the terms of public debate, as well as the content of the agreement itself. Their impact stands in marked contrast to the minimal influence of Canadian environmental groups with respect to the FTA. What accounts for this difference?

One factor has to do with the relative strength of American nongovernmental organizations vis-à-vis national policy-makers. The U.S. environmental movement is better organized than its Canadian counterpart and, because of the structure of the American political system, enjoys greater access to the policy process at the national level. Moreover, there has generally been much more public concern about environmental issues and more public support for effective environmental regulation in the United States than in Canada.

A second factor has to do with the enormous gap between the levels of economic and political development between Mexico and the United States on the one hand and Canada and the United States on the other. While the GNP of the United States is significantly larger than that of Canada, the per capita income of the two countries is roughly similar. Moreover, the United States and Canada have comparable political systems: they are stable democracies, with independent judiciaries and competent public administration.

Mexico, on the other hand, is a newly industrializing country. The gap in per capita income between the United States and Mexico is substantial: while Mexico's population is more than one-third the size of the United States, its GNP is only about 4 percent as large. Not only are its environmental problems an order of magnitude greater than those of both the United States and Canada, but Mexico does not possess sufficient political or administrative resources to address them adequately, at least in the short run. Indeed, many of the most important differences between Mexican and American environmental policies have to have less to do with regulatory standards—many of which are comparable—than with their enforcement. Never has a free trade agreement been attempted between nations with such different political systems and economic resources. It is in part for this reason that while the cross-border environmental disputes between Canada and the United States were not resolved until after the FTA was signed, those between Mexico and the United States became a integral part of the negotiations surrounding the approval of NAFTA in the United States.

A third factor had to do with the GATT ruling in the tuna-dolphin case. This ruling was made in August 1991, just two months after Congress had renewed the Bush administration's request for fast-track negotiating authority. While the GATT ruling had nothing to do with NAFTA per se, it significantly increased public awareness in the United States both of the potential conflict between trade agreements and domestic environmental regulations and of the magnitude of the gap between Mexican and American environmental standards. Significantly, the tuna-dolphin case figured prominently in the anti-NAFTA literature produced by consumer and environmental groups.

The Politics of Ratification

The debate over NAFTA sharply divided the environmental community, as it did the business community. A number of organizations, including Friends of the Earth, Public Citizen, and the Sierra Club, strongly opposed NAFTA. They viewed the agreement as both too weak and too powerful: they feared that the environmental side agreement would be ineffective in making Mexico enforce its environmental laws, and that at the same time the agreement itself would be highly effective in making the United States lower its regulatory standards.

But just as significant, six major national environmental organizations, including the Natural Resources Defense Council, the Audubon Society, the Environmental Defense Fund, and the World Wildlife Federation, endorsed the agreement. They concluded that the provisions of the supplementary environmental agreement, on which they had insisted and which they helped the Clinton administration negotiate, offered adequate regulatory safeguards, though they were disappointed that it did not include any specific procedure for raising environmental standards or their enforcement to the highest common denominator.[90]

The opposition of some environmental and consumer groups to the agreement was not able to prevent its narrow approval by the United States Congress in November 1993. Moreover, as the vote approached, their concerns were overshadowed by the debate over the agreement's perceived impact on the U.S. economy: it was the trade-union movement, not environmental and consumer groups, that ultimately constituted the most important and influential component of the anti-NAFTA coalition.

Nevertheless, NAFTA marked a new level of environmentalist participation in the making of American trade policies. Previous debates over trade agreements negotiated by the United States had been dominated by interest groups whose primary concern was their *economic* impact. Now, for the first time, the regulatory dimensions of a trade agreement were politically salient, and environmental groups became active participants in the making of American trade policy.[91]

Moreover, American NGOs did have a major impact on the terms of the agreement and specifically on the inclusion of an environmental side agreement.[92] Unlike labor unions, a number of environmental organizations were willing to support free trade with Mexico in exchange for specific provisions in the side agreement. This in part explains why the powers granted to the Commission on Environmental Cooperation far exceed those granted to its counterpart on labor standards. Literally hundreds of meetings took place between executives of large environmental groups and administration officials. And the support of environmentalists was, in turn, critical to the agreement's congressional passage. As a result of the input and influence of American environmental organizations, NAFTA is a far greener trade agreement than either the FTA or the GATT: not only does it make more of an effort to reduce the use of regulations as trade barriers, but it seeks both to maintain existing regulatory standards and to strengthen regulatory enforcement.

In addition, the debate in the United States over the environmental implications of NAFTA itself led to substantial changes in the enforcement of Mexican environmental policies. For example, the Mexican government, which rarely inspected its industrial plants prior to the debate over NAFTA, conducted more than 11,000 such inspections in 1992 and 1993, resulting in the partial or full closure of several hundred facilities, including seventy in Mexico City. It also established the office of environmental attorney-general to prosecute both domestic and foreign industries. The budget of the Mexican Secretariat of Social Development (SEDESOL), the agency responsible for formulating and implementing Mexican development policy, increased from 4.3 million dollars in 1988 to 88.4 million dollars in 1992. Moreover, annual government spending on environmental protection grew tenfold between 1988 and 1991.[93] Mexico also significantly tightened its automobile emission standards, bringing them into closer alignment with those of the United States. And Mexico's willingness to change the practices of its fishing fleet so as to further reduce dolphin mortality after its victory in the GATT against the United States was a direct response to the NAFTA negotiations.

In a sense, what the debate over the environmental impact of NAFTA accomplished was to make Mexico's access to the American market contingent on improvements in Mexican environmental quality. Thanks to the influence of American environmental organizations, the United States not only pressured Mexico into strengthening the enforcement of its current environmental regulations, but increased its long-term influence over Mexican environmental policies. By agreeing to the supplementary environmental agreement, Mexico has subjected its environmental policies to continuous scrutiny from American producers and American environmental groups. Moreover, because the U.S. market is so much larger, trade liberalization is likely to promote the adoption of American product standards, just as they are being increasingly adopted by Canadian producers as a result of the FTA.

Indeed, this has already begun: in order to promote automotive exports to the United States, Mexico has matched American automotive fuel economy standards; and in 1993, in anticipation of NAFTA's approval, Mexican trucking firms began to order new diesel engines from the United States which meet the emission requirements of the 1990 Clean Air Act Amendments. Thanks both to pressures from American environmentalists as well as their own interest in having identical standards throughout North America, U.S. multinationals are likely to require their Mexican subsidiaries to adhere to product standards similar to those of the United States, once again illustrating the market dimensions of the California effect.

NAFTA remains essentially a trade agreement. The United States, Canada, and Mexico have not created a common market, let alone a North American equivalent of the European Union. Nevertheless, thanks to the provisions of the environmental side agreement and the much larger size of its domestic market, NAFTA has provided the United States with the potential to play a role in strengthening Mexican regulatory policies analogous to Germany's role in strengthening European regulatory standards. On one hand, the institutions created by NAFTA are far weaker than those of the European Union, thus giving the United States much less legal leverage over Mexico than Germany has been able to exercise over its southern neighbors. But on the other hand, the relative size of the U.S. market within North America is far greater than that of Germany's within the EU, thus giving the United States considerably more economic leverage. Accordingly, "The environmental parallel accord for NAFTA is the beginning, not the end, of negotiations on natural resources issues in North America."[94] It is worth recalling that it took the EC more than fifteen years to begin to have a significant impact on the environmental policies of the Community's less green and poorer member states. NAFTA's impact on Mexican environmental regulation is likely to look considerably different fifteen years from now.

There is another even more important parallel between NAFTA and the EU. Like the EU, NAFTA is likely to expand its number of signatories. Chile has already expressed interest in joining, as have a number of other Latin American nations. And just as the EU has insisted that future member states adopt its regulatory standards, so is the United States likely to insist that any nation joining NAFTA agree to a Supplementary Agreement on the Environment similar to that negotiated with Mexico.[95] Thus, just as the expansion of the EU to central Europe will help strengthen those nations' regulatory standards, so will the expansion of NAFTA southward become an important vehicle for the upward harmonization of third world regulatory standards within the Americas. Though overshadowed by the controversy surrounding the greening of the GATT, in the long run both regional trade agreements are likely to play a much more important role in promoting the export of stricter regulatory standards.

-8-

The California Effect

The tensions between protective regulation and free trade could, in theory, be leading to one of two opposite and exclusive outcomes: either free trade will triumph at the expense of protective regulation, or the opposite will occur. According to the first scenario, trade liberalization will steadily undermine national regulatory standards. Finding that the costs of compliance with the strict standards demanded by their citizens have made their products uncompetitive on global markets, and no longer able to protect their industries by tariffs, national governments will be forced to progressively weaken their consumer and environmental regulations. Their competitors would then respond by lowering their standards still further, thus producing a downward spiral of regulatory standards. Likewise, the increasingly powerful international institutions established by trade agreements and treaties will become progressively more vigilant in their scrutiny of protective regulations that "interfere" with trade, thus inhibiting many nations from enforcing regulatory standards stricter than those of their trading partners. Consequently, the influence of consumer and environmental organizations over regulatory policies would decline.

Alternatively, precisely the opposite outcome may occur. Nations may enact an increasing number of regulatory standards that disadvantage importers, including making access to their domestic markets contingent upon other nations adopting production standards similar to their own. According to this scenario, dispute settlement mechanisms would become toothless in the face of these ecoprotectionist challenges to trade liberalization. Correspondingly, protectionist producers and their environmental and consumer allies would increase their political influence over both trade and regulatory policies.

A number of the developments described in this book are consistent with each of these scenarios. In some cases, increased international scrutiny of domestic regulatory policies has expanded, while in others international institutions have proven unable or unwilling to exert effective discipline over national regulatory standards that restrict trade. The decisions of the GATT dispute panels in the tuna-dolphin case, the GATT's success in preventing restrictions on imports of hardwoods from South Asia, and the European Union's Luxembourg, food additive, and packaging directives illustrate the role of trade agreements in weakening some national regulations. Alternatively, Ontario's beer can tax, Denmark's recycling laws, the paper recycling regulations of American states, and the EU's hormone ban demonstrate the growing importance of protective regulations as nontariff barriers.

Not only are there important conflicts between trade and regulatory policies, but their number and significance is likely to increase as regional and international efforts to promote economic integration clash with the continued disparity of national consumer and environmental regulations. The constantly changing and continually expanding regulatory agenda poses a never-ending challenge to trade liberalization. But at the same time, these cases belie a broader and rather counter-intuitive pattern—a third theoretical outcome of the conflict between trade and regulatory policies. True, the steady growth of regulation has interfered with trade, while trade agreements are increasingly interfering with regulation. But what is more significant is that, on balance, both global and regional economic integration has *increased* while consumer and environmental standards have become *stronger*. Given the reasonable expectation that the strengthening of one should result in the weakening of the other, what has made this non-zero-sum outcome possible?

The Impact of Regulation on Trade

Local, national, and, in the case of the EU, regional environmental and consumer regulations do continue to represent important obstacles to trade. Doubtless in the absence of the substantial expansion of health, safety, and environmental regulation over the last three decades, the current level of both regional and international trade would be greater. In addition, the growing participation of consumer and environmental organizations in the making of trade policies has strengthened political opposition to trade liberalization. However, the impact of both developments on liberal trade policies has been limited by three factors: the political influence of internationally oriented producers, the structure and authority of international institutions, and the ability of countries to cooperate in addressing common environmental problems.

First, producers who operate in many markets have a strong interest in making national product standards more similar, in order to reduce their production costs.[1] For this reason, agreements reducing the disparity of regulatory standards for the production and marketing of chemicals, automobile emissions, and health protection measures for agricultural products has been strongly supported by the export-oriented producers in these sectors. Correspondingly, the reduction of nontariff barriers in these sectors constitutes a political defeat for more domestically oriented producers, for whom distinctive national product standards represented a way of restricting imports.

This dynamic helps explain not only the important decision of the European Union to harmonize emission requirements for automobiles in the late 1980s, but why the harmonized standards the EU selected were the ones preferred by Europe's most export-oriented producers—namely, the German manufacturers of medium and large cars. These standards not only made it easier for German manufacturers to sell their vehicles throughout the EU, but because these standards were similar to those of one of their major export markets, they made it easier for the Germans to produce vehicles for sale in the United States as well.

The power and preferences of internationally oriented producers also accounts for both the EU's relatively rapid progress in harmonizing regulations for the marketing of chemicals within Europe as well as the subsequent agreement between the EU and the United States to harmonize their respective testing procedures for chemicals under the auspices of the OECD. None of the major chemical producers in Germany, Britain, or the United States stood to benefit by national regulations that restricted trade. On the contrary, all had a common stake in assuring access to one another's markets.

The influence of producers also played a critical role in the EU's success in reducing nontariff barriers to trade in food and food processing. This effort has been strongly supported by Europe's export-oriented food producers, processors, and distributors, all of whom hoped to benefit from the removal of national regulatory barriers to trade in animals, plants, food, and beverages. The same dynamic accounts for the decision to restrict the use of sanitary and phytosanitary measures as nontariff trade barriers in the Uruguay Round GATT agreement. The initial pressure for incorporating an agreement on S&P standards into the GATT came from American grain processors, among the world's most important agricultural exporters. But their initiative was supported by a number of other nations, whose food producers and processors also wanted enhanced access to one another's markets, including that of the United States. Likewise, the restrictions on the use of food processing standards as nontariff barriers in the North American Free Trade Agreement reflected the interests of both Mexican and American agricultural exporters.

Moreover, the limited success of NGOs in the United States, acting either alone or in cooperation with producers, on restricting American exports of various "hazardous" product was largely due to the greater political influence of American exporters. Thus it was the opposition of the American chemical industry which prevented congressional passage of the "circle of poison" legislation. And the influence of export-oriented American manufacturing and service firms helped defeat proposals to "tax" imports of manufactured products produced according to laxer environmental standards.

The interests of particular firms or the structure of particular economic sectors is not, however, sufficient to explain the extent to which the use of national regulations as trade barriers has been constrained. For example, the decision of the European Court of Justice in *Cassis de Dijon* can hardly be attributed to the political or economic influence of the French liqueur industry, let alone the German alcoholic beverage importer whose complaint initiated the case. Moreover *Cassis* preceded the Single European Act, which did have substantial business support. And while export-oriented European firms undoubtedly played a critical role in the passage of the SEA, their influence does not adequately explain the EU's subsequent progress in reducing nontariff barriers for so many products in so many sectors.

The second explanation for the compatibility between trade expansion and protective regulation has to do with the structure and authority of international institutions.[2] Thus the success of the EU's 1992 program owes much to the fact that the Union created a set of institutions, in which norms, legal principles, and decision-making rules have significantly facilitated both the harmonization of national regulatory standards and the reduction of national protective regulations that restrict trade. In particular, the European Court of Justice has emerged as a powerful institution, comparable in many respects to the Supreme Court of the United States.[3] Its articulation of the principle of mutual recognition, and its application of this principle to strike down numerous national product regulations, have made an immeasurable contribution to European economic integration. Likewise, the EU's decision to establish a system of weighted voting for directives affecting the single market has played a critical role in facilitating the adoption of Union-wide regulatory standards.

Moreover, the EU's 1992 program helped change the outlook of both large and small firms throughout Europe. By encouraging them to think about markets in regional rather than national terms it affected the way they defined their interests. Instead of focusing on the maintenance of domestic regulations and standards that restricted imports, they began to increasingly challenge the regulations of other member states which limited their exports. The result was to create a degree of business support that did not exist before for the idea of the single market and the removal of trade barriers.[4]

The GATT is a much weaker institution than the EU. Nonetheless, it too has played a role in limiting the use of regulations as trade barriers. Significantly, no GATT signatory has yet imposed a tax on imported products which are produced according to laxer environmental standards, in spite of substantial domestic political support for such a measure from protectionist producers and environmentalists in a number of countries, including the United States. Governments have resisted such a tax—and domestic pressures for it—because it would undermine the logic of liberalized global trade and threaten the broad range of benefits provided by open markets.

The response of the international community to the decision of the tuna-dolphin dispute panel provides another indication of the importance of institutional rules. Although this panel's ruling was widely criticized on both environmental and legal grounds, and not officially adopted by the GATT Council, it nonetheless has affected a number of national policies. Even the United States, which chose to ignore the panel's ruling with respect to Mexican tuna imports, has since hesitated to impose additional trade restrictions which would be inconsistent with the panel ruling. Moreover, when the EU subsequently issued its own directive to reduce dolphin deaths caused by tuna fishing methods, in deference to the ruling of the GATT dispute panel, it did not extend its scope to non-EU-owned fishing vessels. Likewise, it was the European Commission's unwillingness to be subject to GATT dispute settlement proceedings that led it to resist the pressures of the European Parliament to impose restrictions on imports of wood from tropical forests. Austria also withdrew its labeling requirement for imports of tropical wood because of pressure from the GATT. And the United States carefully structured its ban on exports of unprocessed logs to make it GATT-consistent.

The FTA has had less impact on removing regulatory barriers to trade between the United States and Canada in part because these barriers were less significant to begin with. However, NAFTA is likely to play a much more important role in reducing national regulations that restrict trade, in large measure because of the relative importance of existing regulatory trade barriers between Mexico and the United States.

The third reason why the increase in regulation has not been more disruptive of trade has to do with the increasing importance of international environmental treaties and agreements.[5] These accords establish minimum, relatively uniform regulatory standards for both products and processes, thus enabling nations to cooperate in addressing common environmental problems while preventing free-riding. They now encompass a wide range of regulatory policies formerly under the control of national governments, including trade in endangered species of both plants and animals, hazardous waste, fishing methods and fisheries management, the production of CFCs, sulphur emissions (acid rain), and the pollution of international waters. While their enforcement is uneven, they have established rules which have significantly contributed to reducing trade conflicts stemming from divergent domestic environmental standards and cross-national environmental spillovers.[6] Although these treaties and agreements are most important at the international level, they have also played a role in the coordination of environmental standards and their enforcement in North America.

Finally, it is important to note that freer trade does not require that nations adopt uniform production standards, since differences in national production costs are an important reason why trade occurs in the first place. Nor does it require that nations adopt identical product standards for traded goods. They can, for example, also agree to recognize one another's standards, consider them to be equivalent, or accept one another's tests. Rather, the compatibility of trade and regulation primarily requires that national regulatory standards for traded products be designed in such a way as to minimize the obstacles they impose on imports.

The Impact of Trade on Regulation

What has been the impact of trade liberalization and agreements to promote it on national regulatory standards? Has the reduction in both tariff and nontariff barriers undermined national efforts to protect consumers and improve the environment?

International trade as a proportion of GNP has significantly increased in every industrial nation since the late 1960s.[7] Yet during this same period, environmental and consumer regulations have become progressively stricter. All industrial nations and a number of industrializing ones now devote substantially more resources both in absolute and relative terms to environmental and consumer protection than they did in 1970.

Compatibility

Since the early 1970s few major economies have experienced a greater increase in their exposure to international competition than that of the United States: between 1970 and 1980 both its imports and exports as a share of GNP more than doubled.[8] And yet American regulatory standards have become substantially stronger during the last quarter-century. The proportion of American GNP devoted to pollution control stood at 1.5 percent in 1972; it has been higher every year since, averaging more than 1.7 percent between 1980 and 1986 and increasing to 2.2 percent in 1992.[9] Annual expenditures on compliance with federal environmental regulations totaled $90 billion in 1990 and increased by approximately $30 billion following passage of the 1990 Clean Air Act Amendments.[10]

Similarly, across the Atlantic the Single European Act's goal of creating a single European market was in large measure motivated by the interests of European business managers and political leaders in strengthening the ability of European industry to compete successfully in the global economy. Yet this same amendment to the Treaty of Rome also authorized and has contributed to a significant strengthening of EU environmental and consumer regulations. Likewise, since the early 1970s Japan has both emerged as a major international exporter and has significantly increased its environmental expenditures.[11]

The compatibility between increased exposure to the global economy and the strengthening of domestic regulatory efforts is also borne out by the experience of Mexico, a developing nation. Since 1986 Mexico has significantly opened up its economy to foreign competition, while between 1988 and 1991 government spending on environmental protection increased ten-fold.[12] The approval of NAFTA will serve to re-enforce both, especially to the extent that Mexico's per capita GNP moves above the level at which the World Bank estimates that national per capita emission levels begin to decline due to an increase in resources devoted to pollution control.[13]

The United States itself provides the clearest example of the compatibility of strict regulatory standards and extensive economic interdependence. As a union of member states, the United States itself is a highly integrated market whose Constitution permits few restrictions on interstate commerce, especially for traded goods. While many regulatory standards are set by the federal government, a number of federal regulatory statutes only set minimum standards. For example, states are permitted to enact stricter controls on automobile emissions than those required for the nation as a whole. States also are free to impose tougher standards on stationary sources of pollution and restrictions on land use. Furthermore, recycling requirements are set by state and local governments.

While states do compete with one another to attract investment, they have generally not chosen to do so by lowering their standards for environmental or consumer protection. On the contrary, many state standards are stricter than federal ones. A number of states have enacted more stringent controls over the use of pesticides, beef hormones, and CFCs than the federal government. Several state and local governments have also established ambitious recycling programs, bans on the use of specific materials in packaging, and strict standards for solid waste disposal and incineration. A number of states also have established their own, stricter air pollution control standards; those imposed on both individuals and businesses by the Southern California Air Quality Management District are among the strictest in the world.

Nor is the United States unique. Subnational governments in other federal systems, including Canada and Australia, have enacted consumer and environmental regulations stricter than those required by their central governments. Indeed, it was precisely the increasing propensity of local governments to establish their own tougher regulatory standards that led the drafters of the GATT agreement on sanitary and phytosanitary standards to include a provision holding central governments responsible for the regulatory standards of subnational political units.

The Costs of Compliance

To be sure, some national regulatory standards have been lowered or delayed as a result of international competitive pressures. For example, in the United States the automobile emission standards of the 1977 Clean Air Amendments were modified by Congress as a response to the American automobile industry's competitive difficulties, while in the early 1980s automobile safety requirements were delayed for similar reasons.[14] And in 1993, the German government agreed to modify its recycling requirements following complaints from German firms that some of these requirements were placing them at a competitive disadvantage. There is also growing concern in Europe that some Union environmental standards have reduced the international competitiveness of European firms and that this may well temper the EU's willingness to impose new regulations on industry.[15] Indeed, California is also finding itself under pressure to modify some of its environmental standards in order to retain and attract investment.

There are undoubtedly trade-offs between international competitiveness and domestic expenditures on protective regulations. Global competition does constrain domestic regulatory policies as it constrains both national fiscal and monetary policies. But these constraints have still left governments with substantial discretion to enact regulations stricter than those of their trading partners. Thus, in spite of several cases of trade regulation conflict, over the long run economic interdependence has been positively associated with the strengthening of regulatory standards.

Why hasn't increased regional and international competition led regions, nations, or subnational governments to compete with one another by enacting *less* stringent consumer and environmental regulations? In other words, why don't national health, safety, and environmental regulations exhibit the "Delaware effect?" In light of recent trends in labor markets, it seems puzzling that regulatory policies have not followed the same pattern as wages—which have been adversely affected by increased international competition in most industrial nations. To take one important example, why have real wages, fringe benefits, and employment security for American automobile workers declined, in part due to increased international competition, while over the same time period automotive safety, emission, and fuel economy standards have been progressively strengthened?

One important reason is that for all but a handful of industries, the costs of compliance with stricter regulatory standards have not been sufficient to force relatively affluent nations, or subnational governments, to chose between competitiveness and consumer or environmental protection. For in marked contrast to labor costs, the costs of compliance with protective regulations have been modest. According to Martin Houldin, the environmental director at the consulting firm KPMG Peat Marwick in London, "The international differences in the cost of labor are generally so much more important that the environment pales into insignificance."[16] This is not to say they are nonexistent: many expenditures to improve environmental quality do reduce output and lower the rate of productivity growth. But in the aggregate, increases in national levels of pollution control expenditures have had little effect on the growth of economic output.[17] Nor have American states with stronger environmental policies experienced inferior rates of economic growth and development.[18]

While production standards obviously can and do affect corporate plant location decisions, for all but a handful of industries the effects are not significant.[19] Within the United States, differences in environmental standards have not been a major factor in plant siting or expansion decisions.[20] Studies of international corporate location decisions reach similar conclusions: only a relatively few heavily polluting industries have shifted their production from the United States largely because pollution control expenses are generally not large enough a share of total costs to make relocation economical.[21] Environmental control costs comprise less than 2 percent of total production cost for most U.S. industries, even though American standards are relatively stringent.[22]

Likewise, expenditures on environmental compliance have not had a significant impact on the trade performance of most American industries.[23] Significantly, Japan, with which the United States has its largest trade deficit, has relatively strict environmental regulations.[24] The OECD reports that "very little evidence exists of firms being transferred abroad in order to escape the more stringent environmental regulations at home."[25] In fact, "multinational companies are increasingly adopting the same environmental standards for their plants, regardless of the country in which they operate."[26] Accordingly, Stewart concludes, "There is no reason to suppose that international competition for comparative advantage will lead nations to adopt inappropriately low environmental standards."[27]

Finally, just as industrial production often imposes public costs, so do protective regulations produce public benefits. Thus expenditures on air pollution may increase agricultural output while improvements in water quality may result in better fishing yields or increased tourism. Equally important, improvements in environmental quality and product safety can improve the health, and thus the productivity, of a nation's workforce and thus reduce national health-care expenditures. They can also create opportunities for export markets for pollution control equipment.[28] In short, while the economic benefits of regulation are difficult to measure, and have often been exaggerated, they are far from inconsequential.

This does not mean that nations are free to impose whatever environmental regulations they wish on firms engaged in international competition. For while stricter environmental standards may not make a nation poorer, neither do they make it richer; greater wealth leads to a preference for strong regulatory standards, not the reverse. But the fact that laxer regulatory standards are not, for all but a handful of industries, an important source of competitive disadvantage, only helps explain why the reduction of tariff and other trade barriers has not resulted in a Delaware effect, that is, movement toward lower regulatory standards. It does not explain why or how trade liberalization and agreements to promote it has contributed to *raising* them; that is, it does not explain the "California effect."

The California Effect

The Delaware effect does apply to some public policies, but the evidence suggests that protective regulations have not usually been among them. On the contrary, a number of national consumer and environmental regulations exhibit the California effect: they have moved in the direction of political jurisdictions with stricter regulatory standards.

The California effect can be seen literally in the history of American automobile emission standards. The 1970 Clean Air Act Amendments specifically permitted California the option of enacting stricter emissions standards than those required for the rest of the United States, an option which California chose. Consequently its standards remained stricter than those of any other state. In 1990, Congress brought national emission standards up to California's and once again permitted California to impose stricter standards. It also gave other states the option of choosing either national or California standards.[29] In 1994 twelve eastern states requested that the federal government permit them to adopt California's new standards.[30] These standards in turn are likely to become the basis for the next round of minimum federal requirements. California has now had America's strictest automotive pollution control standards for more than three decades. Thus, instead of states with laxer standards undermining those with stricter ones, in the case of automobile emissions precisely the opposite has occurred: California has helped make American mobile emissions standards steadily stronger.

The term "California effect" is meant to connote a much broader phenomenon than the impact of American federalism on federal and state regulatory standards. The general pattern suggested by this term, namely, the ratcheting upward of regulatory standards in competing political jurisdictions, applies to many national regulations as well. This pattern has three components: two relate to market forces, and the third has to do with politics. First, to the extent that stricter regulations represent a source of competitive advantage for domestic firms, the latter may be more likely to support them. Second, rich nations which have enacted greener product standards force foreign producers to adjust to them in order to continue to enjoy market access, thus helping in turn to raise foreign product standards. Third, agreements to reduce trade barriers can provide richer and more powerful greener nations with the opportunity to pressure other nations into adopting stricter product *and* production standards.

The Interests of Domestic Producers

How can international competition turn industrial opponents of tougher standards into self-interested promoters of them? First, knowing or anticipating that the burdens of compliance will fall disproportionately on their international competitors may well make domestic producers more willing to support stricter regulations than they would have in the absence of foreign competition. For example, the beer bottlers of both Denmark and Ontario would probably not have supported stricter recycling requirements had not these regulations also served to help protect their domestic markets. Similarly, the success of European consumer groups in persuading the EU to completely ban the use of growth hormones in beef production was facilitated by the support the ban received from Europe's small, relatively inefficient but politically powerful cattle farmers. Likewise, Germany's willingness to support stricter domestic and EU standards for automobile emissions and packaging stemmed in part from the extent to which these standards benefited domestic producers. And the Thai government would not have imposed such severe restrictions on cigarette marketing in the absence of competition from American cigarette companies.

From this perspective, more liberal trade policies, rather than pressing nations to lower their regulatory standards, may actually provide nations with an economic incentive for strengthening them. By contrast, since relatively closed economies can rely on tariffs and quotas to restrict imports, they have less need to adopt protective regulations that advantage domestic producers. In some cases, these regulations may amount to little more than disguised forms of protectionism. Nor do stricter standards necessarily improve consumer or environmental protection. Nonetheless, the self-interest of producers can play a role in strengthening regulatory standards for a number of internationally traded products. In short, Baptist–bootlegger coalitions can serve to advance the legitimate interests of both Baptists *and* bootleggers.[31]

The Lure of Green Markets

The second way in which international trade can drive national regulatory standards upward has to do with market access. The argument that trade promotes the strengthening of environmental standards has primarily rested on the impact of trade on promoting domestic economic growth, hence increasing both the demand for regulation and the ability to pay for it. The evidence demonstrates that another important factor enabling greener countries to promote the export of stricter standards to less green countries has to do with the size and importance of the former's domestic markets.

Political jurisdictions which have developed stricter product standards force foreign producers in nations with weaker domestic standards either to design products that meet those standards or sacrifice export markets. This, in turn, encourages those producers to make the investments required to produce these new products as efficiently as possible. But having made these initial investments, they now have a stake in encouraging their home markets to strengthen its standards as well, since their exports are already meeting those standards.[32]

Thus, the willingness of Germany's automobile manufacturers to support stricter EU standards was in part due to their previous experience in producing vehicles for the American market. It was precisely the firms supplying the largest, wealthiest automobile market in Europe who took the lead in pressuring the EU to adopt the product standards already set by the world's largest, richest market, the United States. They made common cause with German environmentalists to demand the adoption of "US 83" standards by the EU. Significantly, half of German automobile sales in the United States are in California, the political jurisdiction with the world's strictest automotive emission standards.

Indeed, German producers stood to benefit from the EU's adoption of American standards, since they could then produce similar vehicles for both markets at lower cost. Likewise, the subsequent willingness of the French and Italian manufacturers to support the stricter standards of the Small Car Directive stemmed in part from the experience they had gained in producing cars for export to greener markets in Europe and the United States as well as their fear of losing additional export markets to their greener competitors. Significantly, the one European country whose bottlers welcomed Germany's strict packaging law was Denmark, whose producers enjoyed a competitive advantage in recycling their own products due to Denmark's previously enacted recycling legislation.

The pull of greener markets has also served to drive regulatory standards upward in North America. The expansion of trade between the United States and Canada following the Free Trade Agreement prompted Canada in 1993 to establish automobile emission requirements similar to those imposed on vehicles sold in America three years earlier. As barriers to imports of Mexican products to the United States gradually decline as a result of NAFTA, Mexican producers will be forced to redesign their products to meet American regulatory standards. And those producers who do so will then have an interest in pressuring the adoption of similar standards by Mexico, since this will provide them with a competitive advantage over their more domestically oriented competitors. At the same time, American exporters to Mexico may also become a source of political support for making Mexican regulatory standards more similar to those of the United States, since that will enable them to design similar products for both markets.

The pattern of chemical regulation also illustrates the role of international trade and competition in strengthening regulatory standards. It was the enactment of the Toxic Substances Control Act by the United States that prompted the European Union to enact the Sixth Directive. The EU feared that unless its standards were comparable to those of the United States, it would be deprived of access to one of the world's largest chemical markets. As a result, it established a much stricter system for the introduction and marketing of chemical products. Once again, stricter American standards drove those of its major trading partner *upward*.

In the area of conservation, both the United States and the EU have repeatedly used restrictions, or the threat of restrictions, on access to their large domestic markets to force their trading partners to upgrade their regulatory standards. It was the economic pressure of the EU which forced Canada to end its killing of baby seals and which persuaded both the United States and Canada to end the use of leg-traps to catch fur-bearing animals. Likewise, the large size of its domestic market has provided the United States with the leverage to influence the fishing practices of several of its trading partners, thus helping to protect a variety of species, including whales, turtles, and dolphins.

The impact of both these effects of trade liberalization is limited. Specifically, trade liberalization is most likely to encourage a nation to raise its domestic regulatory standards when doing so provides domestic producers with a competitive advantage. This is often the case, but not always. Likewise, the impact of greener markets on promoting the export of stricter standards primarily applies to product standards. While this encompasses virtually all consumer protection regulations as well as those environmental regulations which apply to products, it excludes those environmental standards that seek to address the harms caused by how products are produced. And the latter are extremely significant: thus there are a number of environmental problems in less developed nations, ranging from deforestation to hazardous levels of urban air pollution, which will not be improved by global market forces. This is, however, another mechanism by which trade liberalization can raise standards, one capable of affecting a much broader range of domestic regulatory policies. This has to do with the terms of trade agreements and treaties.

The Politics of Integration

To the extent that treaties or trade agreements provide formal mechanisms for establishing harmonized or equivalent standards, they provide an opportunity for richer, more powerful countries to play a greater role in setting those standards. If the five trade treaties and agreements discussed in detail in this book were ranked in terms of the extent to which their signatories have agreed to reduce the use of regulation as trade barriers, the most powerful would the Single European Act, followed by the Treaty of Rome, the North American Free Trade Agreement, the Free Trade Agreement, and the various rounds of the General Agreement on Tariffs and Trade. If these same five treaties and agreements were to be ranked in terms of the extent to which they contain provisions designed to either maintain or strengthen the regulatory standards of their signatories or members, *the rankings would be identical.* Paradoxically, the more authority nations concede over the making of national regulatory standards, the more likely these standards will be *strengthened.*

The reason for this relationship is *not* that international agreements to promote trade liberalization automatically strengthen regulatory standards; in principle, they can just as easily weaken them. It is politics that makes the difference. Specifically, trade agreements and treaties are likely to maintain or raise regulatory standards when a powerful and wealthy nation insists that they do so. In turn, the powerful nation's willingness to demand that trade liberalization be accompanied by the maintenance or strengthening of health, safety, and environmental standards is in large measure due to the influence of its domestic NGOs and, in many cases, its domestic producers as well. But the ability of a powerful nation to impose its preferences on its trading partners is also dependent on the degree of integration: the more integration, the greater its influence.

Thus, the most important factor driving EU environmental standards steadily, if unevenly, upward has been the power and preferences of Germany, the member state with the largest economy and Europe's most powerful environmental movement. By strengthening the power of the Union over the regulatory policies of its member states, the SEA has in turn increased the leverage of Germany, along with the Netherlands and Denmark, over the environmental policies of the rest of the Union. The SEA could have attempted to promote integration at the expense of stricter consumer and environmental standards. That it did not do so was a reflection of the political and economic power of those member states which wanted both policy objectives to be achieved simultaneously.

Similarly, NAFTA is a much greener trade agreement than the FTA for one simple reason: the United States insisted upon a Supplementary Agreement which extends international supervision over the enforcement of Mexican domestic production standards as well as over the content of a wide range of product standards. It did so primarily because powerful domestic environmental constituencies, whose support the Clinton administration needed to persuade Congress to support NAFTA, demanded it. But the United States in turn was able to insist upon this condition because it was wealthier and more powerful than Mexico. The impact of NAFTA on Mexican regulatory policies and preferences will continue to be strongly influenced by the United

States, the North American nation with both the largest economy and the most influential environmental pressure groups. However, because the international institutions established by NAFTA are weaker than those of the EU, the United States will have less influence over Mexican regulatory policies than Germany, Denmark, and the Netherlands have had over those of Italy or Greece. But at the same time, NAFTA gives the United States more leverage over Mexican regulatory policies than it had under the GATT.

The frustration of environmentalists with the GATT stem in large measure from the extent to which GATT rules limit the ability of nations in which green pressure groups are especially influential to use trade policies to change the environmental policies of their trading partners. Accordingly, "greening the GATT" essentially means expanding the legal basis on which the United States, but also the EU and a number of other countries, can use their economic power to influence the regulatory policies of countries with a weaker commitment to environmental protection. This, however, has not yet occurred, in part due to a lack of consensus regarding the appropriateness of such a shift by the international community in general and the EU, the United States, and Japan in particular. Accordingly, the scope of the California effect remains weakest at the global level. But at the same time, compared with both NAFTA and the EU, the GATT also has much less authority to *weaken* national regulatory standards.

International agreements and treaties to reduce the role of regulatory standards as trade barriers have constrained the ability of greener countries to establish and enforce regulatory standards as strict as their NGOs and some domestic producers have preferred. But what is striking is how infrequently this has occurred and how little it has adversely affected consumer or environmental quality. With the partial exception of British Columbia's fish landing requirements, the Free Trade Agreement between the United States and Canada has not required either nation to weaken its regulatory policies. In the case of every other FTA trade dispute—including the American restriction on sales of lobsters below a certain size, American states' recycling requirements, Puerto Rico's milk processing standards, the American asbestos ban, and Ontario's tax on beer cans—the nation with the stronger regulation was allowed to maintain it, notwithstanding its impact on trade. If anything, the FTA has probably been too differential to Canadian and American regulatory policies: surely the United

States could have been required to devise a less trade-restrictive way of protecting its small, sexually immature lobsters from unethical American lobstermen than restricting the sales of *all* small lobsters.

In the case of the GATT, dispute panels have issued decisions in only seven cases involving the use of regulations as nontariff trade barriers. In two cases, the dispute over America's Superfund tax and American CAFE standards, the stricter national regulation was found to be GATT-consistent. In the case of the five other disputes that came before dispute settlement panels, national rules were successfully challenged. But two of these essentially involved commercial disputes between Canadian and American fishermen with few environmental consequences. In the case of the complaint brought by the United States against Thailand's restriction on sales of American cigarettes, the dispute panel found the import ban to be inconsistent with the GATT, but it upheld Thailand's much more important marketing restrictions on all cigarettes.

This leaves the two cases involving American restrictions on imports of tuna, both of which were decided against the United States, along with a variety of other more informal efforts on the part of the GATT to discourage import restrictions based on production standards. But the GATT's constraints have as much to do with the unilateral nature of these restrictions as with their extrajurisdictional scope. As the unanimous support of GATT signatories for Mexico in its dispute with the United States reveals, the GATT places a high value on multilateralism. In practice, it is highly unlikely that the newly established World Trade Organization would uphold a complaint against an environmentally related trade restriction that was strongly supported by both the United States and the European Union, let alone one taken pursuant to an international environmental treaty. Moreover, trade restrictions represent only one mechanism that countries can employ to influence the regulatory policies of other nations. They are much less effective than international environmental agreements, especially when the latter include subsidies.

The international institution that has played the most important role in challenging national environmental and consumer regulations has been the European Union. EU directives have frequently prevented the Union's greener member states—most notably Germany, the Netherlands, and Denmark—from enacting stricter regulations for traded products on the grounds that these threaten the single market.

But these ceilings have been more than counter-balanced by the Union's role in progressively strengthening the regulatory standards of the EU's other member states. Moreover, in some cases, most notably the beef hormone ban and the small car directive, the EU's interest in preserving the single market has led it to adopt the regulations of the member state with the strictest standards. Thus, on balance the EU has strengthened both environmental and consumer standards within western Europe. Equally important, the EU's regulatory directives cover *all* consumer and environmental standards which directly affect the health, safety, or environment of its member states and their citizens.

Any assessment of the impact of trade agreements and treaties on national regulatory standards must distinguish between regulations that actually protect the public and those which are actually disguised forms of protectionism. Virtually all of the protective consumer regulations that have actually been eliminated or modified as a result of national obligations under an international agreement or treaty fall into the latter category. This is true of the literally thousands of food labeling and composition standards of the member states of the EU, as well as Japanese S&P standards that have been modified as a result of pressures from its trading partners. Subjecting these regulations to international scrutiny has made consumers better, not worse, off. In these cases, the benefits of trade liberalization have paralleled those of domestic economic deregulation.

It is true that as the authority of international institutions over national regulatory standards increases, so does the possibility that legitimate national regulatory policies will be undermined. Moreover, the distinction between consumer and environmental protection and consumer and environmental protectionism is not always obvious: it is not always possible to sharply distinguish between the California and Delaware effects. Thus, both NAFTA and the WTO's Agreement on Sanitary and Phytosanitary Standards could result in weakening some regulations that arguably do enhance consumer protection. But if the experience of the EU is any guide, on balance they are much more likely to improve public welfare by forcing the elimination or modification of the large number of national regulations which mainly benefit producers. And if the experience of the FTA is any indication, highly visible national regulations that are strongly supported by NGOs will often manage to escape international review.

Indeed, it is more likely that regulations which are barely disguised forms of protectionism will be maintained than it is that regulations which provide clear public benefits will be weakened.

Finally, it is important not to equate the California effect with regulatory convergence. The ratcheting upward of regulatory standards is a dynamic process. As the standards of regulatory laggards are strengthened, so are the standards of the regulatory leaders likely to change as well. The regulatory agenda of green countries is highly unstable: new issues, and new regulations, keep emerging. As a result, the California effect may not reduce the disparity among national regulatory standards; indeed, it may even increase them. What it does do is ratchet national regulatory standards upward.

Regulation and Political Power

The argument that rich, powerful countries can strengthen the regulatory standards of their trading partners through both economic and political mechanisms is premised on the association between national wealth and power, and national preferences for stricter environmental and consumer regulations. The California effect requires both that political jurisdictions with stronger regulatory standards be rich and powerful, and that nonstate actors in rich and powerful political jurisdictions prefer stronger regulatory standards. Accordingly, it is unlikely that Delaware would have been able to insist on its own stricter automobile emission standards, let alone serve as a model for the rest of the United States. California's impact on both American and European regulatory standards is a function of the size of its "domestic" market.

Thus, had Portugal been the EU's greenest member state and Germany been indifferent to stronger regulatory standards, the impact of the EU on European environmental standards would have been rather different; they might well have been driven downward. A similar outcome might be expected to occur in North America if Mexican environmental pressure groups were relatively strong and those in the United States relatively weak. Likewise, relatively few of their trading partners would care if India or Finland, rather than the United States or the EU, had made access to their domestic market contingent on improvements in the international or domestic conservation practices of their trading partners. Likewise, if support of Germany and the

United States for stronger regulatory standards were to diminish, their trading partners would find themselves under less pressure to raise their regulatory standards.

Nor is their anything automatic about the commitment of richer countries to improve the regulatory standards of their trading partners. The former's policy preferences are dependent on the preferences of domestic constituencies. For example, it is unlikely that an Asian common market or free trade zone dominated by Japan, a rich nation with a weak environmental movement, would exhibit the same pattern of regulatory policy-making that has occurred in Europe or is beginning to occur in North America. While Japan does have extremely strict domestic product standards which its trading partners have to meet, it has not played a leadership role in seeking to address global environmental issues. Nor has it attempted to use its considerable economic and political leverage to link Asian economic integration to the strengthening of environmental standards in other Asian nations. Indeed, it is Japan itself which has been subject to pressures from its trading partners, most notably the United States, to improve its environmental practices, especially in the area of wildlife protection.[33] Moreover, while Japan has relatively strict product standards, their international impact is limited by the fact that Japan imports relatively few manufactured goods from its less green trading partners in Asia.

The future regulatory impact of an organization such as the Asia-Pacific Economic Cooperation group will primarily depend on whether Japan chooses to use its political and economic influence to improve the environmental practices of its trading partners. And this in turn will depend in part on the preferences and political influence of Japanese environmental organizations, which to date have been both less influential and less interested in environmental problems outside their nation's borders than their counterparts in the United States and the EU. By the same token, were China to replace the United States as the world's largest economy and its regulatory policies to remain unchanged, the dynamics of global regulatory policy-making would be altered significantly. In sum, the impact of increased integration on regulatory standards depends on the policy objectives of powerful nations, which are largely determined domestically.

To date, increased economic integration has, on balance, contributed to strengthening national regulatory policies, especially for traded goods and—in the case of the EU and, to a lesser extent, NAFTA—for domestic production standards as well. Whether or not it continues to do so depends on the preferences of the world's richest and most powerful nation states. The increased integration of regional and global markets in a "borderless world" has not led to a decline in the importance of national power. On the contrary, the globalization and regionalization of regulatory policy-making has extended the influence of both producers and nongovernmental organizations in rich and powerful countries over the regulatory policies of nations with whom they trade and with which their economies have become integrated. In the final analysis, the impact of trade and trade agreements on regulatory standards is determined by the interaction of domestic and international politics.

Notes

Preface

1. U.S. Congress, Office of Technology Assessment, *Trade and Environment: Conflicts and Opportunities* (Washington, D.C.: U.S. Government Printing Office, May 1992). *The Greening of World Trade: A Report to EPA from the Trade and Environment Committee of the National Advisory Council for Environmental Policy and Technology* (Washington, D.C.: U.S. Government Printing Office, 1993). *Environmental Effects of Trade* (Paris: Organization for Economic Co-Operation and Development, 1994). F. Schmidt-Bleek and H. Wohlmeyer, *Trade and Environment: Report on a Study Performed by the International Institute for Applied Systems Analysis and the Austrian Association for Agricultural Research* (Laxenburg, Austria: 1991). Patrick Low, ed., *International Trade and the Environment: World Bank Discussion Papers* (Washington, D.C.: World Bank, 1992.)

2. Durwood Zaelke, Paul Orbuch, and Robert Housman, eds., *Trade and the Environment: Law Economics and Policy* (Washington, D.C.: Island Press, 1993). Kym Anderson and Richard Blackhurst, eds., *The Greening of World Trade Issues* (Ann Arbor: University of Michigan Press, 1992). Heraldo Muñoz and Robin Rosenberg, eds., *Difficult Liaison: Trade and the Environment in the Americas* (New Brunswick: Transaction Publishers, 1993). C. Ford Runge, *Freer Trade, Protected Environment: Balancing Trade Liberalization and Environmental Interests* (New York: Council on Foreign Relations, 1994). Daniel C. Esty, *Greening the GATT: Trade, Environment and the Future* (Washington, D.C.: Institute for International Economics, 1994).

3. For comprehensive bibliographies, see *Bibliography of Trade and Environment Literature* (Paris: OECD, 1993), and Esty, *Greening*, pp. 281–306.

1. National Regulation in the Global Economy

1. See, for example, Lynton Keith Caldwell, *International Environmental Policy* (Durham and London: Duke University Press, 1990).

2. William L. Cary, "Federalism and Corporate Law: Reflections upon Delaware," *Yale Law Journal*, 83 (1974): 663–705. In fact, students of corporate law disagree as to whether Delaware's standards for corporate chartering are actually weaker. I use the "Delaware effect" as a metaphor.

3. See "California Sunshine" in Curtis Moore and Alan Miller, *Green Gold* (Boston: Beacon Press, 1994), pp. 105–124.

4. This paragraph is based on Steve Charnovitz, "Exploring the Environmental Exceptions in GATT Article XX," *Journal of World Trade, 25*, no. 3 (October 1991): 40.

5. According to a study by Gene Grossman and Alan Krueger, "environmental quality tends to improve as a nation's per capita gross domestic product approaches $8,000 in 1985 dollars on a purchasing-power basis." Gene Koretz, "A Robust Economy Can Help Cure a Sick Environment," *Business Week*, May 23, 1994.

6. Steve Charnovitz, "The World Trade Organization and Environmental Supervision," *International Environment Reporter*, 17, no. 2 (January 26, 1994): 92.

7. Robert A. Leone, *Who Profits? Winners, Losers, and Government Regulation* (New York: Basic Books, 1986), p. 44.

8. Edward Luttwak, "From Geopolitics to Geo-Economics," *National Interest*, Summer 1990, p. 18.

9. Martin Shapiro, "The European Court of Justice," in *Euro-Politics*, ed. Alberta Sbragia (Washington, D.C.: Brookings Institution, 1992), p. 131.

10. This phrase was by coined by Bruce Yandle, "Bootleggers and Baptists," *Regulation, 7* (May/June 1982): 12–16.

11. For an account of the enactment of this law, see Gabriel Kolko, *The Triumph of Conservatism* (Chicago: Quadrangle Paperbacks, 1963), pp. 99–108. For Kolko, the support of beef processors for federal meat inspection reveals that this legislation was not a "genuine" example of consumer protection. My interpretation differs.

2. Protectionism versus Consumer Protection in Europe

1. Paolo Cecchini et al., *The European Challenge, 1992* (Aldershot, England: Wildwood House, 1988), pp. 57–58.

2. Paul Gray, "Food Law and the Internal Market," *Food Policy,* April 1990, p. 111.

3. Quoted in T. R. Stocker, "Food Law and 1992," unpublished paper

prepared for Worldwide Information Conference on Food Law: Current Changes and Their Implications (1990), p. 2.

4. Jacques Pelkmans, "Regulation and the Single Market: An Economic Perspective," in *The Completion of the Internal Market,* ed. Horst Siebert (Tubingen: Institüt für Weltwirtschaft an der Universitat Kiel, 1989), p. 94.

5. Quoted in Diana Welch, "From 'Euro Beer' to 'Newcastle Brown': A Review of European Community Action to Dismantle Divergent Food Laws," *Journal of Common Market Studies,* 22, no. 1 (September 1983): 48.

6. Quoted in Commission v. Italian Republic, Case 193/80, 9.12.81.

7. Quoted in Stocker, "Food Law and 1992," p. 2.

8. Quoted in Welch, "From 'Euro Beer,'" p. 48.

9. Ibid., p. 522.

10. C. Burke, "EEC Law and the Food Manufacturer," *RHS,* 97, no. 6, p. 266.

11. Quoted in Gray, "Food Law," p. 112.

12. Ibid., p. 111.

13. Shawn Tully, "Europe Gets Ready for 1992," *Fortune,* February 1, 1988, p. 83.

14. David Brooks, "Jam Sessions," *New Republic,* November 4, 1991, p. 20.

15. Quoted in Welch, "From 'Euro Beer,'" p. 55.

16. Ibid.

17. John Abraham and Erik Millstone, "Food Additive Controls: Some International Comparisons," *Food Policy,* 14, no. 1 (February 1989): 43–57.

18. John McCarthy, "Protectionism and Product Harmonization in the EEC," *Economic and Social Review,* April 1979, p. 191.

19. Stephen George, *Politics and Policy in the European Community* (Oxford: Oxford University Press, 1991), p. 159.

20. Tully, "Europe Gets Ready," p. 83.

21. McCarthy, "Protectionism," pp. 188–189.

22. Karen Atler and Sophie Meunier-Aitsahalia, "Judicial Politics and Commission Entrepreneurship: European Integration and the Pathbreaking *Cassis de Dijon* Decision," *Comparative Political Studies,* 26, no. 4 (January 1994): 551.

23. Quoted in Alan Swinbank, "EEC Food Law and Trade in Food Products," *Journal of Agricultural Economics,* September 1982, p. 345.

24. Mitzi Elkes, "Europe 1992: Its Impact on Nontariff Barriers and Trade Relations with the United States," *Food, Drug and Cosmetic Law Journal,* September 1989, p. 471.

25. Ibid.

26. G. Chambers, *Food Hygiene Policy and 1992,* Scientific and Technological Options Assessment, European Parliament, May 17, 1990, p. 36.

27. Quoted in Welch, "From 'Euro Beer,'" p. 60.

28. Ibid., p. 61.

29. Quoted in ibid., p. 60.

30. Quoted in ibid., p. 62.

31. Quoted in "Environmental Protection and the Free Movement of Goods: The Danish Bottles Case," *Journal of Environmental Law*, 2, no. 1 (1990): 93.

32. Quoted in Alter and Meuiner-Aitsahalia, "Judicial Politics," p. 5.

33. Quoted in T. Venables, "The Impact of Consumer Protection on International Trade," presented at an OECD Symposium on Consumer Policy and International Trade, Paris, November 1984, p. 15.

34. Frank Fine, "Foodstuffs with Additives: Free Movement within the EC," *British Food Journal*, 94, no. 8 (1992): 26.

35. Welch, "From 'Euro Beer,'" p. 64.

36. Renaud Dehousse, "Integration v. Regulation? On the Dynamics of Regulation in the European Community," *Journal of Common Market Studies,* 30, no. 4 (December 1992): 397.

37. Quoted in ibid.

38. Alan Dashwood, "Hastening Slowly: The Community's Path towards Harmonization," in *Policy-Making in the European Community,* ed. Helen Wallace, William Wallace, and Carole Webb (New York: John Wiley & Sons, 1983), p. 182.

39. Quoted in Atler and Meunier-Aitsahalia, "Judicial Politics," p. 545.

40. *Completing the Internal Market* (Luxembourg: Commission of the European Communities, 1985).

41. Quoted in Henk Folmer and Charles Howe, "Environmental Problems and Policy in the Single European Market," *Environmental and Resource Economics,* 1 (1991): 19.

42. P. S. Gray, "EEC Food Law and International Trade," unpublished paper, Brussels, June 1991, p. 8.

43. *Completing,* p. 6.

44. For more detailed discussion and analysis of the EC's new approach to technical standards, see Jacques Pelkmans, "The New Approach to Technical Harmonization and Standardization," *Journal of Common Market Studies,* 25, no. 3 (March 1987): 181–192. Also Michelle Egan, "'Associative Regulation' in the European Community: The Case of Technical Standards," prepared for the ECSA Biennial Conference, May 22–24, 1991.

45. Chambers, *Food Hygiene*, p. 39.

46. Gray, "EEC Food Law," p. 13.

47. Quoted in Elkes, "Europe 1992," p. 568.

48. Quoted in Kalypso Nicolaidis, "Mutual Recognition: The New Frontier of Multilateralism?" *Promethee,* June 1989, p. 29.

49. Martin Shapiro, "The European Court of Justice," in *Euro-Politics,* ed. Alberta Sbragia (Washington, D.C.: Brookings Institution, 1992), p. 137.

50. Cecchini, *The European Challenge, 1992.*

51. Ibid., pp. 57–61.

52. "The European Community without Technical Barriers," CEPS Working Paper No. 5, Centre for European Policy Studies, March 1992, p. 12.

53. Cecchini, *The European Challenge,* p. 61.

54. Charles Arthur, "Prawn Crisps and Politics," *Financial Times,* November 10, 1992, p. 10.

55. Nicholas Colchester and David Buchan, *Europe Relaunched* (London: Economist Books Ltd, 1990), p. 240.

56. Gray, "EEC Food Law," p. 3.

57. Quoted in John Weinkopf, "Pure Beer Law and Free Movement of Beer in the Common Market after *Commission v. Germany:* A Case Note on the *Reinheitsgebot Decision for the Beer Lover,*" prepared for European Community Law Seminar, Boalt Hall, 1989, p. 33.

58. "Communication on the free movement of foodstuffs within the Community," *Official Journal of the European Communities,* October 24, 1989, C. 271 4.

59. Philip Revzin, "Italians Must Change Their Business Style in Integrated Europe," *Wall Street Journal,* November 21, 1988, p. 1.

60. "Court of Justice Bans Some National Food Laws," *Europe,* no. 285, p. 42.

61. "Community-Food," *Reuters Library Service,* February 23, 1989.

62. "Our Good Food in Danger," *Le Point,* February 13–19, 1989, passim.

63. "Why Brussels Sprouts," *Economist,* January 8, 1993, p. 71.

64. Marlise Simons, "The Message from Camembert to Europe: Don't Mess with Cheese," *New York Times,* November 29, 1991, p. B1.

65. Ibid.

66. "Cheesed Off," *Economist,* December 7, 1991, p. 78.

67. "Runny, Smelly and Safe," *Economist,* June 27, 1992, p. 60.

68. Ibid.

69. Ibid.

70. Brooks, "Jam Sessions," p. 20.

71. "People's Europe: A Consumer Viewpoint," *EIU European Trends,* no. 2 (1990): 78.

72. Ibid.

73. Ibid.

74. Gray, "Food Law," p. 118.

75. J. A. Papadakis, "The Control of Foodstuffs in the Context of the

Completion of the E.C. Internal Market," Scientific and Technological Options Assessment, European Parliament, Strausbourg, May 17, 1990, p. 1.

76. Gray, "Food Law," p. 119.

77. G. Chambers, "Food Hygiene Policy and 1992," p. 30.

78. Colchester and Buchan, *Europe Relaunched,* p. 240.

79. "Mad, Bad and Dangerous to Eat," *Economist,* February 3, 1990, p. 89.

80. Ibid.

81. Nigel Dudley, Robert Melcher, and Tony Paterson, "Shoppers Snub the Experts in Mad Cow Crisis," *The European,* June 8–10, 1990, p. 1. See also Marianne McGowan, "In Britain, Concern Grows about Cattle Disease," *New York Times,* June 21, 1990, p. B7.

82. "Protecting Beef-Eaters," *The Times,* June 1, 1990, p. 13.

83. Michael Hornsby and Susan MacDonald, "France Defies EC on Beef Ban," *The Times,* June 1, 1990, p. 1.

84. "Protecting," p. 13.

85. E. J. Dionne Jr., "Europeans Squabbling over Food: Is Their Produce Free of Radiation?" *New York Times,* May 10, 1986, p. 5.

86. "EEC Confirms Ban on Food Imports from East Europe," *Financial Times,* May 13, 1986, p. 3.

87. Paul Cheeseright, "EEC to Set N-Safety Level in Food," *Financial Times,* May 5, 1986, p. 3.

88. Quoted in Ved Nanda and Bruce Bailey, "Export of Hazardous Waste and Hazardous Technology: Challenge for International Environmental Law," *Denver Journal of International Law and Policy,* 17, no. 1 (1988): 174.

89. Quentin Peel and Alison Maitland, "Fact's Fall Victim to the Butcher's Knife," *Financial Times,* May 14-15, 1994, p. 9.

90. Quentin Peel, "Commission Calls for Stricter Limits on Radiation in Food," *Financial Times,* May 21, 1987, p. 2.

91. William Dawkins, "EC Ministers Agree on Radiation Safety Levels for Food," *Financial Times,* December 15, 1987, p. 2.

92. Quentin Peel, "EC in Deadlock over Food Radiation Limits," *Financial Times,* October 21, 1987, p. 4.

93. "Irradiated Food Row Splits European Community," *Reuters Library Service,* December 13, 1990.

94. Ibid. See also "EC Commission Rejects Call for Ban on Food Irradiation," *Reuters Library Service,* March 10, 1987.

95. T. R. Stocker, "Food Law and 1992," pp. 1, 5.

96. Richard Owen and Michael Dynes, *The Times Guide to 1992* (London: Times Books, 1989).

97. Interview with S. Van Caenagem, Brussels, October 23, 1991.

98. Charles Arthur, "Prawn Crisps and Politics," *Financial Times,* November 10, 1992, p. 10.

99. Natalie Avery, "Fears over Food Quality Standards," *Pesticides News,* 20 (June 1993): 3.

100. Arthur, "Prawn Crisps," p. 10.

101. Joann Lublin, "U.S. Food Firms Find Europe's Huge Market Hardly a Piece of Cake," *Wall Street Journal,* May 15, 1990, p. 1.

102. Giandomenico Majone, "Market Integration and Regulation: Europe after 1992," *Metroecemica,* 43, nos. 1–2 (1992): 131–156.

103. Giandomenico Majone, "The European Community between Social Policy and Social Regulation," *Journal of Common Market Studies,* 31, no. 2 (June 1993): 63.

104. Quoted in Dehousse, "Integration vs. Regulation," p. 388.

3. Environmental Regulation and the Single European Market

1. Nigel Haigh, *EEC Environmental Policy and Britain,* 2nd ed. (Harlow, Essex: Longman, 1989).

2. Angela Liberatore, "Problems of Transnational Policymaking: Environmental Policy in the European Community," *European Journal of Political Research,* 19 (1991): 289.

3. Giandomenico Majone, "Cross-National Sources of Regulatory Policymaking in Europe and the United States," *Journal of Public Policy,* 11 (1991): 95.

4. Jackson Diehl, "Choking on Their Own Development," *Washington Post National Weekly Edition,* May 29–June 4, 1988, p. 9.

5. Ludwig Kramer, "The Single European Act and Environmental Protection: Reflections on Several New Provisions in Community Law," *Common Market Law Review,* 24 (1987): 651.

6. Ibid., p. 681. This provision only applied to directives approved by a qualified majority of the Council, i.e., under Article 100(a). See also Dirk Vandermeersch, "The Single European Act and the Environmental Policy of the European Community," *European Law Review,* 12 (December 1987): 407–429.

7. Commission of the European Communities, Task Force on Environment and the Internal Market, *1992: The Environmental Dimension* (Bonn: Economica Verlag, 1990).

8. *Environmental Policy in the European Community,* 4th ed. (Luxembourg: Office of Official Publications on the European Communities, 1990), p. 5.

9. Ibid., p. 15.

10. Alberta Sbragia, "Environmental Policy in the Political Economy of the European Community," prepared for the Workshop of The Consortium for 1992, Stanford, California, May 1992, p. 4.

11. Elizabeth Bomberg, "European Community Environmental Policy: The Role of the European Parliament," presented at Eighth Annual Conference of Europeanists, March 1992, fn. 31.

12. See Haigh, *EEC Environmental Quality and Britain.* Also David Judge, *Environmental Politics* (London: Frank Cass, 1992).

13. David Wilkinson, "Maastricht and the Environment: The Implications for the EC's Environment Policy of the Treaty on European Union," *Journal of Environmental Law,* 4, no. 2 (1992): 221, 223.

14. Eckard Rehbinder and Richard Stewart, "Legal Integration in Federal Systems: European Community Environmental Law," *American Journal of Comparative Law,* 33 (1985): 77.

15. Stanley P. Johnson and Guy Corcelle, *The Environmental Policy of the European Communities* (London: Graham and Trotman, 1989), p. 124.

16. Haigh, *EEC Environmental Policy and Britain,* p. 203.

17. Turner T. Smith Jr. and Pascale Kromarek, *Understanding US and European Environmental Law: A Practitioner's Guide* (London: Graham and Trotman, 1989), p. 71.

18. Haigh, *EEC Environmental Policy and Britain,* p. 204.

19. "Agreement on New Auto Emission Standards Starting in 1988 Called Major Breakthrough," *International Environmental Reporter,* April 4, 1985, p. 109.

20. "Auto Industry Environmentalists Disagree over Need for U.S. Auto Emission Standards," *International Environmental Reporter,* November 13, 1985, p. 368.

21. This section draws extensively on Henning Arp, "Interest Groups in EC Legislation: The Case of Car Emission Standards," presented in the workshop "European Lobbying towards the Year 2000" at the ECPR Joint Session of Workshops, University of Essex, March 22–28, 1991.

22. The Japanese had in fact chosen to adopt emission standards similar to those of the United States for precisely this reason: a major portion of their cars were exported to the United States. "So closely did [the standards adopted by the Environmental Agency in October 1972] parallel the standards of the U.S. Clean Air Act of 1970 that they came to be called the Nipponban Masukh (Japanese Muskie Law)." Susan Pharr and Joseph Badaracco Jr., "Coping with Crisis: Environmental Regulation" in *America versus Japan,* ed. Thomas McCraw (Boston: Harvard Business School Press, 1986), p. 246.

23. Kevin Done, "A Two-Speed Europe on Exhaust Fumes," *Financial Times,* July 18, 1988, p. 11.

24. "Government Says It Stands Firm on Refusal to Require Catalytic Converters on New Cars," *International Environmental Reporter,* April 9, 1986, p. 114.

25. "France, Britain Oppose German Attempt to Win Agreement in Emission Standards," *International Environmental Reporter,* February 13, 1985, p. 40.

26. "Trade Association of Automakers Opposes Use of Catalytic Converters to Meet Limits," *International Environmental Reporter,* November 13, 1985, p. 39.

27. "France, Britain," pp. 40–41.

28. "Auto Industry," p. 368.

29. "Commission to Consider Legal Proceedings on West German Incentives for Cleaner Cars," *International Environmental Reporter,* February 13, 1985, p. 39.

30. Ibid.

31. Jonathan Story and Ethan Schwartz, "Auto Emissions and the European Parliament: A Test of the Single European Act," INSEAD-CEDEP, 1990, pp. 23–24.

32. Ibid., p. 24.

33. Ibid., p. 25.

34. Ibid.

35. "Franco-German Row Looms over Car Emission Rules," *Reuters Library Service,* July 25, 1988.

36. *Le Monde,* August 4, 1988.

37. "European Community Environment Ministers Agree on New Emission Level for Small Cars," *International Environment Reporter,* June 1989, p. 283.

38. Quoted in Elizabeth Bomberg, "EC Environmental Policy: The Role of the European Parliament," prepared for delivery at the Eighth International Conference of Europeanists, Chicago, March 27–29, 1992, p. 23.

39. Story and Schwartz, "Auto Emissions," p. 27.

40. "Green Greener Greenest?" *Economist,* May 6, 1989, p. 67.

41. "European Community Environment Ministers Agree on New Emission Levels for Small Cars," *International Environment Reporter,* June 1989, p. 283.

42. Quoted in Bomberg, "EC Environmental Policy," p. 25.

43. Ibid.

44. "France Ready to Ban Big West German Cars, Minister Says," *Reuters Library Service,* September 12, 1990.

45. Ibid.

46. "Danish Car Emission Law in the EEC Spotlight," *Europe Information Service,* November 6, 1990.

47. David Gardner, "EU to Recycle the Issues at Fresh Talks on Waste," *Financial Times,* December 2, 1993, p. 2.

48. Eckard Rehbinder and Richard Stewart, "Environmental Protection Policy," in *Integration through Law: Europe and the American Experience,* vol. 2, ed. Mauro Cappelletti, Monica Secombe, and Joseph Weiler (Berlin: Walter de Gruyter, 1985), p. 92.

49. Cynthia Whitehead, "E.C. Environmental Policy Is Model for Other Nations," *European Affairs,* September/October 1985, p. 30.

50. George B. Wilkinsen, "The Sixth Amendment: Toxic Substance Control in the EEC," *Law and Policy in International Business,* 12 (1980): 465.

51. Ronald Brickman, Sheila Jasanoff, and Thomas Ilgen, *Controlling Chemicals: The Politics of Regulation in Europe and the United States* (Ithaca: Cornell University Press, 1985), p. 286.

52. Ibid., p. 276.

53. Wilkinsen, *The Sixth Amendment,* p. 483.

54. Whitehead, "E.C. Environmental Policy," p. 30.

55. Patrick Kenis and Volker Schneider, "The EC as an International Corporate Actor: Two Case Studies in Economic Diplomacy," *European Journal of Political Research,* 15 (1987): p. 48.

56. Whitehead, "E.C.," p. 31.

57. Brickman, Jasanoff, and Ilgen, *Controlling Chemicals,* p. 279.

58. Giandomenico Majone, "Market Integration and Regulation Europe after 1992," *Metroeconomica,* 43, nos. 1–2 (1992): 239.

59. "Environmental Protection and Free Movements of Goods: The Danish Bottles Case," *Journal of Environmental Law,* 2, no. 1 (1990): 90.

60. Hanna Nolan and H. Landis Gabel, "Environmental Policy in the European Community," INSEAD, Paris, France, 1990, p. 10.

61. Paolo Cecchini, *1992: The Benefits of a Single Market* (Aldershot: Wildwood House, 1988), p. 60.

62. Ibid.

63. "Environmental Protection," p. 96.

64. Ida Koppen, "The Role of the European Court of Justice in the Development of the European Community Environmental Policy," EUI Working Papers, European Policy Unit, Florence, European University Institute, p. 21.

65. Benoit Laplante and Jonathan Garbutt, "Environmental Protectionism," *Land Economics,* 68, no. 1 (February 1992): 118–119.

66. Ibid., p. 97.

67. Ibid., p. 95.

68. Quoted in "Danish Bottles" (A) A case prepared by John Clark for the

Management Institute for Environment and Business, 1992, p. 7 (italics in original).

69. Ibid., p. 94.

70. Ibid., p. 6.

71. Ibid., p. 104.

72. Damien Geradin, "Free Trade and Environmental Protection in an Integrated Market: A Survey of the Case-Law of the United States Supreme Court and the European Court of Justice," *Florida State University Journal of Transnational Law and Policy,* April 1983, p. 48.

73. Nolan and Gabel, "Environmental Policy," p. 10.

74. Ibid., pp. 102–103.

75. "Environmental Protection," p. 105.

76. John Clark and Matthew B. Arnold, "The Danish Bottles Case," in *The Greening of World Trade: A Report to EPA from the Trade and Environment Committee of the National Advisory Council for Environmental Policy and Technology* (Washington, D.C.: U.S. Government Printing Office, 1993), p. 167.

77. C. Foster Knight, "Effects of National Environmental Regulation on International Trade and Investment—Selected Issues," *Pacific Basin Law Journal,* 10, no. 1 (Fall 1991): 213.

78. Tim Dickson, "Bonn Bottle Scheme Wins EC Backing," *Financial Times,* November 16, 1989.

79. "A Wall of Waste," *Economist,* November 30, 1991, p. 73.

80. Christopher Parkes, "Survey of Packaging and the Environment," *Financial Times,* May 28, 1992, p. 34.

81. "Waste and the Environment," *Economist,* May 29, 1993, p. 12.

82. "Free Trade's Green Hurdle," *Economist,* June 15, 1991, p. 61.

83. Ibid.

84. John Thornhill, "Wasting Time over Recycling," *Financial Times,* March 31, 1992, p. 12.

85. Ibid.

86. Ibid.

87. Christopher Boerner and Kenneth Chilton, "Recycling's Demand Side: Lessons from Germany's 'Green Dot,'" Center for the Study of American Business, Contemporary Issues Series 59, August 1993, p. 11.

88. Marilyn Stern, "Is This the Ultimate in Recycling?" *Across the Board,* May 1993, p. 31.

89. Alison Maitland, "Germany Rebuts Criticism of Its Waste Recycling Laws," *Financial Times,* October 19, 1993, p. 3.

90. "Take It Back," *Economist,* May 1, 1993, p. 64.

91. Maitland, "Germany Rebuts," p. 3.

92. Richard Weiner and Stefan Tostmann, "What Can the EC Learn from

Germany's Bold Legislation on Packaging Waste?" *International Environmental Affairs,* 3, no. 4 (Fall 1991): 282–291.

93. Ibid.

94. Frances Cairncross, "How Europe's Companies Reposition to Recycle," *Harvard Business Review,* March–April 1992, p. 38.

95. "EU Packaging Directive Passed." *Financial Times,* December 15, 1994, p. 3.

96. "Tied Up in Knots," *Economist,* January 28, 1995, p. 62.

97. Neil Buckley, "EU Ministers Wrap Up Agreement on Packaging," *Financial Times,* December 29, 1993, p. 2.

98. "The Unrubbishing," p. 64.

99. Ariane Genillard, "Germans to Ease Laws on Waste Burning," *Financial Times,* June 30, 1993, p. 2.

100. Christopher Boerner and Kenneth Chilton, "Recycling: What a Waste?" *American Enterprise,* March/April 1994, p. 18. Michael Rose and David Perchard, "When Waste Is Not Wanted," *Financial Times,* January 25, 1994, p. 12.

101. "Member of Parliament Warns of 'Pyrrhic' Victory for EC Applicants," *International Environment Reporter,* January 16, 1994, p. 49.

4. Greening the GATT

1. *The Text of the General Agreement on Tariffs and Trade* (Geneva: The GATT, 1986), pp. 37, 38.

2. Ibid.

3. Ibid.

4. *The Texts of the Tokyo Round Agreements* (Geneva: The GATT, 1986), p. 1.

5. See, for example, Ralph Nader et al., *The Case against Free Trade* (San Francisco: Earth Island Press, 1993), and Harold Gilliam, "The Real Price of Free Trade," *San Francisco Examiner: The World,* January 2, 1994, pp. 13–14.

6. Both this and the following two cases are discussed in detail in Congress of the United States, Office of Technology Assessment, *Trade and Environment: Conflicts and Opportunities* (Washington, D.C.: U.S. Printing Office, 1992), pp. 82–85. See also John Manard Jr., "GATT and the Environment: The Friction between International Trade and the World's Environment—The Dolphin and Tuna Dispute," *Tulane Environmental Law Journal,* 5, no. 2 (May 1992): 400–404.

7. *International Trade 1990–91,* vol. 1 (Geneva: GATT, 1992), p. 26.

8. *Trade and Environment,* pp. 83–84.

9. Stan Sesser, "Opium War Redux," *New Yorker,* 69, no. 29 (September 13, 1993): 87.

10. Unless otherwise noted, this section is based on National Research Council, *Dolphins and the Tuna Industry* (Washington, D.C: National Academy Press, 1992), pp. 1–22, and Kerry L. Holland, "Exploitation on Porpoise: The Use of Purse Seine Nets by Commercial Tuna Fishermen in the Eastern Tropical Pacific Ocean," *Syracuse Journal of International Law and Commerce,* 17 (Spring 1991): 267–279.

11. "Congress Approves Moratorium on Sea Mammal Killings," in *1972 Quarterly Congressional Almanac* (Washington, D.C.: Congressional Quarterly Press, 1993), p. 9.

12. Robert Housman and Durwood Zaelke, "The Collision of the Environment and Trade: The GATT Tuna/Dolphin Decision," *Environmental Law Reporter,* April 1992, p. 10271.

13. Andrew Taylor, "Canner's 'Dolphin-Safe' Vows Spur Tuna Labeling Bill," *Congressional Quarterly Weekly Report* (May 19, 1990): 1553.

14. "Labeling of 'Dolphin-Safe' Tuna Regulated," in *1990 Congressional Quarterly Almanac* (Washington, D.C.: Congressional Quarterly Press, 1991), p. 399.

15. Taylor, "Canner's," p. 1553.

16. David Colson, "U.S. Policy on Tuna-Dolphin Issues," *U.S. Department of State Dispatch,* August 24, 1992, p. 668.

17. James Brooke, "America—Environmental Dictator?" *New York Times,* May 3, 1992, p. 7.

18. Housman and Zaelke, "The Collision," p. 10272.

19. Brooke, "America," p. 7.

20. Federic Kirgis, "Environment and Trade Measures after the Tuna/Dolphin Decision," *Washington and Lee Law Review,* 29 (1992): p. 1222 (emphasis in original).

21. GATT panel ruling, quoted in Joel Trachtman, "GATT Dispute Settlement Panel," *American Journal of International Law,* 86, no. 1 (January 1992): 151.

22. Trachtman, "GATT Dispute," p. 149.

23. Housman and Zaelke, "The Collision," p. 10274.

24. Frances Williams, "GATT Members Set to Oppose U.S. on Tuna Import Curb," *Financial Times,* February 19, 1992, p. 6.

25. Keith Bradsher, "U.S. Ban on Mexico Tuna Is Overruled," *New York Times,* August 23, 1991, p. C1.

26. John Maggs, "EC Will Protest U.S. Tuna Embargo against 20 Nations," *Journal of Commerce,* February 4, 1992, p. 3A.

27. Stuart Auerbach, "Endangering Laws Protecting the Endangered," *Washington Post National Weekly Edition,* October 7–13, 1991, p. 22.

28. Brooke, "America," p. 7.

29. John Vidal, "Global Conservation Threatened as GATT Declares War," *Guardian,* September 6, 1991, p. 29.

30. Auerbach, "Endangering," p. 22.

31. Ibid.

32. Ibid.

33. Quoted in Ted McDorman, "The U.S.—Mexico GATT Panel Report on Tuna and Dolphin: Implications for Trade and Environmental Conflicts," *North Carolina Journal of International Law and Commercial Regulation,* 17 (1992): 488.

34. Quoted in Matthew Hurlock, "The GATT, U.S. Law and the Environment: A Proposal to Amend the GATT in Light of the Tuna/Dolphin Decision," *Columbia Law Review,* 92 (1992): 2133.

35. Laura Lones, "The Marine Mammal Protection Act and International Protection of Cetaceans: A Unilateral Attempt to Effectuate Transnational Conservation," *Vanderbilt Journal of International Law,* 22 (1989): 1018.

36. "Divine Porpoise," *Economist,* October 5, 1991, p. 31. For a more detailed analysis of the administration's strategy, see George Mitchell Jr., "Between Compliance and Defiance: Executive Branch Disposition of 'Unwanted' Legislation," paper presented at the 1993 Annual Meeting of the American Political Science Association, Washington, D.C., September 1993, p. 24.

37. "Divine Porpoise," p. 34.

38. Ibid.

39. "Congress Considers New Bill to Save Dolphins," *Dolphin Alert,* Fall 1992, p. 2.

40. "Must Try Harder," *Economist,* August 21, 1993, p. 22.

41. Steve Charnovitz, "Exploring the Environmental Exceptions in GATT Article XX," *Journal of World Trade,* 5 (October 1991): 52.

42. Housman and Zaelke, "Collision," p. 10276.

43. Steve Charnovitz, "GATT and the Environment: Examining the Issues," *International Environmental Affairs,* 4, no. 3 (Summer 1992): 210.

44. Jeffrey Dunhoff, "Reconciling International Trade with Preservation of the Global Environment: Can We Prosper and Profit?" *Washington and Lee Law Review,* 49 (1992): 1417.

45. Ibid.

46. Charnovitz, "GATT and the Environment," pp. 205–209.

47. "The Environment," *Economist,* May 30, 1992, p. 14.

48. Matthew Hurlock, "The GATT, U.S. Law and the Environment: A Proposal to Amend the GATT in Light of the Tuna/Dolphin Decision," *Columbia Law Review,* 92 (1992): 2100.

49. Naomi Roht-Arriaza, "Precaution, Participation and the 'Greening'

of International Trade Law," *Journal of Environmental Law and Litigation,* 7 (1992): 77.

50. Steven Shrybman, "Trading Away the Environment," *World Policy Journal,* Winter 1991–1992, p. 103.

51. Ibid.

52. Ibid.

53. Housman and Zaelke, "Trade, Environment, and Sustainable Development: A Primer," *Hastings International and Comparative Law Journal,* 15 (1992): 548–549.

54. Housman and Zaelke, "Collision," p. 10276.

55. Steve Charnovitz, "GATT and the Environment," p. 207.

56. Patti Goldman, "Resolving the Trade and Environment Debate: In Search of a Neutral Forum and Neutral Principles," *Washington and Lee Review,* 49 (1992): 1293.

57. Peter Passell, "Tuna and Trade: Whose Rules?" *New York Times,* February 19, 1992, p. C2.

58. Keith Schneider, "Balancing Nature's Claims and International Free Trade," *New York Times,* January 16, 1992, Section 4, p. 5.

59. Piritta Sorsa, "Environment—A New Challenge to GATT," paper prepared for the 1992 World Development Report, World Bank, June 1991, pp. i, 25.

60. GATT press release, February 11, 1992.

61. Christopher Joyce, "U.S. Environmentalists Oppose World Trade Deal," *New Scientist,* February 15, 1992, p. 16.

62. Bruce Stokes, "The Road from Rio," *National Journal,* May 5, 1992, p. 1287.

63. "Trade and the Environment," *International Trade 90–91,* vol. 1 (Geneva: The GATT, 1992), pp. 19–39. The author of this chapter is cited in Pater Passell, "Tune and Trade: Whose Rules?" *New York Times,* February 19, 1992, p. C2. For the background papers prepared for the GATT report, see Kym Anderson and Richard Blackhurst, eds., *The Greening of World Trade Issues* (Ann Arbor: University of Michigan Press, 1992).

64. "Trade and the Environment," pp. 21–22.

65. Ibid., pp. 21–22, p. 33.

66. Ibid., p. 30.

67. Ibid., pp. 86–87.

68. Ibid., p. 24.

69. Ibid., pp. 6, 20.

70. Ibid., p. 22.

71. Ibid., p. 23.

72. Patrick Low, ed., *International Trade and the Environment* (Washington, D.C.: The World Bank, 1992).

73. Ibid., p. 43.

74. Piritta Sorsa, "GATT and the Environment," *World Economy* 15, no. 1 (January 1992): p. 123.

75. Quoted in William Brown, "Trade Deals a Blow to the Environment," *New Scientist,* November 10, 1990, p. 21.

76. Nancy Birdsall and David Wheeler, "Trade Policy and Industrial Pollution in Latin America: Where Are the Pollution Havens?" in Low, *International Trade,* pp. 159–168.

77. David Wheeler and Paul Martin, "Prices, Policies and the International Diffusion of Clean Technology: The Case of Wood Pulp Production," in Low, *International Trade,* pp. 197–224.

78. "Action Urged on Tuna Panel Report," *GATT Focus,* 88 (March 1992): 5.

79. "First Submission of the United States to the Panel on United States-Restriction on Imports of Tuna," p. 37.

80. Ibid., p. 33.

81. Michael Bergman, "U.S. Says Secondary Tuna Ban Is Covered by GATT Exception Rules," *Inside U.S. Trade,* 11, no. 15 (April 16, 1993): 2.

82. Ibid.

83. Frances Williams, "Boycott Ruling Irks US Greens," *Financial Times,* May 27, 1994, p. 7.

84. Quoted in J. Owen Saunders, "Trade and Environment: The Fine Line between Environmental Protection and Environmental Protectionism," *International Journal,* 1992, p. 939 (italics added).

85. Ted McDorman, "The GATT Consistency of U.S. Fish Import Embargoes to Stop Driftnet Fishing and Save Whales, Dolphins and Turtles," *George Washington Journal of International Law and Economics,* 24 (1991): 496.

86. Matthew Hunter Hurlock, "The GATT, U.S. Law and the Environment: A Proposal to Amend the GATT in Light of the Tuna/Dolphin Decision," *Columbia Law Review,* 92 (1992): 2112.

87. Steve Charnovitz, "Encouraging Environmental Cooperation through the Pelly Amendment," *Journal of Environment & Development,* 1, no. 3 (Summer 1964): pp. 1–26.

88. "Mortal Turtles," *In These Times,* January 11, 1983, p. 8.

89. Ibid.

90. Thomas Friedman, "U.S. Puts Sanctions on Taiwan," *New York Times,* April 12, 1994, p. C1.

91. The following two paragraphs are based on David Freestone, "European Community Environmental Policy and Law," in *Law, Policy and the Environment,* ed. Robin Churchill, Lynda Warren, and John Gibson (Oxford: Basil Blackwell, 1991), p. 141. See also Paul Demaret, "Environmental Policy and Commercial Policy: The Emergence of Trade-Related Environmental Mea-

sures in the External Relations on the European Community," in *The European Community's Commercial Policy after 1992: The Legal Dimension,* ed. M. Maresceau (Netherlands: Kluwer Academic Publishers, 1993), pp. 328–329.

92. Demaret, "Environmental Policy," p. 330.

93. Ibid., p. 396.

94. "Spare That Tree," *Economist,* November 14, 1992, p. 40; Frances Williams, "ASEAN Condemns Timber Labelling," *Financial Times,* November 6, 1992, p. 4.

95. Williams, "ASEAN Condemns," p. 4.

96. Ibid.

97. Demaret, "Environmental Policy," pp. 334–335.

98. Ibid.

99. Barbel Hegenbart, "Systematics of Interdependencies: Trade Instruments and Their Impact on Environment," in *Trade and the Environment,* ed. F. Schmidt-Bleek and H. Wohlmeyer (Laxenburg, Austria: International Institute for Applied Systems Analysis and the Austrian Association for Agricultural Research, 1991), p. 231.

100. "Now for the Hard Part," *Economist,* April 17, 1993, p. 8.

101. Ibid.

102. Marianne Lavelle, "Free Trade vs. Law," *National Law Journal,* March 29, 1993, p. 39.

103. Brian Shaffer, "Regulation, Competition, and Strategy: Evidence from the Auto Industry," doctoral dissertation, Haas School of Business, University of California, Berkeley, 1992, p. 177.

104. Jim Henry, "Imports Fear Higher CAFE Would Boost Fines, Lower Sales," *Automotive News,* May 1, 1989, p. 26.

105. Ibid.

106. Ibid.

107. Nancy Dunne, "EC Challenge over US Fuel Economy Tax," *Financial Times,* May 11, 1993, p. 5.

108. "U.S. Auto Fuel-Efficiency Taxes to Be Examined by GATT Panel," *Trade and the Environment: News and Views from the GATT,* June 3, 1993, p. 4.

109. Ibid.

110. Charles Arden-Clarke, *The General Agreement on Tariffs and Trade: Environmental Protection and Sustainable Development,* A World Wildlife Fund Discussion Paper, June 1991, p. 9.

111. Ibid., p. 23.

112. Steve Charnowitz, "Environmental and Labor Standards in Trade," *World Economy,* 15, no. 3 (May 1992): 336.

113. Ibid.

114. William Lash III, "Green Gang's GATT Holdup," *Journal of Commerce,* December 10, 1993.

115. Ibid.

116. "Can GATT GO Green?" *New Scientists,* November 10, 1990, p. 11.

117. Ibid.

118. Richard Steinberg, "The Uruguay Round: A Legal Analysis of the Final Act," *International Quarterly,* 6, no. 2 (April 1994): 35 (italics added).

119. Ibid.

120. Quoted in Daniel Esty, *Greening the GATT* (Washington, D.C.: Institute for International Economics, 1994), p. 170.

121. Quoted ibid., p. 50.

122. Ibid.

123. "Several Countries Urge Quick Start to GATT Environment Work," *GATT Newsletter,* 80 (April 1991): 9.

124. "Decisions Adopted by Ministers in Marrakesh," *Focus: The GATT Newsletter,* May 1994, p. 9.

125. Ibid.

126. "Several Countries," p. 23.

127. Laura Kosloff and Mark Trexler, "The Convention on International Trade in Endangered Species: No Carrot, But Where's the Stick?" *Environmental Law Reporter,* 17 (1987): 10221–10236.

128. Quoted in "The Environment," *Economist,* May 30, 1992, p. 13.

129. "Several Countries," p. 9. See also U.S. Congress, Office of Technology Assessment, *Trade and Environment: Conflicts and Opportunities,* OTA-BP-ITE (Washington, D.C.: U.S. Government Printing Office, May 1992), pp. 44–46.

130. Quoted in Steve Charnovitz, "GATT and the Environment," p. 206.

131. Quoted in Housman and Zaelke, "Trade, Environment," p. 588.

132. Steven Globerman, "The Environmental Impacts of Trade Liberalization" in *NAFTA and the Environment,* ed. Terry Anderson (San Francisco: Pacific Research Institute for Public Policy, 1993), p. 38.

133. Bronwen Maddox, "Ecology Worry Is Dismissed," *Financial Times,* April 25, 1994, p. 6. "Trade and the Environment," a draft prepared by the Trade Committee of OECD, June 27, 1989.

134. Esty, *Greening,* p. 102.

135. Ibid., p. 189.

5. Food Safety and International Trade

1. Ann Tutwiler, "Food Safety, the Environment and Agricultural Trade: The Links," International Policy Council on Agricultural and Trade, Discussion Papers, series no. 7, June 1991, p. 2.

2. Robert Sweeney Jr., "Technical Analysis of the Technical Barriers to

Trade Agreement," *Law and Policy in International Business,* 12, no. 1 (1980): 185.

3. R. W. Middleton, "The GATT Standards Code," *Journal of World Trade Law,* 14 (1980): 202.

4. J. H. J. Bourgeois, "The Tokyo Round Agreements on Technical Barriers And on Government Procurement in International and EEC Perspective," *Common Market Law Review,* 19 no. 1 (1982): 32.

5. Joseph Grieco, *Cooperation among Nations: Europe, America and Non-Tariff Barriers to Trade* (Ithaca: Cornell University Press, 1990), p. 61.

6. Quoted in Adrian Rafael Halpern, "The U.S.-EC Hormone Beef Controversy and the Standards Code: Implications for the Application of Health Regulations to Agricultural Trade," *North Carolina Journal of International Law and Commercial Regulation,* 14, no. 1 (Winter 1989): 130.

7. Jacques Nusbaumer, "The GATT Standards Code in Operation," *Journal of World Trade Law,* 18 (1984): 545.

8. Quoted in Halpern, "US-EC Hormone," p. 140.

9. Steven Rothberg, "From Beer to BST: Circumventing the GATT Standards Code's Prohibition on Unnecessary Obstacles to Trade," *Minnesota Law Review,* 75 (1990): 515.

10. Halpern, "U.S.-EC Hormone," p. 142.

11. Quoted in Grieco, *Cooperation among Nations,* p. 88.

12. Todd Thurwachter, "Japan's Non-Tariff Barriers: Case Studies from Files of U.S. and Foreign Commercial Service," *Journal of the American Chamber of Commerce in Japan,* 25, no. 11 (November 1988): 42.

13. Quoted in Grieco, *Cooperation,* p. 89.

14. Quoted ibid., p. 87.

15. Andre Brand and Amanda Ellerton, *Report on Hormone-Treated Meat* (Brussels: Club de Bruxelles, 1989), p. 2.9.

16. Mark Hunter, "Francois Lamy: How France's Nader Won Ban on Hormone-Tainted Meat," *Washington Post,* December 25, 1988, p. H3.

17. John Peterson, "Hormones, Heifers and High Politics: Biotechnology and the Common Agricultural Policy," *Public Administration,* 67, no. 4 (Winter 1989): 461.

18. The quotation is from Brand and Ellerton, *Report,* p. 3.6; the EC's response to the second inquiry is discussed in *The Effects of Greater Economic Integration within the European Community on the United States: First Follow-Up Report* (Washington, D.C.: United States International Trade Commission, Publication 2268, March 1990), pp. 6–50.

19. Brand and Ellerton, *Report,* p. 3.4.

20. Quoted in Brand and Ellerton, *Report,* p. 3.4.

21. Rene Barents, "Hormones and the Growth of Community Agricultural Law: Some Reflections on the Hormones Judgment (case 68/86)," *Law Review of the Europa Institüut, University of Amsterdam,* no. 1 (1988): 7.

22. Brand and Ellerton, *Report,* p. 4.3.

23. Janet Shaner, "The Beef Hormone Trade Dispute," Harvard Business School Case no. 9-590-035, Rev. 12/89, p. 6.

24. Quoted in Halpern, "The U.S.-EC Hormone Beef Controversy," p. 137.

25. Hunter, "Francois Lamy," p. H3.

26. Shaner, "The Beef Hormone Trade Dispute," p. 5.

27. Ibid.

28. Quoted in *The Effects of European Integration,* pp. 6–51.

29. Ibid.

30. Walter Mossberg, "Dispute over Meat Imports Threatens New Snarl in U.S.-E.C. Trade Links," *Wall Street Journal,* December 23, 1988, p. A4.

31. Shaner, "The Beef Hormone Trade Dispute," p. 8.

32. Ibid.

33. Mossberg, "Dispute," p. A4.

34. Quoted in "European Officials Emphasize Hormone Ban Is a Consumer Protection Issue, Not a Trade Barrier," *International Trade Reporter,* February 15, 1989, p. 197.

35. "European Officials," p. 196.

36. Brand and Ellerton, *Report,* p. 3.3.

37. "European Officials," p. 197.

38. Quoted in William Sheeline, "What's the Beef?" *Fortune,* January 30, 1989, p. 8.

39. Quoted in Peterson, "Hormones, Heifers and High Politics," p. 461.

40. "Brie and Hormones," *Economist,* January 7, 1989, p. 21.

41. Ibid.

42. Ibid.

43. Clyde Farnsworth, "Trade Retaliation Readied If Europe Bars Meats of U.S.," *New York Times,* December 27, 1988, p. D6.

44. "European Officials," p. 197.

45. Quoted in Mossberg, "Dispute," p. A4.

46. Peterson, "Hormones, Heifers, and High Politics," p. 461.

47. Ibid., p. 460.

48. Brand and Ellerton, *Report,* p. 3.6.

49. Quoted in Halpern, "US-EC Hormone," p. 146.

50. Quoted ibid., p. 148.

51. Quoted ibid., p. 149.

52. Ibid.

53. Werner Meng, "The Hormone Conflict between the EEC and the United States within the Context of GATT," *Michigan Journal of International Law,* 11, no. 3 (Spring 1990): 836.

54. "USTR Formally Announces Sanctions to Retaliate against EC Meat Hormones Ban," *International Trade Reporter,* January 4, 1989, p. 7.

55. "EC to Talk Further with Texas Farm Official about Offer to Export Hormone-Free U.S. Meat," *Journal of Commerce,* January 25, 1989, p. 94.

56. Ibid.

57. Bruce Barnard, "Cease-Fire Ends in Hormone War between US, EC" *Journal of Commerce,* February 7, 1990, p. 5A.

58. "Note," *Food Chemical News,* December 12, 1988, p. 10.

59. Shaner, "Beef Hormone Dispute," p. 9.

60. Nancy Dunne, "Phoney Peace Breaks Out in US-EC Clash over Farm Trade," *Financial Times,* April 27, 1989, p. D6.

61. Shaner, "Beef Hormone Dispute," p. 13.

62. Keith Rockwell, "US Says EC Milk Ban Would Set Bad Precedent," *Journal of Commerce,* August 7, 1989, p. 6A.

63. Rockwell, "US Says," p. 6A.

64. Ibid.

65. Quoted in "Trading Our Future?" Press Release, League of Rural Voters (undated), p. 4.

66. Ibid.

67. *News of the Uruguay Round,* GATT Secretariat, Geneva, April 19, 1990.

68. *1992: The Effect of Great Economic Integration within the European Community on the United States,* First follow-up report, March 1990, Investigation no. 332–267 (Washington, D.C.: United States International Trade Commission), pp. 6–49.

69. Christopher Culp, "Small Farmers Have Regulators Cowed," *Wall Street Journal,* September 2, 1992, p. A10.

70. "Adulteration Controllee," *Economist,* September 22, 1990, p. 23.

71. Patti Goldman, "The Legal Effect of Trade Agreements on Domestic Health and Environmental Regulation," *Journal of Environmental Law and Litigation,* 7 (1992): 47.

72. Goldman, "The Legal Effect," p. 47.

73. "Ban on Some European Wines May End," *New York Times,* February 2, 1991, p. 10.

74. Jimmy S. Hillman, *Technical Barriers to Agricultural Trade* (Boulder: Westview Press, 1991), p. 83.

75. Roy Garner, "More a Barrier than a Force for Reform," *Far Eastern Economic Review,* June 11, 1987, p. 67.

76. Susan Chira, "Diffuse Goals Set by Naders of Japan," *New York Times,* July 14, 1986, p. D10.

77. Jocelyn Ford, "Groups Say Harmful Food Additives Sanctioned Here," *Asahi Evening News,* June 14, 1986, reprinted in *Revealing Japan,* July 1986, no. 94, p. 5.

78. "Food Additives: A Matter of Consumer Concern," *Mainichi Daily*

News, June 10, 1986, p. 12, reprinted in *Japan Resources,* May/June 1986, p. 16.

79. Maurine A. Kirkpatrick, "Consumerism and Japan's New Citizen Politics," *Asian Survey,* 15, no. 3 (March 1975): 242.

80. "Health and Welfare Ministry Is Asked to Approve Nine Food Additives," reprinted in *Japan Resources,* June 1983, p. 7.

81. "Export Product Review, Country Report, Japan," Foreign Agricultural Service, High Value Products Division, USDA, September 1988, p. 3.

82. Interview with Department of Agriculture officials, April 5, 1989.

83. "The Problems of the Artificial Sweetener Aspartame," *Japan Resources,* August–September 1984, p. 2.

84. Ford, "Groups Say," p. 5.

85. Ibid.

86. "Now It's Compulsory for Food Makers to Indicate All Additives in Products," *Japan Economic Journal,* September 20, 1983, p. 59.

87. "Panel Recommends List of Additives for Mention on Labels," *Japan Times,* November 11, 1987, p. 2.

88. "Evian Travels 600 km in France to Meet Japan's Heat Sterilization Rule," *Japan Economic Journal,* May 28, 1985, p. 4.

89. "Thirsty, Trendy Consumers," *Japan Economic Journal,* July 18, 1987, p. 24.

90. Stefan Wagstyl, "Row Erupts over Ban by Japanese on Wines from Italy," *Financial Times,* April 22, 1992, p. 6.

91. Ibid.

92. David Cohen and Karen Martin, "Western Ideology, Japanese Product Safety Regulation and International Trade," *University of British Columbia Law Review,* 19 (1985): 363.

93. Kyoko Sato, "Agriculture Ministry Called Unwilling to Cut Apple Ban," *Japanese Times Weekly International Edition,* June 14–20, 1993, p. 13.

94. Ibid.

95. Timothy Egan, "Angered by Japan's Barriers, U.S. Apple Growers Retaliate," *New York Times,* August 17, 1993, p. 1.

96. Ibid., p. A7.

97. Warren Brookes, "On Earth Day Thank God for Technology," *San Francisco Chronicle,* April 12, 1990, p. A16.

98. "Synthetic Chemical Pesticides," in *Risk Management in the U.S. and Japan: A Comparative Perspective,* Vanderbilt University, Management of Technology Program, May 1986, p. 139.

99. Koichiro Hidaka, "Many Fear U.S. Rice Chemically Tainted: Consumer Advocates," *Japan Times,* July 2, 1987, p. 4.

100. Ibid.

101. Takamatsu Osamu, "California Rice Is Full of Agricultural Chemicals: Far More Dangerous than Imported Flour," *Japan Resources,* November–December 1988, pp. 1–4.

102. Takamatsu, "California Rice," pp. 1–4.

103. Naomi Ono, "Pesticide Limits Relaxed As Trade Pressure Intensifies," *Nikkei Weekly,* February 15, 1992, reprinted in *Japan Resources,* January–March 1992, p. 8.

104. Ibid.

105. "Japanese Farmers Push Video Slamming U.S. Farm Imports," *Asahi Evening News,* August 4, 1988, reprinted in *Revealing Japan,* September 1988, p. 10.

106. Carol Luffy, "The Docile Charm of the Japanese Consumer," *Far Eastern Economic Review,* November 3, 1988, p. 79.

107. Ibid.

108. Ibid.

109. Ibid.

110. Gary Mead, "Farmers Reap Rich Public Relations Crop," *Financial Times,* January 21, 1993, p. 8.

111. "Dairy Ads Targeting in Probe," *Japan Times,* February 10, 1991, p. 1.

112. Mead, "Farmers Reap," p. 8.

113. "Safety of Imported Food Big Worry for Women," *Asahi Evening News,* March 19, 1993, reprinted in *Revealing Japan,* April 1993, p. 2.

114. Tutwiler, "Food Safety, the Environment and Agricultural Trade," p. 2.

115. Steven Rothberg, "From Beef to BST: Circumventing the GATT Standards Code's Prohibition on Unnecessary Obstacles to Trade," *Minnesota Law Review,* 75 (1990): 530.

116. Natalie Avery, "Fears over Food Quality Standards," *Pesticides News,* no. 20 (June 1993): 3.

117. "Trade and Environment," *Nature,* 359 (September 17, 1992): 174.

118. Quoted in Mark Ritchie, "Impact of GATT Trade Negotiations on the Environment," issued by the European Environmental Bureau, July 3, 1988, p. 34.

119. "Environmental Protection Agency Pursuing 'More Aggressive' Role in Pesticide Trade," *International Trade Reporter,* 7 (April 1990): 468.

120. Maury Bredahl and Kenneth Forsythe, "Harmonizing Phyto-sanitary and Sanitary Regulations," *World Economy,* 12, no. 2 (June 1992): 190.

121. "'Big Green'-Style Pesticide Laws Could endanger Uruguay Round, EC Warns U.S.," *Bureau of National Affairs,* August 13, 1990.

122. Larry Waterfield, "Yeutter Jabs at California during Farm Bill Testimony," *The Packer,* February 25, 1990. See also Virginia Postrel, "The Big

Green Trade-Killing Machine," *Wall Street Journal,* September 21, 1990, p. A14.

123. "Understanding the Proposed GATT Agreement on Sanitary and Phytosanitary Measures," a background paper prepared by the GATT Secretariat, April 1993, p. 2.

124. Ibid.

125. Steve Charnovitz, "The World Trade Organization And Environmental Supervision," *International Trade Reporter,* January 26, 1994, p. 89. The following paragraphs draw heavily on Charnovitz's analysis.

126. Ibid., p. 90.

127. Ibid.

128. Ibid.

129. Ibid.

130. Ibid.

131. Frances Williams, "Uruguay Deal Boosts World Standardization," *Financial Times,* February 4, 1994, p. 5.

132. Jacques Pelksman and Michelle Egan, *Tackling Technical Barriers* (Brussels: Centre for European Policy Studies, 1992), p. 4.

133. Quoted in Ursula Kettlewell, "GATT: Will Liberalized Trade Aid Global Environmental Protection?" *Denver Journal of International Law and Policy,* 21, no. 1 (1992): 67.

134. Quoted in *The Greening of World Trade: A Report to EPA from the Trade and Environment Committee of the National Advisory Council for Environmental Policy and Technology* (Washington, D.C.: U.S. Government Printing Office, 1993), p. 187.

135. Oliver Gillie, "Trade Agreement Raises Fears over Food Safety," *Independent,* April 19, 1993, p. 13.

136. Avery, "Fears over Food Quality Standards," pp. 3–5.

137. Testimony to the Senate Finance Committee by Ambassador Michael Kantor, February 8, 1994, "The Uruguay Round: Growth for the World, Jobs for the U.S.," p. 18.

138. Ibid.

139. Ibid.

140. *International Food Safety: A Comparison of U.S. and Codex Pesticide Standards,* US GAO, August 1991, p. 4.

141. Ibid., p. 27.

142. Ibid., p. 28.

143. In fact, the EC's ban on the use of hormones for both beef and dairy cows represents one of the few cases in which European regulatory standards have been stricter, and based on less scientific evidence, than those of the United States. See David Vogel, *National Styles of Regulation: Environmen-*

tal Policy in Great Britain and the United States (Ithaca: Cornell University Press, 1986).

144. Harvey Sapolsky, "The Politics of Risk," in *Risk,* ed. Edward J. Burger Jr. (Ann Arbor: University of Michigan Press, 1990), p. 93.

145. Ibid., pp. 92–93.

146. Ann Reilly Dowd, "Envionmentalists Are on the Run," *Fortune,* September 19, 1994, p. 96.

147. For a description of how the Codex Commission operates, see Liora Salter, *Mandated Science: Science and Scientists in the Making of Standards* (Dordrecht, Holland: Kluwer Academic Publishers, 1988).

148. Executive Summary, Twentieth Session of the Joint FAO/WHO Codex Alimentarius Commission, July 13, 1993, p. 3.

6. Baptists and Bootleggers in the United States

1. Mark Dowie, "The Corporate Crime of the Century," *Mother Jones,* November 1979, pp. 23–39.

2. Karen Goldberg, "Efforts to Prevent Misuse of Pesticides Exported to Developing Countries: Progressing Beyond Regulation and Notification," *Ecology Law Quarterly,* 12, no. 4, p. 1032.

3. David Weir, "The Boomerang Crime," *Mother Jones,* November 1979, pp. 40–48.

4. Goldberg, "Efforts," p. 1035.

5. Ibid.

6. Robert Richter, "Pesticides and Pills for Export Only," transcript of television broadcast on Public Broadcasting Service, October 5, 1991, reproduced in *Pills, Pesticides and Profits,* ed. Ruth Norris, A. Karim, S. Jacob Scherr, and Robert Richter (Croton-Hudson, N.Y.: North River Press, 1982), p. 97.

7. Mark Willen, "Senate Panel Takes a Swing at Pesticides," *Congressional Quarterly Weekly Report,* February 20, 1988, pp. 368–369.

8. "EPA Strengthens US Pesticide Export Notification," *Pesticides News,* 19 (March 1993): 20.

9. Peter Schmeisser, "Pushing Cigarettes Overseas," *New York Times Magazine,* July 10, 1988, p. 20.

10. Philip Hilts, "Thailand's Cigarette Ban Upset," *New York Times,* October 4, 1990, pp. D1–D3.

11. U.S. Congress, Office of Technology Assessment, *Trade and Environment: Conflicts and Opportunities,* OTA-BP-ITE-94 (Washington, D.C.: U.S. Government Printing Office, 1992), p. 86.

12. John Burgess, "Cigarette Sales Overseas Light a Fire under U.S.

Tobacco's Tail," *Washington Post National Weekly Edition,* December 24–30, 1990, p. 21.

13. "Complaint against Thai Cigarette Barriers Trade Issue, No Health Matter, Exports Say," *International Trade Reporter,* September 20, 1990, p. 1181.

14. Ibid.

15. Pete Engardio, "Asia: A New Front in the War on Smoking," *Business Week,* February 25, 1991, p. 66.

16. Burgess, "Cigarette Sales Overseas," p. 21.

17. Paul Magnusson, "Uncle Sam Shouldn't Be A Travelling Salesman for Tobacco," *Business Week,* October 9, 1989, p. 61; "Medical Association Assails U.S. Policy on Tobacco Exports," *New York Times,* June 21, 1990, p. A5.

18. Burgess, "Cigarette Sales Overseas," p. 21.

19. Schmeisser, "Pushing Cigarettes," p. 22.

20. "Bush Administration Export Policies at Odds with Public Health Goals, GAO Report Says," *International Trade Reporter,* May 5, 1990, p. 726.

21. "Bush Administration Export," p. 726.

22. "Medical Association," p. A5.

23. Schmeisser, "Pushing Cigarettes," p. 22.

24. "Complaint against Thai Cigarette Barriers," p. 1181.

25. Chris Bright, "Pesticide Export Reform Act Tries to Break the Circle of Poison," *In These Times,* May 9–15, 1990, p. 3.

26. Marlise Simons, "Concern Rising over Harm from Pesticides in Third World," *New York Times,* May 30, 1989, p. C4.

27. Ibid.

28. For criticisms of American exports of pesticides to less developed nations, see Raymond Hill, "Problems and Policy for Pesticide Exports to Less Developed Countries," *Natural Resources Journal,* 28, no. 4 (Fall 1988): 699–720; Charlotte Uram, "International Regulation of the Sale and Use of Pesticides," *Northwestern Journal of International Law and Business,* 10 (1990): 460–478; Karen Goldberg, "Efforts to Prevent Misuse of Pesticides Exported to Developing Countries: Progressing Beyond Regulation and Notification," *Ecology Law Quarterly,* 12, no. 4 (1985): 1025–1051.

29. Bright, "Pesticide Export," p. 3.

30. Ibid.

31. David Weir, "The Boomerang Crime," *Mother Jones,* November 1979, pp. 40–48.

32. See, for example, David Weir and Mark Shapiro, *Circle of Poison: Pesticides and People in a Hungry World* (Washington, D.C.: Institute for Food and Development Policy, 1981).

33. Barry Meier, "As Food Imports Rise, Consumers Face Peril from Use of Pesticides," *Wall Street Journal,* March 26, 1987, p. 1.

34. Ibid.

35. Ibid.

36. Fred Powledge, "Toxic Shame," *Amicus Journal,* Winter 1991, p. 39.

37. Crowe, "Breaking the Cycle," pp. 320–321.

38. "1990 Farm Bill to Focus on Export Issues, 'Circle of Poison' Legislation Is Priority," *International Trade Reporter,* April 4, 1990, p. 467.

39. Weir, "The Boomerang Crime," p. 44.

40. Frank Horton, "Pesticide Residues in Imported Products: A Menace to American Public Health," *Environmental Forum* (November 1984): 19.

41. Harold V. Semling Jr., "Getting Tough on Imported Food Safety," *Food Processing* (June 1987): 12.

42. Barry Meier, "As Food Imports Rise," p. 1.

43. David Cloud, "Attacking the 'Circle of Poison,'" *Congressional Quarterly Weekly Report,* June 9, 1990, p. 1783.

44. "Bills Offered in Senate, House Would Ban Overseas Sales of Unregistered Pesticides," *International Trade Reporter,* March 7, 1990, p. 331.

45. Bright, "Pesticide Export Reform," p. 3.

46. Powledge, "Toxic Shame," p. 43.

47. Quoted in Andrew Davis, "Can Congress Close Off the Circle of Poison?" *Business and Society Review,* Summer 1992, p. 39.

48. Quoted in Mark Ritchie, "Agricultural Trade Liberalization," in Ralph Nader et al., *The Case against Free Trade* (San Francisco: Earth Island Press, 1993), p. 184.

49. Letter to author, August 24, 1990.

50. Quoted in C. Ford Runge, "Trade Protectionism and Environmental Regulations: The New Nontariff Barriers," *Northwestern Journal of International Law and Business,* 11 (1990): 48.

51. See also *Food Safety and Quality: Five Countries' Efforts to Meet U.S. Requirements on Imported Produce,* U.S. General Accounting Office, March 22, 1990. For evidence of increased public concern, see Meier, "As Food Imports Rise," p. 1.

52. Ronald Elving, "Congress Ships Trade Bill to Bush for Signature," *Congressional Quarterly Weekly Report,* August 4, 1990, p. 2490.

53. "Logging on Protectionism," *Wall Street Journal* December 6, 1990, p. A14.

54. Robert Houseman and Durwood Zaelke, "The Collision of the Environment and Trade: The GATT Tuna/Dolphin Decision," *Environmental Law Report,* 22 (1992): 10275.

55. Arvind Subramanian, "Trade Measures for Environment: A Nearly Empty Box," *World Economy,* 15 (January 1992): 135.

56. Patrick Low and Raed Safadi, "Trade Policy and Pollution," in *International Trade and the Environment,* ed. Patrick Low (Washington, D.C.: The World Bank, 1992), p. 39.

57. Quoted in Craig Obey, "Trade Incentives and Environmental Reform: The Search for a Suitable Incentive," *Georgetown International Law Review,* 4, no. 2 (1992): 443.

58. Ibid.

59. Quoted in Matthew Hunter Hurlock, "The GATT, U.S. Law and the Environment: A Proposal to Amend the GATT in Light of the Tuna/Dolphin Decision," *Columbia Law Review,* 92 (1992): 2114–2115.

60. Hurlock, "The GATT," p. 2115.

61. Quoted in Obey, "Trade Incentives," p. 426.

62. Quoted in ibid., pp. 439–440.

63. For a discussion of this issue in the context of both international and domestic law, see Kenneth Komoroski, "The Failure of Governments to Regulate Industry: A Subsidy under the GATT?" *Houston Journal of International Law,* 10, no. 1 (Summer 1988): 189–209.

64. Nancy Dunne, "US Sees A Health Hazard in GATT" *Financial Times,* August 1, 1990.

65. Press Release, May 15, 1990.

66. Ardith Maney, "Business, Consumers and the Protective State," paper prepared for delivery at the Annual Meeting of the American Political Science Association, Chicago, Illinois, September 3–6, 1992, p. 16.

67. Brian Ahlberg, "Administration Trade Proposal Endangers US Health, Food-safety Standards," Press release, National Family Farm Coalition, Washington, D.C.

68. Ralph Nader, "GATT Could Get Us," *National Forum,* July 16–22, 1990, p. 1.

69. "Environmental Consumer Group's Letter on Uruguay Round," *Inside U.S. Trade,* January 17, 1992, p. 13.

70. "Sierra Club Letter on Waxman-Gephardt Resolution," *Inside U.S. Trade,* February 21, 1992, p. S5.

71. "Gephardt-Waxman Letter on GATT and the Environment," *Inside U.S. Trade,* February 28, 1992, p. S12.

72. "Sabotage of America's Health, Food, Safety and Environmental Laws," *San Francisco Chronicle,* May 29, 1992, p. A20 (advertisement) (emphasis in original). Similar ads appeared in 1993 and again in 1994 following the Uruguay round GATT agreement. See "Will a Mad Rush to a False Deadline Lead to a GATT Failure in Congress?" *Financial Times,* December 9, 1993, p. 4; and "Jeopardized by GATT—*100* U.S. Environmental Laws," *New York Times,* June 20, 1994 (advertisment), p. A5.

73. "Leahy Skeptical over U.S. Assurances to Protect the Global Environment," *Inside U.S. Trade,* July 10, 1992, p. S2.

74. "EPA Letter on GATT Food Safety Rules," *Inside U.S. Trade,* August 3, 1990, p. S4.

75. Ibid.

76. Leslie Kaufman, "America's New Mr. International," *The International Economy,* July–August 1991, p. 36.

77. Ibid.

78. Marianne Lavelle, "Free Trade vs. Law," *National Law Journal,* March 29, 1993, p. 38.

79. Marian Burros, "A Debate Rages over Whether International Trade Agreements Imperil Food Safety," *New York Times,* April 28, 1993, p. B4.

80. Stewart Hudson, "Coming to Terms with Trade," *Environmental Action,* Summer 1992, p. 35.

81. Burros, "A debate," p. B4.

82. C. Ford Runge, "Environmental Risk and the World Economy," *American Prospect,* Spring 1990, p. 117.

83. Hudson, "Coming to Terms with Trade," p. 33.

7. Reducing Trade Barriers in North America

1. Elizabeth Wehr, "U.S.-Canada Free-Trade Pact Seen Likely to Win Approval," *Congressional Quarterly Weekly Report,* March 5, 1988, pp. 581–584.

2. Elizabeth Wehr, "Mulroney Victory Clears Way for Free-Trade Pact," *Congressional Quarterly Weekly Report,* November 26, 1988, p. 3397.

3. Marcia Valiante and Paul Muldoon, "Annual Review of Canadian-American Environmental Relations—1988," *International Environmental Affairs,* 1, no. 4 (Fall 1989): 290.

4. Ibid.

5. Steven Shrybman, "Trading Away the Environment," *World Policy Journal,* 9, no. 1 (Winter 1991–1992): 105.

6. Quoted ibid., p. 95.

7. Antoine St-Pierre, "Business and the Environment: The International Dimensions," *Global Business Issues,* 2, no. 3 (September 1990): 3.

8. Ibid.

9. Kyle McSlarrow, "International Trade and the Environment: Building a Framework for Conflict Resolution," *Environmental Law Reporter,* 21 (October 1991): 10596.

10. Candice Stevens, "Harmonization, Trade and the Environment," *International Environmental Affairs,* 5, no. 1 (Winter 1993): 44.

11. Patti Goldman, "The Legal Effect of Trade Agreements on Domestic Health and Environmental Regulation," *Journal of Environmental Law and Litigation,* 7 (1992): 52.

12. Ibid.

13. See U.S. Congress, Office of Technology Assessment, *Trade and Environment: Conflicts and Opportunities,* OTA-BP-ITE-94 (Washington, D.C.: U.S. Government Printing Office, May 1992), pp. 87–88; Marcia Valiante and Paul Muldoon, "Annual Review of Canada-U.S. Environmental Relations—1989," *International Environmental Affairs,* 2, no. 3 (Summer 1990): 253–254.

14. C. Ford Runge, "Trade Protectionism and Environmental Regulations: The New Nontariff Barriers," *Northwestern Journal of International Law & Business,* 11, no. 1 (Spring 1990): 56.

15. Ibid.

16. Quoted ibid., p. 57.

17. Runge, "Trade Protectionism," p. 57.

18. Jennifer Lewington, "Trade Mechanism Little Help in U.S. Fish Dispute," *Toronto Globe and Mail,* November 10, 1989, p. B4.

19. Ibid.

20. Ibid., p. B1.

21. Ibid.

22. Ibid.

23. Madelaine Drohan, "Canada Agrees to Allow Fish to Be Sold Directly for Export," *Toronto Globe and Mail,* November 7, 1989, p. B1.

24. Quoted in Steven Shrybman, "Selling the Environment Short," *Canadian Environmental Law Association,* January 1991, p. 8.

25. Shrybman, "Trading Away," p. 101.

26. Quoted in John Manard Jr., "GATT and the Environment: The Friction between International Trade and the World's Environment—the Dolphin and Tuna Dispute," *Tulane Environmental Law Journal,* 5, no. 3 (May 1992): 409.

27. Konrad von Moltke, "Dispute Resolution and Transparency," in *The Greening of World Trade: A Report to EPA from the Trade and Environment Committee of the National Advisory Council for Environmental Policy and Technology* (Washington, D.C.: U.S. Government Printing Office, 1993), p. 122.

28. Ibid., p. 410.

29. Naomi Rohi-Arriaza, "Precaution, Participation and the 'Greening' of International Trade Law," *Journal of Environmental Law and Litigation,* 7 (1992): 70.

30. Ibid.

31. Quoted in Shrybman, "Trading Away," p. 105.

32. David Palmeter, "Environment and Trade," *Journal of World Trade,* 26, no. 2 (April 1992): 36.

33. Quoted ibid., p. 39.

34. Quoted in Shrybman, "Selling the Environment Short," p. 13.

35. Ibid., p. 36.

36. Testimony of Ellen Haas before Senate Subcommittee on Labor of the Senate Committee on Labor and Human Resources, April 23, 1989, p. 7.

37. Kristin Dawkins and William Carroll Muffett, "The Free Trade Sell-out," *The Progressive,* January 1993, p. 19.

38. Quoted in Shrybman, "Selling the Environment Short," p. 7.

39. James McCarthy, "The Trade Implications of Recycled Content in Newsprint: The US View," in *Life-Cycle Management and Trade* (Paris: Organization for Economic Co-Operation and Development, 1994), p. 145.

40. James Rusk, "Green Concerns Color Trade Disputes in the '90s," *Toronto Globe and Mail,* August 10, 1992, p. B3.

41. Nancy Dunne and Bernard Simon, "Canada-US Beer War Gets Green Tinge," *Financial Times,* July 31, 1992, p. 5.

42. Steve Charnovitz, "GATT and the Environment: Examining the Issues," *International Environmental Affairs,* 4, no. 3 (Summer 1992): 219.

43. Rusk, "Green Concerns," p. B1.

44. Quoted in "Beer Blast," *Wall Street Journal,* August 4, 1992, p. A14.

45. Keith Bradsher, "U.S. and Canada Make Deal on Beer amid Trade Talks," *New York Times,* August 6, 1993, p. D1.

46. Marianne Lavelle, "Free Trade vs. Law," *National Law Journal,* March 29, 1993, p. 39.

47. "In the Matter of Puerto Rico Regulations on the Import, Distribution and Sale of U.H.T. Milk from Quebec," Panel No. USA-93-1807-01 (June 3, 1993), 5.2.

48. Ibid., 5.5.

49. Elaine Dodge and Christy Law, "Poisoned Meat from Canada," *New York Times,* May 31, 1991, p. A15.

50. Lori Wallach, "The Consumer and Environmental Case against Fast Track," ITC Testimony, April 12, 1991, p. 11.

51. Ibid. See also Elaine Dodge and Christy Law, "Poisoned Meat from Canada," *New York Times,* May 13, 1991, p. A 15.

52. U.S. General Accounting Office, July 6, 1990, p. 4.

53. Shrybman, "Selling the Environment Short," p. 19.

54. George Holberg, "Sleeping with an Elephant: The American Influence on Canadian Environmental Regulation," *Journal of Public Policy,* 11, no. 1 (1991): 118.

55. Ibid., p. 120.

56. Ibid., p. 122.

57. See J. Owen Saunders, "Trade and Environment: The Fine Line between Environmental Protection and Environmentalism Protectionism," *International Journal,* 47 (Autumn 1992): 733–750.

58. Barrett Walker, "International Cooperation: The Role of Free Trade in Conservation," in *Environmental Gore,* ed. John A. Baden (San Francisco: Pacific Research Institute for Public Policy, 1994), p. 203.

59. Dennis Leaf, "Intergovernmental Cooperation: Air Pollution from an U.S. Perspective," *Canada–United States Law Journal,* 18 (1992): 245–250.

60. "Federal Government, Industry Agree on Tougher Auto Emission Standards," *International Environment Reporter,* 15, no. 5 (March 11, 1992): 132.

61. Robert Pastor, "NAFTA as the Center of an Integration Process: The Non-trade Issues," in *Assessing the Impact of North American Free Trade,* ed. Nora Lustig et al. (Washington, D.C.: Brookings Institution, 1992), p. 182.

62. Eva Regnier, "Trade Policy and the Environment: U.S.-Mexico Free Trade," *Journal of the IES,* 35, no. 2 (March–April 1992): 83.

63. Pastor, "NAFTA as the Center," p. 182.

64. Ibid.

65. William Burke, "The Toxic Price of Free Trade in Mexico," *In These Times,* May 22–28, 1991, p. 2.

66. Jonathan Marshall, "How Ecology Is Tied to Mexico Trade Pact," *San Francisco Chronicle,* February 25, 1992, p. A8.

67. Richard Rothstein, "Exporting Jobs and Pollution to Mexico," *New Perspectives Quarterly,* 8, no. 1 (Winter 1991): 23.

68. "The Consumer and Environmental Case against Fast Track," ITC Testimony of Lori Wallach, Public Citizen's Congress Watch, April 12, 1991, p. 13.

69. Ibid., p. 16.

70. Ibid. See also Ralph Nader and Michael Waldman, "Off-Track," *New Republic,* June 3, 1991, pp. 15–16.

71. Roberto Suro, "In Search of a Trade Pact with the Environment in Mind," *New York Times,* April 14, 1991, p. E4

72. Ibid., p. E20.

73. Ibid., p. E4.

74. Letter to President George Bush from Congressmen Richard Gephardt, March 27, 1991.

75. Keith Bradsher, "U.S. and Mexico Draft Plan to Fight Border Pollution," *New York Times,* April 2, 1991, pp. C1, C6.

76. Ibid., p. C6.

77. Jane Kay, "Environmentalists Urge Tough Mexico Trade Law," *San Francisco Examiner,* September 9, 1991.

78. Diana Solis, "Mexico Cracks Down on Pollution, Spurred in Part by Trade Talks," *Wall Street Journal,* February 10, 1992, p. A10.

79. Ibid.

80. Jonathan Marshall, "How Ecology Is Tied to Mexico Trade Pact," *San Francisco Chronicle,* February 25, 1992, p. A8.

81. Damian Fraser, "Environment Hit by Too Much Free Trade," *Financial Times,* July 2, 1992, p. 4.

82. Nancy Dunne, "US Political Sands Shift under NAFTA," *Financial Times,* June 12, 1992, p. 5.

83. Marshall, "How Ecology," p. A8.

84. William Reilly, "Mexico's Environment Will Improve with Free Trade," *Wall Street Journal,* February 10, 1992, p. A10.

85. Michelle Swenarchuk, "NAFTA and the Environment," *Canadian Forum,* 71 (January–February 1993): 13.

86. Roberto Salinas-Leon, "Green Herrings," *Regulation,* Winter 1993, p. 31.

87. Ibid.

88. Gary Hufbauer, Jeffrey Schott, *North American Free Trade: Issues and Recommendations* (Washington, D.C.: Institute for International Economics, 1992), p. 156.

89. Quoted in James Sheehan, "Nafta—Free Trade in Name Only," *Wall Street Journal,* September 9, 1993, p. A21.

90. For criticisms of the environmental provisions of both NAFTA and the side agreement, see Gary Hufbauer and Jeffrey Scott, *NAFTA: An Assessment,* rev. ed. (Washington, D.C: Institute for International Economics, 1993), pp. 92–97.

91. Stephen Mumme, "Environmentalists, NAFTA, and North American Environmental Management," *Journal of Environment and Development,* 2, no. 1 (Winter 1993): 215.

92. Keith Bradsher, "Side Agreements to Trade Accord Vary in Ambition," *New York Times,* September 19, 1993, pp. 1, 15.

93. Lash, *NAFTA and the Greening,* p. 11.

94. Jan Gilbreath and John Benjamin Tonra, "The Environment: Unwelcome Guest at the Free Trade Party," in *The NAFTA Debate,* ed. M. Delal Baer and Sidney Weintrab (Boulder: Lynne Reinner, 1994), p. 88.

95. David Pilling, "NAFTA Accord Back on Chile's Agenda: Environmental and Labor Issues Are Expected to Dominate Talks with the US," *Financial Times,* May 27, 1994, p. 7.

8. The California Effect

1. Helen Milner employs a similar argument to explain business support for liberal trade policies during the 1970s and 80s. See Helen Milner, *Resisting Protectionism: Global Industries and the Politics of International Trade* (Princeton: Princeton University Press, 1988). For an analysis of the role of

industrial structures in explaining patterns of international regulatory convergence, see Dale Murphy, "Open Economies' Competition for Comparative Advantage," unpublished paper, MIT Center for International Studies, November 1993. See also Charles Pearson, "Environmental Standards, Industrial Relocation, and Pollution Havens," in *Multinational Corporations, Environment, and the Third World,* ed. Charles Pearson (Duke University Press, 1987), p. 116.

2. This analysis parallels theories on the formation and maintenance of international regimes. See Stephen Krasner, ed., *International Regimes* (Ithaca: Cornell University Press, 1983); and Robert Keohane, *After Hegemony* (Princeton: Princeton University Press, 1984).

3. See Anne-Marie Burley and Walter Mattli, "Europe before the Court: A Political Theory of European Integration," *International Organization,* 47, no. 1 (Winter 1993).

4. This analysis is consistent with the neofunctionalist explanation of European economic integration put forward by Ernst Haas. See Ernst Haas, *The Uniting of Europe* (Stanford: Stanford University Press, 1958).

5. For a discussion of the increasing importance of international environmental institutions, see Peter M. Haas, Robert O. Keohane, and Marc A. Levy, eds., *Institutions for the Earth: Sources of Effective International Environmental Protection* (Cambridge: MIT Press, 1993).

6. See, for example, John Carroll, ed., *International Environmental Diplomacy* (Cambridge: Cambridge University Press, 1988); Nazli Choucri, ed., *Global Accord* (Cambridge: MIT Press, 1993); Lawrence Susskind, *Environmental Diplomacy* (New York: Oxford University Press, 1994); and Oran Young, *International Cooperation* (Ithaca: Cornell University Press, 1989).

7. Michael Piore and Charles Sabel, *The Second Industrial Divide* (New York: Basic Books, 1994), p. 185.

8. Ibid.

9. *Pollution Control Expenditures in Selected OECD Countries 1972–1986* (Paris: Organization for Economic Cooperation and Development, 1989), p. 39; "When Green is Good," *Economist,* November 20, 1993, p. 19.

10. Raymond Kopp, Paul Portney, and Diane DeWitt, *International Comparisons of Environmental Regulations* (Washington, D.C: Resources for the Future, 1990), p. 3.

11. See Susan Pharr and Joseph Badaracco Jr., "Coping with Crisis: Environmental Regulation," in *America versus Japan,* ed. Thomas McCraw (Boston: Harvard Business School Press, 1986), pp. 229–260.

12. William Lash III, *"NAFTA and the Greening of International Trade Policy"* (St. Louis: Center for the Study of American Business, 1993), p. 11.

13. Globerman, "Environmental Impacts of Trade Liberalization," p. 34; see also Gene Koretz, "A Robust Economy Can Help Cure a Sick Environment," *Business Week,* May 23, 1994, p. 20.

14. David Vogel, "A Case Study of Clean Air Legislation 1976–1981," in *The Impact of the Modern Corporation,* ed. Betty Bock et al. (New York: Columbia University Press, 1984), pp. 340–354.

15. Bronwen Maddox, "Black Skies, Red Tape, Green Fields, Grey Area," *Financial Times,* March 3, 1994, p. 8.

16. Ibid.

17. Frances Cairncross, *Costing the Earth* (Boston: Harvard Business School Press, 1991), p. 23.

18. Stephen Meyer, "Environmentalism and Economic Prosperity: Testing the Environmental Impact Hypothesis," MIT Project on Environmental Politics and Policy.

19. For a summary of the literature on environmental regulation, trade, and corporate location decisions, see Richard Stewart, "Environmental Regulation and International Competitiveness," *Yale Law Journal,* 102, no. 8 (June 1993): 2077–2079, and Judith Dean, "Trade and the Environment: A Survey of the Literature," in *International Trade and the Environment,* ed. Patrick Low (Washington, D.C.: World Bank, 1992), pp. 16–20. See also Robert Lucas, David Wheeler, and Hemamala Hettige, "Economic Development, Environmental Regulation and International Migration of Toxic Industrial Pollution: 1960–1988," in Low, *International Trade and the Environment,* pp. 67–86; Patrick Low and Alexander Yeats, "Do 'Dirty' Industries Migrate?" in Low, *International Trade,* pp. 89–103; James A. Tobey, "The Effects of Domestic Environmental Policies on Patterns of World Trade: An Empirical Test," *Kyklos,* 43 (1990): 191–209; Konrad von Moltke, "Environmental Protection and Its Effects on Competitiveness," in *Difficult Liaison: Trade and the Environment in the Americas,* ed. Heraldo Muñoz and Robin Rosenberg (New Brunswick: Transaction Publishers, 1993), pp. 5–20.

20. See Timothy Bartik, "The Effects of Environmental Regulation on Business Location in the United States," *Growth and Change,* no. 19 (1988): 22–44.

21. Hilary F. French, "Reconciling Trade and the Environment," *State of the World 1993,* ed. Linda Starke (New York: Norton, 1993), p. 166.

22. Stewart, "Environmental Regulation," p. 2077.

23. Ibid., p. 2076.

24. Charles Pearson and Robert Repetto, "Reconciling Trade and Environment: The Next Steps," in *The Greening of World Trade: A Report to EPA from the Trade and Environment Committee of the National Advisory Council for Environmental Policy and Technology* (Washington, D.C.: U.S. Government Printing Office, 1993), p. 97.

25. "Trade and the Environment," A draft prepared by the Trade Committee of OECD, June 27, 1989, p. 6.

26. Edith Brown Weiss, "Environmentally Sustainable Competitiveness: A Comment," *Yale Law Journal,* 102 (**1993**): 2135.

27. Stewart, "Environmental Regulation," p. 2058.

28. Michael Porter, *The Competitive Advantage of Nations* (New York: Free Press, 1990), pp. 685–588. See also U.S. Environmental Protection Agency, *International Trade in Environmental Protection Equipment* (Washington, D.C.: U.S. Government Printing Office, 1993), and Curtis Moore and Alan Miller, *Green Gold* (Boston: Beacon Press, 1994).

29. Gary Bryner, *Blue Skies, Green Politics* (Washington, D.C.: Congressional Quarterly Press, 1993), pp. 149–150.

30. Matthew Wald, "Harder Auto Emission Rules Agreed to by Eastern States," *New York Times*, February 2, 1994, p. 1, A6.

31. Baptist-bootlegger coalitions have also played an important role in strengthening international environmental agreements. For example, the strong support of the United States for the Montreal Protocol reflected a convergence of interests between American environmental organizations and Dupont. The latter supported international restrictions on the production of CFCs because it was more easily able to produce a substitute product than its European competitors. See Richard Elliot Benedick, *Ozone Diplomacy* (Cambridge: Harvard University Press, 1991).

32. This latter point is made by John Braithwaite in "Transational Regulation of the Pharmaceutical Industry," *ANNALS, AAPSS*, 525 (January 1993): 29.

33. Hanns W. Maull, "Japan's Global Environmental Policies," in *The International Politics of the Environment*, ed. Andrew Hurrell and Benedict Kingsbury (Oxford: Clarendon Press, 1992), pp. 354–372.

Abbreviations

BEUC	Bureau of European Consumer Unions
BSE	Bovine spongiform encephalopathy
BST	Bovine somatotropin
CAFE	Corporate average fuel economy
CFC	Chlorofluorocarbons
CITES	Convention on International Trade in Endangered Species of Wild Fauna and Flora
CLEAR	Campaign for Lead-Free Air
CUJ	Consumer Union of Japan
EC	European Community
ECE	United Nations Economic Commission for Europe
ECJ	European Court of Justice
EDB	Ethyl dibromide
EEC	European Economic Community
EFTA	European Free Trade Association
EPA	United States Environmental Protection Agency
ETP	Eastern tropical Pacific, a triangle of the Pacific ocean extending from southern California to northern Chile
EU	European Union
FDA	United States Food and Drug Administration
FIFRA	Federal Insecticide, Fungicide, and Rodenticide Act
FTA	Free Trade Agreement between the United States and Canada. Also referred to as CFTA, the Canadian Free Trade Agreement
GAO	United States General Administration Organization
GATT	General Agreement on Tariffs and Trade
GNP	Gross national product
IWC	International Whaling Commission
MEP	Member of European Parliament
MHW	Japanese Ministry of Health and Welfare

MMPA   The United States Marine Mammal Protection Act
NAFTA North American Free Trade Agreement
NGO   Nongovernmental organization
NRDC   Natural Resources Defense Coucil
NTB   Nontariff trade barrier
OECD   Organization for Economic Cooperation and Development
PPM   Process and production methods
S&P   Sanitary and phytosanitary
SCF   European Community (Union) Scientific Committee for Foodstuffs
SEA   Single European Act
TSCA   Toxic Substances Control Act
TBT   Technical barrier to trade
USDA   United States Department of Agriculture
USTR   United States Trade Representative

Index

309